Critical Voices on Special Education

Critical Voices on Special Education

Problems and Progress
Concerning the Mildly Handicapped

Edited by
Scott B. Sigmon

State University of New York Press

LC
3981
C75
1990

Published by
State University of New York Press, Albany

© 1990 State University of New York

For information, address State University of New York
Press, State University Plaza, Albany, N.Y. 12246

Library of Congress Cataloging-in-Publication Data

Critical voices on special education : problems and progress
    concerning the mildly handicapped / edited by Scott B. Sigmon.
        p.   cm.
    Includes bibliographical references.
    ISBN 0-7914-0319-X. — ISBN 0-7914-0320-3 (pbk).
    1. Special education—United States. 2. Educational sociology—
United States. 3. Handicapped children—Education—United States.
I. Sigmon, Scott B.
LC3981.C75   1990
371.9'0973—dc20   89-38707
                                                                            CIP

10 9 8 7 6 5 4 3 2 1

To Lyle

Contents

Part II: Progress

Preface

Since the beginning of the twentieth century, psychological theory—along with the medical model of individual pathology—has formed the cornerstone of special education practice. When engaged in this model, the justification for placing students into educational programs for the handicapped has been impairment inherent to the youngster. Lately, because of the multitudes of the so-called mildly impaired, many people have become critical of reigning practices relative to special needs education. The basis for this book is such criticism by a group of professional special educators.

Most "mildly impaired" students are actually victimized by faulty instruction within regular education programs or social problems unrelated to education. William Ryan's (1971) "blaming the victim" syndrome has re-emerged today more blatantly than ever in the education for the handicapped field! Due to the misidentification of millions of children as handicapped, we must re-examine the purpose and practices of special education. Moreover, as a result of concerns over such special educational programing, that is, who is placed into it, what has emerged is a growing body of literature which could be called *the sociology of special education*.

John L. Johnson's (1969) "Special education and the inner city: A challenge for the future or another means for cooling the mark out?" may by the first significant article on the sociology of special education. Previous work critical of special education dealt with the efficacy of programs, whereas Johnson was concerned with the socio-educational mistreatment of a particular group, the Afro-Americans. Later, some books (e.g., Sigmon, 1987; Tomlinson, 1982) have specifically dealt with special education's maltreatment of the poor. There is emerging today a *reconstruction of knowledge* pertaining to special education, and the book you are holding is an effort to further that end.

It seems whenever divergent opinion arises over existing practice and its related theory, at minimal, perfunctory homage is paid to Thomas S. Kuhn's (1962) very important ideas on scientific paradigms. This is done again here. Kuhn propounded the notion that scientific knowledge is not merely a cumulative linear progression; instead, after a period consolidation and quiescence, scientific change takes place when old theories and methods are broken down and replaced. Hence, advances in thought occur via spasmodic paradigmatic change, which are then followed by another period of stability, only to be completely replaced at some later date.

Perhaps special education's major problem is that it has been too efficient. It has absorbed so well those youngsters who cannot fit easily into the ordinary educational apparatus that it has been called upon to take more and more of those with problems. Inasmuch as the schools are assigned the task of preserving culture, they are very resistant to change. Therefore, we can anticipate no quick resolution from within the schools to special education's problem of constant expansion—or even from the outside, unless society changes. Nevertheless, having recognized the problems, we must be prepared to implement new solutions as soon as opportunities arise.

To avoid confusion, a brief note on the usage of "critical" is necessary. One ordinarily associates this word with "critical theory" or the "radical humanist" perspective. And, while my work can be considered as such, most of the other authors' chapters in this book are not critical in the critical theory sense; but, they all, in varying degrees, find fault with and therefore seek change in prevailing special education procedures concerning the mildly handicapped.

In *Radical Analysis of Special Education: Focus on Historical Development and Learning Disabilities* (Sigmon, 1987)—a book dealing with the historical, philosophical, psychological, and especially the sociological foundations of the education for the handicapped—a solid foundation was prepared for the advancement of current theory and practice for students with special needs.

Toward that end, *Critical Voices on Special Education: Problems and Progress Concerning the Mildly Handicapped* takes the next step forward.

Scott B. Sigmon, Ed.D.

Acknowledgments

The editor wishes to thank all those authors, organizations, and publishers who granted permission to reproduce their work. (The source of material previously published is cited on the first page of each chapter or appendix.) I particularly want to thank Tom Skrtic, Gerry Coles, Diane Ganeles and Priscilla Ross—whose support helped make possible the publication of this work.

Introduction: Critical Voices on Special Education

Scott B. Sigmon

On the most basic level, any form of schooling is predicated upon a set of beliefs, values, or ideology. The Kindergarten through twelfth grade (K-12) configuration that has evolved in the United States is a prime example. Sound arguments could easily be made favoring other arrangements; e.g., pre-K through tenth grade. The K-12 configuration is based more on tradition than logic; and to change it would be quite difficult—but it probably will be different sometime in the future. The same holds true with special education. At first, there was no education for the handicapped, then institutionalization, then special classes, etc. Therefore, changing special education's arrangements will be difficult, because educational programs are a function of ideology and tradition.

One need not be a "zeitgeist detective" to realize that the growing numbers of children classified as mildly handicapped indicates two significant points: (a) the increasing practice of labeling children as impaired learners is an attempt to preserve the rigid K-12 system, and (b) stating that most of these impaired students have mild learning disabilities is a form of pneumatology (a ludicrous study of spirits applied to education). For the mildly handicapped, special education of any type provides a warm supportive environment where, unfortunately, academic standards are lowered; and, at the same time, such students' standardized group test scores—if they take these tests—are not included in the official regular class, school, or district averages. Thus, not only does special education nurture the individual mildly handicapped student, it also preserves the integrity of the K-12 schooling arrangement.

This book examines some of special education's current problems; moreover, it shows the way toward their solution with some new thoughts on theory, policy, and, most importantly, substantial ideas about more efficacious school practice. Contained within this volume of collected papers are previously published journal articles, several of which are from obscure periodicals; but also, some original work by the editor. Additionally, there are short position papers pertaining to special education; these, along with some very brief articles, are appended at the end. The critical voices represented in this tome are not only those of researchers and scholars, but also large national practitioner organizations representing thousands of other critical but unnamed voices. All of the authors or organizations whose work was selected to appear in this edited book represent much of the vanguard of thought about special education today—although not all of them consider themselves to be exclusively special educators, as their ideas could be applied to all students. What all of these authors have in common is their critical posture toward today's system of education for the "classified" exceptional learner.

Although there is little doubt over who is a seriously impaired youngster, there is major concern over the millions of students who are classified as being educationally handicapped because of mild to moderate problems. Those pupils who are blind, deaf, orthopedically disabled, severely to profoundly retarded, and autistic clearly have special educational needs which in most cases require differential educational treatment. On the other hand, for those students with no obvious physical, sensory, or behavioral/ emotional disorder, and who do poorly in school, there is grave critical concern. Today, there are serious critics of special education who believe many students of the latter group, the so-called mild to moderate handicapped, should not be part of special education. And this second group constitutes most of the current population of classified exceptional students. These mild to moderate handicaps are in most cases more a product of the educational institutions or the society which produces them—most students are placed into special education because they read poorly or exhibit behavior considered too disruptive for ordinary classes. Furthermore, in most instances, there is no difference between the instruction which these pupils received in regular education—

and did poorly with — to that provided in segregated special classes.

Those school professionals responsible for placing students with no obvious disability into special education do so with good intent; they believe these students will be better helped this way, as ordinary education has failed them. But in order to justify the special placement, psychoeducational tests—most of which have little or no real relationship to instruction or academics—will be administered until the search for some alleged psychopathology or neuropathology is found. And when this occurs, a nurturant change to a less demanding special program is made. Almost all of these machinations are done, really, because of the failure of the regular school program to serve many of today's children; and this is a result of socio-political problems outside the school. But it appears, as things are now done in the schools, that there are millions of children with mild to moderate *internal* handicaps. (Refer to Sigmon [1987a] for an extensive discussion of this problem.) This is what the criticism toward special education today is primarily directed. The problem of the (mis)treatment of the so-called mild to moderate handicapped student remains an "open secret" to a growing number of research-educators at the university level; but this notion is not really known, by and large, within the schools where nothing has yet changed. The lag time between the development of new pedagogic ideas and their implementation in the schools can be as much as fifty years.

Special education must be de-emphasized as soon as possible in favor of re-emphasizing remedial education. Ivan Illich (1970) proposed "deschooling society" so that schools could be re-made to better meet human needs. I propose that most (mild to moderate) educationally handicapped students be immediately deprogrammed from special education and be placed into regular education with remedial instruction.

It is thought that all the authors here believe the key to better education for all students is threefold: More attention to their individual human needs, a solid foundation for learning how to learn, and good instruction. The following chapters address this tripartite notion directly or indirectly. This is done through diverse topics such as different public policy, developmental theory, learning strategy instruction, the "activity model" of reading assessment, and counseling.

In Part I, we primarily discuss the current mistreatment of the
mild educationally handicapped. In Part II, different outlooks and
methods for dealing with the so-called mildly handicapped are
pointed out. (There is, of course, some unavoidable overlap
between Parts I and II.) Thus, the emphasis in the second part—
the bulk of the book—is on services prior to classification. So rather
than using the time of school professionals to "confirm" with
questionable inferential psychoeducational test findings a child's
mild handicap, children who have difficulty in school are first provided a myriad of helpful services. Hence, professional resources
are utilized prior to special educational placement, there is a major change of emphasis in professional practice under the existing
special ed arrangements, many at-risk students benefit individually,
and the regular education K-12 configuration continues to function. In essence, this service delivery model—being primarily based
upon pre-referral interventions—serves as both a way to change
special services/education from within and maintains the K-12
schooling configuration. It may be possible to humanely preserve
the K-12 regular education arrangement by merely changing the
curriculum (Sigmon, 1987b); and this would reduce the need of
regular education to place many students into special education.
Nevertheless, special ed's current regulations (US federal statute
P.L. 94-142) must be changed, especially in regard to the present
noxious labels and their lenient eligibility (as handicapped) criteria.

Part I opens with a chapter by Scott B. Sigmon, whose
emphasis is on problems pertaining to the mild or educable
mentally retarded (EMR) label, social class, racial minorities, IQ
and standardized tests. Next, Christine E. Sleeter provides her
interpretation as to why the learning disability (LD) category is
a social construct and how it came about. Then, Sigmon discusses
the mildly learning disabled from the radical perspective of the
educational foundations field. Lynn M. Gelzheiser shows the
relationship of dysfunctional LD policy to current practices, and
she proposes alternatively a policy which advocates "a minority
view of disability." Part I concludes with a chapter by George J.
Hagerty and Marty Abramson on obstacles to policy change for
the mildly handicapped.

Part II starts with chapter 6 where Sigmon proposes a
qualitative, interactive "methodology for rational discourse on

special education" knowledge, research, and theory. Sigmon follows with a piece on orthopedically disabled children illustrating how actual impairment is not necessarily handicapping, and how each person, with obvious or suspected impairment, must be viewed individually. Larry Maheady, Richard Towne, Bob Algozzine, Jane Mercer, and James Ysseldyke, in a classic article, make an appeal for "alternative practices prior to [formal special education] referral" because of "minority overrepresentation." Inasmuch as almost all students considered learning disabled have reading problems, Peter H. Johnston offers a fresh, "Vygotskian perspective on assessment in reading." Steven A. Carlson outlines "nonnormative" assessment procedures as an alternative to those currently in vogue. The University of Kansas Institute for Research in Learning Disabilities (KU-IRLD) had, as its "major mission," the development of "a validated intervention model for LD adolescents" (Schumaker, Deshler, Alley, & Warner, 1983, p. 69). Two significant pieces based on the KU-IRLD work are included within this collection. The first, by Jean B. Schumaker and Donald D. Deshler, explains how the consideration of "setting demand variables" are a part of good "program planning." The second, by Deshler and Schumaker, focuses on "learning strategies" as "an instructional alternative for low-achieving adolescents." At this juncture, Sigmon addresses counseling as an essential, and oft neglected, prereferral intervention. Part II ends with a chapter by Alan Gartner and Dorothy Kerzner Lipsky in which they delineate—actually, they reiterate elegantly and succinctly much of what was previously discussed within this edited collection—and reconceptualize seven crucial areas of special education.

There are six short appendices. The first by Sigmon is a framework for counseling related to his counseling chapter in Part II; it suggests who should be counseled in the schools and relates this to special education. Appendix B, by Sigmon, looks at racial/gender factors regarding special ed placement locally and state-wide. In Appendix C, Sigmon offers an example of school practitioner research on classroom behaviors, which, in their extreme, could lead to special placement. "Rights Without Labels" (Appendix D) is a position statement by three national organizations regarding school services and noxious special ed rubrics. Appendix E is a published letter by Sigmon commenting on

Appendix D. This book closes with another position paper (Appendix F) authored by two of the same three national organizations who penned Appendix D; it is "apropos" to close *Critical Voices on Special Education* with "Advocacy for Appropriate Educational Services for All Children"—it should be the bottom line on education in a democracy.

Finally, I have come to realize that problems regarding the schooling of the "mildly educationally handicapped"—the bulk of the special education population—are complex and *always* involve regular education. This book makes an attempt to change special ed in the short-term, by showing some things that can be done now. Future work in special ed must be more far reaching, it must be systemic and organizational.

Part I

Problems

Overview

Scott B. Sigmon

A study of the historical development of American special education finds a benevolent, progressive inclusion of more and more handicapped students of various types. The first area for large-scale controversy in special education was the misdiagnosis of mild or educable mental retardation (EMR), especially in regards to the excessive inclusion of ethnic or racial minorities. Moreover, there has also been some concern during the last three decades over who should receive segregated education due to emotional disturbance (ED). However, there has never been the sort of mass protest and litigation associated with the ED classification as there has been over that of EMR. Perhaps more of a stigma is attached to being dull as it is thought of as being permanent, whereas ED may, in fact, only be temporary, and, in some perverse way, glamorous to some extent. In addition, very little academic achievement is either offered to or expected from the EMR youngster in too many instances. Furthermore, the number of students classified ED has always been far less than that of MR; but the numbers seem to be reversing, and this could signal protestation with the ED label. Today, however, the specific learning disability (LD) classification has burgeoned to include almost two million American students; this far exceeds the highest yearly current total of any other classification ever. LD is the newest category, and although it suggests a specific area or areas of retarded performance—due to brain damage—as the term was originally intended, there has not yet been the clamour regarding it by the parents of LD students as there has been with EMR or even ED to some extent. An LD label is not nearly as noxious as EMR or ED. Nevertheless, some professionals are now very seriously involved in an effort against the prevailing misuse of the LD category.

9

Chapter 1

Remarks on Social Inequality and Measured Cognitive Abilities in the Schools*

Scott B. Sigmon

> Truth is more complex, multifaceted and value-determined than is the usual fact. Fact is empirical while truth is interpretative. Fact is, in itself, unrelated to value; it merely is. Truth, as the understanding—in the fullest sense—of fact, is related to value and, for that reason, more fully human.
>
> Kenneth B. Clark (1965, p. xxiv)

[The thesis of this chapter is that social class profoundly affects performance on IQ, aptitude, and specific school learning (dis)-abilities tests; and that a fair quantitative measurement of socio-economically depressed students is only possible with local or comparable norms. The most controversial issue regarding the testing of schoolchildren is resultant educational programming which is usually quite limiting for low social status youngsters, too many of whom are now specially classified as educable mentally retarded and learning disabled. Facts and myths about social inequality and schooling are discussed. The author believes that political action to improve the quality of life for socioeconomically depressed adults will have greater as well as quicker effects on their children's test scores than tinkering with school reforms.]**

*This chapter first appeared in *The Western Journal of Black Studies* (1988), Vol. 12, No. 4, pp. 210–214. Published by Washington State University Press.

**Chapter abstracts within brackets did not appear with the original journal article.

Current Concerns

Conclusive evidence has been gathered in a number of states on the overrepresentation of black and Hispanic children in public school classes for the mild or educable mentally retarded (EMR). In 1979, landmark cases in California (*Larry P. v. Wilson Riles*) and Mississippi (*Mattie T. et al. v. Charles E. Holliday et al.*) highly publicized the extent of the problem, although an important but less well-known study by the Massachusetts Advocacy Center (1978) preceded the resolution of the infamous litigation. Officials with the New Jersey State Department of Education, reacting to the legal issues above, researched—as education officials in other states probably did as well—NJ's status and had the courage to document and distribute their findings (Manni, Winikur, & Keller, 1980). The NJ situation, of which I am most familiar, turned out to be rather serious, as is well-explained below in an article from the popular press.

Although there are four times as many white children as blacks in New Jersey's schools, black children are four times more likely to be placed in classes for mildly retarded students. New Jersey officials, in announcing plans Friday to eliminate the disproportionate racial imbalance in special education programs, also said Hispanic children are three times more likely than whites to be assigned to the special classes. The placement of as many as 5,500 of the more than 10,000 children who have been labeled as "educable mentally retarded" has been questioned. Public Advocate Stanley Van Ness and Education Commissioner Fred Burke said a recent analysis of students classified as "educationally handicapped" will serve as a guide for correcting placement practices in more than 600 school districts. The analysis was made by a task force of representatives of both departments. Van Ness said placement disparities for the mentally retarded were largely the result of reliance by school districts on I.Q. tests which have been ruled discriminatory by the federal courts. ("Racial Balance Eyed," 1981, p. A3) [See also Appendix B, this book.]

To avoid legal problems, guidelines for the EMR classification have been revised—the major changes being a lowered IQ cutoff point (often going from 77 to 69 in most states) and the consideration of "adaptive" social functioning in addition to IQ. As a result of this, both the total number and the percentage of minority students classified as EMR have decreased sharply (U.S. Office of Special Education, 1987).

School battles were fought in the courtroom successfully in the late 1970s and early 1980s which curtailed the use of the EMR label with all its negative self-image and economic ramifications for students. Even earlier, as a result of federal legislation from the impetus of previous litigation, some less restrictive special educational programming was available (Sigmon, 1983a). We must not, however, grow complacent in the glory of previous victories for there is a new education war that could burst forth with fury in the near future (see McKnight, 1982). Many of those children formerly classified as EMR are now considered in some quarters to have "specific learning disabilities," and are being labeled as such (U.S. Office of Special Education, 1987). So instead of having a pervasive mild cognitive problem, a child's learning difficulty is often seen as being in one or more specific areas by many educational diagnosticians—primarily those trained in the learning disabilities orientation over the past decade or two. The rationale for the alleged mild educational handicapping condition has changed, but it is still supposedly caused from something within the child who gets blamed for what usually is a societal or school finance problem—in terms of remedial program funding (Sigmon, 1984). This is not meant to be construed that there are no learning disabilities of actual neurological genesis—these do exist. What we must be skeptical of is the increasing number of American schoolchildren who are now formally classified as having specific learning disabilities which was 1,847,591 as of the 1985-86 schoolyear (U.S. Office of Special Education, 1987). The implications, of course, are not necessarily better for the minority child despite the more palatable label (Collins & Camblin, 1983).

Whatever the special education rubric used or the educational status derived, tests administered to "scientifically" substantiate labels will almost always be unfair to the socioeconomically depressed child, regardless of his/her race or ethnicity; and no matter how culturally fair the test appears (Sigmon, 1983b). Johnson (1969) earlier warned us about the "emotionally disturbed" and "socially maladjusted" labels for "inner city" students. Schools act as a sorting mechanism and have not served as the "great social equalizer" because of unequal opportunity both before and upon finishing one's education. "The relationship of measured intelligence to socio-economic level is one of the best documented findings in mental-test history" (Tyler, 1965, p. 336). Make no mistake, whether looking at global IQ scores, specific school-related learning (dis)abilities, or "college readiness tests" (my phrase for college aptitude examinations), the culturally different minorities who are often socioeconomically depressed in racist American society and the white poor will *always* fare worse as a group when compared to more affluent students. Perhaps nothing could more dramatically point up the role of the school as a social sieve than to examine some figures about the Scholastic Aptitude Test (SAT). The SAT is administered by a company known as the Educational Testing Service and is the most widely used American college admissions test. Table 1 is adapted from a booklet by The College Entrance Examination Board (1974).

Table 1[1]
Parental Annual Income by SAT Average
for 647,031 (1973–4) Respondents[2]

Students' SAT Scores	Students' Mean Family Incomes
750–800	$24,124
700–749	21,980
650–699	21,292
600–649	20,330
550–599	19,481
500–549	18,824
450–499	18,122
400–449	17,387
350–399	16,182
300–349	14,355
250–299	11,428
200–249	8,639
Total Mean Score: 462	Total Mean Income: $17,563

[1] Adapted from The College Entrance Examination Board (1974), Table 21, p. 27; and very similar to a table in de Lone (1979), p. 102.

[2] This table is derived from the students (647,031) who responded to the optional parent annual income question on the SAT application form. Registered for this test were 1,045,273; while 985,247 students actually took it during the 1973–4 schoolyear.

The SAT score is strongly considered by various colleges to whom the pupil seeks admission, and acceptance is often dependent upon the SAT cutoff point established by the particular college. Based on the figures in Table 1, one would need only know a high school senior's family income range to predict with a high level of confidence the probable test outcome. This most clearly is a blatant case of social class bias.

Social Inequality: Myths and Reality

In order to fully understand social inequality, the concepts of social class and stratification need to be analyzed—the latter first. Social stratification implies the existence of social inequality and a hierarchy of societal levels, e.g., social classes. Blumberg (1972) points out that in America there are two pervasive but powerful myths that go side by side: American society is classless, and that if persons have talent and determination they can get to the top. These myths persist despite the fact that they are patently contradictory, for if there is no hierarchy of classes, then there is obviously nothing to get to the top of. Karl Marx was instrumental in pointing out the importance of social classes when studying societies more than 125 years ago. Max Weber discussed stratification in terms of status, power, and class around the turn of the century, emphasizing that class affects one's "life chances in the marketplace." If one believes that America is a land of "equal opportunity" and "free enterprise" (this writer and probably most serious students of our society believe that both are myths), then hard work plus intelligence and some luck should be all it takes "to make it big in America," and that those who fail are lazy, stupid, and probably constitutionally defective because of heredity. There are numerous but evasive opportunities for many but not all. Free enterprise is only for those with the capital. The financial success of a few extraordinarily talented individuals reinforces the myth of the "American dream." This author also believes America is a "closed-class system." Yet simultaneously there appears to be an "open-class ideology" in operation which helps maintain the superstructure of the American system. If a society were really open there would be vertical social mobility between social classes.

Besides the American dream myth, the notion of freedom keeps a closed American society going. Although there are constraints on freedom to Americans, it definitely exists here. However, economic freedom is ultimately more important than political freedom in the USA. Even though every person has only one vote despite one's wealth, it is the wealthy and therefore the powerful who present the limited political choices in terms of which politician/candidates are chosen and what issues are voted upon. Briefly, in America there is limited political freedom and less economic freedom.

The British sociologist Basil Bernstein (1960) has developed a theory of language dealing with "linguistic differences [which he refers to as "codes"], other than dialect," that are transmitted via social class. Bernstein's theory is obviously biased in favor of the middle-class and is another explanation of why these schoolchildren do better in school than those of the "lower working class." He wrote:

> It is suggested that the typical, dominant speech mode of the middle class is one where speech becomes an object of special perceptual activity and a 'theoretical attitude' is developed towards the structural possibilities of sentence organization. This speech mode facilitates the verbal elaboration of subjective intent, sensitivity to the implications of separateness and difference, and points to the possibilities inherent in a complex conceptual hierarchy for the organization of experience. It is further suggested that this is not the case for members of the lower working class. The latter are limited to a form of language-use which although allowing for a vast range of possibilities, provides a speech form which discourages the speaker from verbally elaborating subjective intent and progressively orients the user to descriptive, rather than abstract, concepts. (p. 271)

Bernstein's notion about working-class linguistic differences is based upon his British experience. This author believes that even if his position were true in England—which is doubtful—it surely is not valid in America because: (a) the form of the language used does not indicate an inability to think in the abstract regardless of what biased "measures" he provides as proof; (b) his arguments are really grounded more in social acceptability than anything else; and, (c) the flexibility, adaptability, and creativity of the poor or minority oral language later become incorporated into mainstream speech as an acceptable idiom and eventually into literary form. Offered, for example, is the phrase "rip-off." Bernstein's theory is functional at best, and Entwisle (1970) found:

> contrary to expectation, that slum children are apparently more advanced linguistically than suburban children at first grade. . . . The superiority is short-lived, however, for by third grade, suburban children, whether blue collar or upper middle class, have surpassed the inner city children. (p. 14)

Taking the viewpoint that school is geared today more toward suburban/middle-class children, this is not surprising. The problem of language for black minority students, for example, is nicely explained through an understanding of "Ebonics" (Williams, 1975) which the reader should see for further explication of this topic.

Some writers have proclaimed that social class differences are diminishing and social class is no longer a useful concept in the analysis of American society (Nisbet, 1959), or that Western societies are becoming increasingly classless (Goldthorpe, Lockwood, Bechhofer, & Platt, 1967); but Blumberg (1972) contends these authors gloss over some important areas and that inequalities which remain are significant enough so that social class continues to be one of the most powerful analytical instruments available to the sociologist.

Perhaps even more important than social class per se for studying educational problems is the contemporary concept known as socioeconomic status (SES). The following passage taken from Boocock (1980) explains why SES is perhaps the key concept when looking at variables that affect schooling.

> The family characteristic that is the most powerful predictor of school performance is socioeconomic status (SES): the higher the SES of the student's family, the higher his or her academic achievement. This relationship has been documented in countless studies and seems to hold no matter what measure of status is used (for example, occupation of principal breadwinner, family income, parents' education, or some combination of these). It

holds with a variety of achievement/aspiration variables, including grades, achievement test scores, retentions at grade level, course failures, truancy, suspension from school, dropout rates, college plans, and total amount of formal schooling. It also predicts academic honors and awards, elective school offices, extent of participation in extracurricular activities, and other indicators of "success" in the informal structure of the student society. It holds, moreover, even when the powerful variables of ability and past achievement are controlled. Finally, the relationship between family SES and academic achievement has been found in virtually every Western society for which empirical evidence is available. (p. 40)

Richard de Lone (1979) further accentuates this while looking more specifically at chances for higher education.

School performance—grades and test scores—substantially correlate with the SES of a student's family . . . . The higher the student's social status, the higher the probability that he or she will get high grades. Similarly, the higher the grades and test scores, the more likely an individual from any SES is to get more schooling. (p. 102)

Mr. de Lone credits Jencks et al. (1972) with the idea that higher education admits students on the basis of grades and test scores and in part because those who do well in school develop a taste for more schooling.

Conclusion

Professionals working in the schools must expect to see poor children as a group score lower on tests with national norms. More leeway has to be accorded a lower SES child before placement into a slow track, a retarded class, or a program for the learning disabled is considered. Hence, local norms are necessary and no school test instrument is valid without competent interpretation, especially in the area of knowing where certain tests have built-in biases and for whom (see Williams, 1972).

The educational community needs to ensure that children have developed learning strategies before they are expected to develop subject or task proficiency. Because it is a well-documented fact that poor children lag behind the more affluent academically (and this writer believes it is not because of intelligence), they are, among other things, probably less well-prepared. Bloom (1980) talks about "cognitive entry characteristics." He says these are the specific knowledge, abilities, or skills that are essential prerequisites for the learning of a particular school subject or a particular learning task. It is important that someone so influential as Bloom should emphasize this; but these prerequisites have for years been called study or readiness skills. Boocock (1980) directly addresses the issue of the middle-class having what I call the "mental tools" and preparedness for school.

> The middle-class family is usually better able to provide the books, play materials, trips to zoos and farms, and other stimuli that prepare them for the student role, and they may even provide coaching in school related skills and tasks. (p. 77)

Society as a whole is the major problem with education, not the methods used or the tests administered. The problem is situational. How can a child who lives in squalor be expected to care about school? How can even a master teacher motivate a classroom of students who cannot foresee any personal future benefits from formal education? Band-aid measures of social reform have not really helped to improve educational opportunity or decrease the number of socially disenfranchised poor over the past 150 years in America (de Lone, 1979). Bowles and Gintis (1976) contend that more revolutionary change of the entire social order in the form of a redistribution of wealth is necessary before any real improvements can be made. There are many inequities within our society that need changing. Institutions which are unjust must be changed. Institutions have a way of perpetuating themselves, and changing them will improve society. Nothing will have as great a positive influence on child development as better living conditions, which requires changing the social structure itself. When this happens, educational performance in general and test taking "ability" in particular will improve. This change must be done through politics.

It is within the complex arena of schooling where the intricacies of the closed American society are most telling. A major aspiration of the poor is that their progeny should have better lives than themselves, and their hopes for this rest in the educational institutions. Yet there are a number of contemporary social critics who claim research shows that: the quality of schooling per se is not an effective means of equalizing income (Jencks et al., 1972); socioeconomic status more than anything else most clearly predicts school success plus years of schooling (Boocock, 1980); the type of schooling a student receives is determined by social class (Jencks & Riesman, 1968); and more prestigious schooling goes to high SES students who in turn get the more desired credentials that schools offer (Lasch, 1975)—all combining to perpetuate the closed system.

The public schools teach that royalty does not exist in America. Also taught is that America is a land of freedom and opportunity, which is true to some extent. America is, however, a closed society with stratified social classes, and this fact is rarely a part of the public school curriculum. It is true that the more wealth one has in America the more comfortably one can live and the more freedom one gains—this is a well-recognized fact. Most poor parents do realize the difficulty for their offspring to gain admittance to prestigious professional schools, such as for medicine, but I doubt that they realize just how minuscule their youngsters' chances really are—as was poignantly demonstrated via Table 1.

Because the present educational system has not opened American society, either a massive restructuring of the educational system or a tremendous boost in income for the poor seems necessary (de Lone, 1979). Either way it requires a redistribution of wealth away from those who currently are rich to those who are not. The problem, though, is that those affluent persons who are in the best positions to do this would not want to do it. They must be persuaded to do so, and by so doing will make Grier and Cobbs' (1968) words from their chapter entitled "The promise of education" for all American students less depressing:

> But the black man who has breached so many barriers to achieve academic success must at this writing realize that further doors are open to all save him. His is a blind alley. His achievements are circumscribed by the same impediments of discrimination as are those of his less gifted brother. (pp. 149-150)

Chapter 2

Learning Disabilities:
The Social Construction of a Special
Education Category*

Christine E. Sleeter

This chapter reinterprets the history of learning disabilities, situating it in the context of the movement to reform education after Sputnik. After Sputnik, standards for reading achievement were raised and students were tested more rigorously and grouped for instruction based on achievement level. Students unable to keep up with raised standards were placed into one of five categories. Four of the categories were used primarily to explain the failures of lower class and minority children; learning disabilities was created to explain the failures of white middle class children in a way that gave them some protection from the stigma of failure. Events during the late 1960s and early 1970s prompted a shift in the use of the category of learning disabilities, and subsequently in the category's membership. Implications of this reinterpretation for today's education reform movement are suggested.

Current reports of education reform advocate that schools raise standards for achievement and test students according to those standards more regularly and more rigorously. For example, *A Nation at Risk* (National Commission on Excellence in Education, 1983) recommends that "schools, colleges, and universities adopt more rigorous and measurable standards, and higher expectations,

---

*This chapter first appeared in *Exceptional Children* (1986), Vol. 53, No. 1, pp. 46–54. Copyright © 1986 The Council for Exceptional Children.

22   CRITICAL VOICES ON SPECIAL EDUCATION

for academic performance and student conduct" (p. 27). It goes on to advocate that "standardized tests of achievement . . . should be administered at major transition points from one level of schooling to another" (p.28). Similarly, *Action for Excellence* (Task Force on Education for Economic Growth, 1983) recommends that we "raise both the floor and the ceiling of achievement in America" (p. 18).

These reports have been criticized for their failure to address substantively the needs of handicapped students. For example, the CEC Ad Hoc Committee to Study and Respond to the 1983 Report of the National Commission on Excellence in Education (1984) applauded *A Nation at Risk* for its "efforts to improve curricula and methods to assess the acquisition of required skills and knowledge" (p. 488) but criticized it for its failure to address the diverse capabilities and needs of students. The Committee noted that special education has expanded over the past several decades and advocated its continuing development and provision of services. Implicitly, the CEC reply accepted existing categories of exceptionality and saw reform attempts as delinquent mainly in their failure to address the needs of students who occupy or should occupy those categories. In this chapter it will be argued that the problem in today's reform movement is more than merely overlooking those who are handicapped. Rather, reforms such as those just cited help create handicapped children, and the main category for which this has been true historically is learning disabilities.

Many educators suggest that learning disabilities always has been and continues to be an ill-defined special education category. A full twenty years after the founding of the Association for Children with Learning Disabilities (ACLD), the 1983 *Annual Review of Learning Disabilities* featured a series of articles by prominent scholars in the field still debating its definition and criteria for identification. Recently Ysseldyke, Algozzine, Shinn, and McGue (1982) found little difference between students classified as learning disabled (LD) and non-LD low-achievers on several psychometric tests commonly used to classify students as LD. They concluded that "we must begin to evaluate very carefully the purposes and needs being served by identifying certain students as LD while not identifying others (who are very much their twins)" (p. 84).

Why did the category come about in the first place, and whose interests has it served? This chapter addresses these questions by briefly critiquing the prevailing interpretation of why the category emerged when it did and who it has served, and then by showing that learning disabilities is in part an artifact of past school reform efforts that have escalated standards for literacy. In so doing, this chapter shows the implications of the emergence of the LD category during the early 1960s for debates about school reform in the 1980s.

Prevailing Interpretation of the Emergence of LD

To investigate how the history of the LD field is usually interpreted, I examined fifteen learning disabilities textbooks published between 1980 and 1985 in the U.S. Textbooks were examined because they typically present the field's history in a manner conventionally accepted by professionals in the field. (Several authors drew on the interpretation of the field's history offered by J. L. Wiederholt, "Historical perspectives on the education of the learning disabled," in L. Mann & D. Sabatino [Eds.], *The Second Review of Special Education*; Philadelphia: Journal of Special Education Press, 1974.) The average learning disabilities textbook, which was 403 pages long, devoted 10 pages to explaining how and why the field emerged when it did (range = 6-34 pages). Five did not discuss its history. (See end of reference section for complete list of textbooks reviewed.)

The LD field usually is presented as having developed on the basis of medical research beginning in the 1800s. This research documented links between brain damage and subsequent behavior. More recent advances in our understanding of learning disabilities are presented as having been made by psychologists, neurologists, and physicians studying children who displayed difficulties acquiring language and reading skills, and by educators who experimented with methods for teaching them. These children were believed to have suffered minimal brain dysfunction. Once sufficient research had been conducted and publicized, parents, educators, and physicians began to organize and press for appropriate educational services. Since then, schools have with growing vigor developed and provided these services.

The ideology underlying this interpretation is that schools, supported by medical and psychological research, are involved in a historic pattern of progress. Problems that have always existed are one by one being discovered, researched, and solved. Learning disabilities is essentially a medical problem; it is thought to reside within the child. Progress is brought about mainly by individual thinkers involved in medical and psychological research, and at times by pressure groups who use that research to advance the interests of the underdogs. Once alerted to problems, the American public tends to support their amelioration, and the main beneficiaries are those whose needs are finally recognized and met.

Missing from this interpretation is much analysis of the social context that created conditions favorable to the category's emergence. A sizable body of literature outside special education links school structures and processes with needs of dominant economic and political groups in society (e.g., Apple, 1981; Spring, 1976). This literature suggests that changes in schools are instituted mainly to serve more efficiently existing social and economic structures, although changes may also offer some benefit to students whom schools had previously disserved most. One school structure this literature has examined, which is closely related to special education, is tracking.

While many people see tracking as a way of homogenizing students in classrooms so teachers can teach them better, research studies have found that lower track students consistently fare worse than their nontracked counterparts (Persell, 1977) and rarely achieve upward mobility (Rosenbaum, 1976). Furthermore, those in the upper track are disproportionately from white middle class backgrounds; lower track students disproportionately represent minority and lower social class backgrounds (Shafer & Olexa, 1971). This literature argues that tracking is widely practiced largely for the purpose of sorting and preparing students for a stratified labor market: Students are rank-ordered and classified for instruction such that those from advantaged social groups tend to be prepared for the better jobs, while those from disadvantaged backgrounds tend to be channeled into low pay, low status work.

With a few exceptions (e.g., Coles, 1978; Farber, 1968; Sarason & Doris, 1979; Ysseldyke & Algozzine, 1982), special education usually is *not* examined with relationship to social competition for power, wealth, and prestige. Rather, it usually is presented as a school structure instituted solely to benefit students unable to profit from school because of handicapping conditions. The textbook interpretation of the emergence of learning disabilities is an example. While there is merit to this interpretation for children with obvious handicaps (e.g., severely retarded and physically impaired), it must be questioned for children whose handicaps are not obvious. The remainder of this chapter does that.

Schooling in the Late 1950s and Early 1960s

Learning disabilities was officially founded with the birth of ACLD in 1963. Learning disabled children suffer chiefly from an inability to achieve certain standards for literacy. These standards have changed historically as requirements of the American economy and the race for international supremacy have changed. Let us examine how the raising of reading standards, coupled with social expectations that schools help America's cold war effort and also sort students for future work roles in a stratified economy, led to the creation of learning disabilities.

Before the twentieth century, most information could be exchanged face to face and records were relatively simple. At that time, children with reading difficulties did not present a great social problem because most Americans did not need to be able to acquire new information through reading. Industrial expansion escalated literacy standards, requiring more and more people who could keep and understand increasingly complex records, pursue advanced professional training, and follow written directions in the workplace. As literacy standards in society escalated, schools responded by emphasizing reading more and by expecting students to attain increasingly higher levels of literacy (Chall, 1983; Resnick & Resnick, 1977).

Before the 1980s, the most recent major escalation of reading standards followed the Soviet Union's launching of Sputnik in 1957. Americans reacted to Sputnik by charging schools with failing to produce scientists and technicians needed for the U.S. to remain ahead internationally in technological development. This charge was widely publicized in numerous popular magazines (e.g., *Good Housekeeping, Time*). American schools were compared with Russian schools and found deficient. The chief problem, critics believed, was lax standards. For example, in March of 1958, *Life* magazine compared the schooling of two boys; one in Moscow and one in Chicago. It reported that in the Soviet Union, "The laggards are forced out [of school] by tough periodic examinations and shunted to less demanding trade schools and apprenticeships. Only a third—1.4 million in 1957—survive all 10 years and finish the course" ("School Boys," p. 27). In contrast, American students lounge in classrooms that are "relaxed and enlivened by banter," and in which the "intellectual application expected of [students] is moderate" (p. 33).

Recommendations for reforming American education included (a) toughening elementary reading instruction (Trace, 1961); (b) introducing uniform standards for promotion and graduation and testing students' mastery of those standards through a regular, nation-wide examination system ("Back to the 3 R's?," 1957; "What Went Wrong," 1958); (c) grouping students by ability so the bright students can move more quickly through school and then go on to college and professional careers, while the slower students move into unskilled or semi-skilled labor ("Famous Educator's Plan," 1958; "Harder Work for Students," 1961; Woodring, 1957); and (d) assigning the most intellectually capable teachers to the top group of students (Rickover, 1957). To some extent, all these reforms were implemented in the late 1950s and early 1960s.

In reading, elementary textbooks were toughened and some tests were renormed. Chall (1977) analyzed the readability levels of widely used textbooks published between 1930 and 1973. She found elementary readers to offer progressively less challenge from 1944 until 1962; in 1962 first grade readers appearing on the market were more difficult, a trend that continued into the 1970s. There is also evidence that some widely used achievement tests were renormed shortly after Sputnik to reflect escalated standards for literacy. The 1958 version of the Metropolitan Achievement Tests were renormed in 1964; the new norms reflected average reading levels 2 to 13 months higher for students in grades 2 through 9 (no gain was found for first grade) (Special Report No. 7, 1971). Similarly, the 1957 version of the Iowa Tests of Basic Skills was renormed in 1964. Hieronymus and Lindquist (1974) reported that the average gain in reading was 1.9 months at the 90th percentile, 2.6 months at the 50th, and 1.0 months at the 10th.

Many children were unable to keep up, but few blamed the raising of standards. Instead, students who scored low on reading achievement tests were personally blamed for their failure. By the early 1960s, children who failed in reading were divided into five categories, differentiated by whether the cause of the problem was presumed to be organic, emotional, or environmental, and whether the child was deemed intellectually normal or subnormal. They were called slow learners, mentally retarded, emotionally disturbed, culturally deprived, and learning disabled.

Slow learners and the mentally retarded were distinguished mainly on the basis of IQ: Those scoring between 75 and 90 were considered slow learners, and those scoring below were considered retarded. Both categories included disproportionate numbers of low-income children and children of color. As adults, slow learners were expected to occupy semi-skilled and unskilled occupations, and retarded individuals were expected to occupy unskilled occupations or work in sheltered workshops (Goldstein, 1962). The emotionally disturbed also included large numbers from low-income backgrounds (Dunn, 1963). A subcategory was the "socially maladjusted," who were concentrated in Black, Puerto Rican, and immigrant neighborhoods (Shaw & McKay, 1942). A fourth category, which overlapped considerably with the previous three, was referred to as the culturally deprived. The National Conference on Education and Cultural Deprivation held in 1964 identified them as Puerto Ricans, Mexicans, southern Blacks and whites who moved to urban areas, and the poor already living in inner cities and rural areas (Bloom, Davis, & Hess, 1965). They were believed severely handicapped by home environments that lacked environmental stimuli; systematic ordering of stimuli sequences; language training; and training in the value of intellectual work, delayed gratification, individuality, and the belief that hard work brings success (e.g., Deutsch, 1963; Riessman, 1962).

A fifth category came to be known as the learning disabled. Of the five categories, this is the only one for which descriptions of the kinds of neighborhoods most likely to produce them were virtually absent from literature. The closest statement one finds is that they are essentially "normal" or come from "normal family stock" (Strauss & Lehtinen, 1947, p. 112), whatever that means. (Strauss and Lehtinen, reknown pioneers in the learning disabilities research, reported twelve case studies that give some indication of what "normal family stock" meant to them. Of the eight whose race was specified, all were white, and of the four whose race was not specified, two were of "above average" social standing or home environment. No data were given for the other two.)

The cause of LD reading retardation was believed to be organic. Hypothesized causes included minimal brain damage (e.g., Strauss & Kephart, 1955), a maturational lag in general neurological development (e.g., Bender, 1957; Rabinovitch, 1962), a failure of the brain to establish cerebral dominance (Orton, 1937), or a failure to achieve certain stages of neurological development (Delacato, 1959).

Who Was Classified as Learning Disabled?

National-level statistics were not collected on the student composition of LD classes until the late 1970s. While the category was in name open to children of any background, I suspected it would be populated by a select group during the early years of its existence. To estimate the student composition of LD classes, I examined descriptions of samples of LD students used in research studies published between 1963 and 1973 in the *Journal of Learning Disabilities, Exceptional Children,* and the *Journal of Special Education.* To be included in my analysis, the study had to specify either that sample students were in LD classes, were identified by the school district as learning disabled although they may not yet have been assigned to LD classes, attended a private clinic for LD students, or attended a private reading clinic and were suspected by the clinic or the researcher as being learning disabled. Not included were samples of low achievers in general, retarded readers in general, or samples from programs that combined LD students with students in other special education categories.

A total of 61 studies with LD samples were located. Of these, twelve reported the racial composition of their samples; this made a total of 460 subjects whose race was known. These subjects were overwhelmingly white: 98.5% were white, only 1.5% were of color. In ten of the twelve studies, samples were all white. Sixteen studies reported the social class composition of their samples, totaling 588 subjects whose social class background was known. There was more balance with respect to social class than race: 69% of the subjects were middle class or higher, 31% were lower middle class or lower. Of the sixteen studies, twelve had samples that were at least 90% middle class or above.

The literature offers additional evidence that students in LD classes were overwhelmingly white and middle class during the category's first ten years. White and Charry (1966) studied characteristics of children in special programs in Westchester County, New York, and found those labeled "brain damaged" to have no significant IQ or achievement differences from those labeled "culturally deprived," but to be from significantly higher social class backgrounds. Franks (1971) surveyed Missouri school districts that received state reimbursement for LD and educable mentally retarded (EMR) services during school year 1969-1970. He found the LD classes to be almost 97% white and 3% Black, while the EMR classes were only 66% white and 34% Black. Furthermore, the professional literature during the 1960s and early 1970s discussed failing children of the white middle class and those of lower class and minority families as if they were distinct. For example, volumes 1 and 3 of the *Journal of Learning Disabilities* (1968, 1970) contained twelve articles about culturally "deprived" or "disadvantaged" children. Most of these reported studies; none of the subjects were reported to be in LD classes (many were in Head Start programs), and only two authors suggested they could or should be (Grotberg, 1970; Tarnopol, 1970).

The learning disabilities category probably was not consciously established just for white middle class children, even though it was populated mainly by them. It was established for children who, given the prevailing categories used to describe failing children, did not seem to fit any other category. Since most educators explained the failures of children of color and lower socioeconomic backgrounds with reference to the other four categories, such children tended not to have been placed in LD classes. White middle class parents and educators who saw their failing children as different from poor or minority children pressed for the creation and use of this category. By defining the category in terms of organic causality and IQ score, the white middle class preserved for itself some benefits.

First, the use of IQ to help distinguish LD students from other categories of failing children suggested its members "really" belonged in the middle or upper tracks or ability groups. As proponents of tracking during the late 1950s clearly pointed out, students were to be sorted for differentiated education based on ability, and members of each track were destined to hold different kinds of jobs in the labor market (e.g., Woodring, 1957). White children tend to score about 15 points higher on IQ tests than children of color, ensuring a greater likelihood that they would be seen as intellectually "normal" and thus potentially able to fill higher status positions. The intent of defining the category partly on the basis of IQ score was probably not to disadvantage the "disadvantaged" further, but to provide failing children whom educators saw as intellectually normal their best chance for moving ahead as rapidly and as far as possible.

Second, distinguishing between environmental and organic causes of failure helped legitimate the "superiority" of white middle class culture. The literature during the early 1960s contains much about the failings of low-income homes, and especially those of people of color. For example, readers of *Saturday Review* in 1962 were told that "slow learners appear most frequently in groups whose home environment affords restricted opportunity for intellectual development" ("Slow Learners," p. 53), and that "culturally deprived children" learn "ways of living [that] are not attuned to the spirit and practice of modern life" ("Education and the Disadvantaged American," p. 58). One does not find similar condemnations of the average white middle class home. If one were to accept such homes as normal, organic explanations for failure would seem plausible. One must view this as peculiar, since the main proponents of raising school standards to help America retain economic and political international supremacy were members of the white middle class. Yet rather than questioning the culture that viewed children as raw material for international competition, most educators questioned the organic integrity of members of that culture who could not meet the higher demands.

Third, some viewed minimal brain dysfunction as an organic deficiency that could potentially be cured in the same way diseases can be cured. The cure was hypothesized as involving the training of healthy brain cells to take over functions of damaged cells (e.g., Cruickshank et al., 1961; Frostig & Horne, 1964; Strauss & Lehtinen, 1947), the promoting of overall neurological development (e.g., Doman, Delacato, & Doman, 1964), the training of the brain to assume greater hemispheric dominance (Orton, 1937), or the altering of chemical balances through diet or drugs (e.g., Feingold, 1975; Sroufe & Stewart, 1973). Professionals may have cautioned against over-optimism, but the popular press did not. For example, in 1959, *Newsweek* readers were told about "Johnnies" with "very high IQ's" who can't read due to inherited neurological conditions. These "Johnnies" were described as educationally treatable using the Gillingham reading method; "Of the 79 Parker students taught under the method so far, 96 per cent have become average or above average readers" ("Learning to Read," p. 110). In 1964, *Reader's Digest* provided case descriptions of children who were brain-injured at birth and experienced difficulty learning language, physical movements, and reading. A new program for motor development by Delacato and the Doman brothers was reported to "activate the millions of surviving [brain] cells to take over the functions of the dead ones" (Maisel, 1964, p. 137). Prognosis was reported excellent, and readers were told that it even helped affected children learn to read.

Probably due to these optimistic perceptions, students in LD classes seem to have suffered lesser negative teacher attitudes than other categories of failing students. Research studies have found that regular teachers see the LD student as less different from the "norm" than the ED or EMR student, and as demanding less of their time and patience (Moore & Fine, 1978; Shotel, Iano, & McGettigan, 1972; Williams & Algozzine, 1979), even when they observe behavior that contradicts their expectations for the label (Foster & Ysseldyke, 1976; Salvia, Clark, & Ysseldyke, 1973; Ysseldyke & Foster, 1978). Studies have not compared teacher attitudes toward LD and "culturally deprived" students, but there is evidence that teachers have more negative attitudes toward and lower expectation of children of color and lower class children than white or middle class children (e.g., Anyon, 1981; Jackson & Cosca, 1974; Rist, 1970).

Whether teacher attitudes toward various categories of exceptionality actually affected how students were taught in school has not been reported in the literature. However, there is evidence from outside special education that teacher attitudes toward children based on social class or presumed intellectual ability do affect the quality and amount of instruction they give (e.g., Brookover et al., 1979; Rosenthal & Jacobson, 1968; Rist, 1970). Thus, it is reasonable to assume that teachers gave more and better instruction to low-achieving students labeled as learning disabled than to low-achieving students bearing other labels, even if actual behavioral differences among such students would not in itself warrant differential treatment.

Learning Disabilities in the 1970s

Since the early 1970s, there has been a shift in who has been classified as learning disabled and how the category has been used politically. That shift was propelled by a decline in the late 1960s in school standards for achievement, the civil rights movement and subsequent school responses, and a redefinition of mental retardation.

Although standards for school achievement were raised immediately after Sputnik, student test scores have caused many to believe standards were not maintained, for a variety of reasons (Goodlad, 1984). Declines in SAT scores, beginning in about 1966, have been widely publicized, and some state achievement tests also have shown declines (Boyer, 1983). One would think that if standards for achievement dropped during the late 1960s, fewer students would have been seen as failures and interest in classifying students as learning disabled would have waned. What happened was the reverse, due to other social developments.

During the late 1960s and early 1970s, minority groups pressured schools to discard the notion of cultural deprivation and stop classifying disproportionate numbers of minority children as mentally retarded. In 1973, the category of mental retardation was redefined, lowering the maximum IQ score from one standard deviation below the mean to two (Grossman, 1973), which dissolved the category of slow learner. The intent of these moves was to pressure schools to teach a wider diversity of students more effectively. Instead, many students who previously were or would have been classified as retarded, slow, or culturally deprived were now classified as learning disabled.

For example, based on a study of the racial composition of LD and MR classes in over 50 school districts between 1970 and 1977, Tucker (1980) found Black students overrepresented in MR classes but underrepresented in LD classes until 1972. After 1972, the proportion of the total school population in MR classes declined and Blacks lost some overrepresentation in that category, but they rapidly gained representation in LD classes, where they were over-represented by 1974. Thus, even though pressure may have sub-sided during the late 1960s and early 1970s to provide a protected placement for failing white middle class children, learning disabilities has been used increasingly as a more palatable substitute for other categories to " explain" the failure of lower class children and children of color.

Learning Disabilities and Today's Reform Movement

In the 1980s, educators and the public are again viewing children as raw material for international competition, very much like during the late 1950s. Standards for achievement are again seen as too low, and schools are again being called upon to raise standards for reading, math, science, and computer literacy, and to test students more rigorously based on those raised standards. What will be done with those who do not measure up to the new standards? When standards were raised previously, failing children were defined as handicapped and segregated. Learning disabilities was created to explain the failure of children from advantaged social groups, and to do so in such a way that it suggested their eventual ability to attain relatively higher status occupations than other low achievers.

Schools need to focus much greater attention on how to teach children rather than on how to categorize those who do not learn well when offered "business-as-usual." But it is not enough to search for better ways to remediate those who have the greatest difficulty achieving standards for school success *as long as* society still expects schools to produce "products" with certain kinds of skills developed to certain levels of competence, and to rank-order those "products" based on their achievement of those skills. Those who come out on the bottom will still be destined for the lowest paying jobs or the reserve labor force and will still experience the pain of failure when compared to their peers. And members of advantaged social groups will still advocate treating their failing children in ways that maintain their advantaged status as much as possible. We need to shift our perspective from the failings of individuals or the inefficiencies of schools to the social context of schooling. Rather than attempting to remake children to fit social needs, we must first give greater consideration to the possibility that society's expectations for children and society's reward structure for their performance may need remaking.

Chapter 3

Foundations of Education and the Mildly Learning Disabled: Toward a New Understanding*

Scott B. Sigmon

The purpose of this chapter is to deliberately expand the explanation of why students are considered learning disabled. Although the main focus is formally on mildly learning disabled students, the categories of mild mental retardation and emotional disturbance are discussed as well. The foundations of education literature, e.g., social, philosophic, etc., can help provide a better understanding of the relationship between schooling and culture. With the new, radical perspective—radical connotes root or basic elements—that has recently emerged from the foundations field, an even wider vision of schooling is possible through radical analysis of cultural transmission. The development and method of this new root perspective are discussed. Only infrequently have learning disabilities (LD) or special education been viewed from a radical perspective. An example of the new perspective applied to special education is given. The position taken here is that LD—conceived originally to indicate difficulty learning due to neurologic dysfunction—has become a means for instituting a form of social control.

Overview

It is extraordinary that a notion so diffuse as "learning disability" (LD) has become the major focus of contemporary special

---

*This chapter, as revised in 1987, is available from the U.S. Department of Education (ERIC Document Reproduction Service No. ED 298 687).

35

education in such a relatively short period of time. LD, as recently conventionally defined by the U.S. government, is an amalgam of any number of dysfunctional psychological processes within an individual. The current interest in LD brought special education together in many ways, and simultaneously divided it. It might not be too strong an analogy to suggest that what organized religion did to humanity as a whole, LD has done to special education of late. Obviously, the support of a position such as this requires an argument different from the functional or empirical approach generally found within the social and behavioral sciences. The functional paradigm tends to be a justification of the status quo while the quantitative empirical method provides little real understanding of larger social phenomena. Therefore, we must step out of the more common modes of inquiry and, in a sense, look at the historical, social, and psychological foundations of LD to understand this phenomenon in a new way.

Certain premises must be spelled out before proceeding. The position taken here is that serious learning disabilities in small numbers do exist and require special attention. Therefore, their study is essential and can be used to help children learn. The problem arises, however, when the existence of a supposed psychologically based mild dysfunctional cognitive learning style or syndrome is transformed into a rationale for an educational and institutional arrangement. With this arrangement (i.e., special education schooling) established, very serious social and ethical questions arise, such as: Who should be placed within this sort of track? How is this to be determined? Will those placed there derive more educational benefit than if they remained in a regular educational program, and how can we know this? It is one thing to study a medical syndrome or personality style; it is yet quite another to set aside or make special educational arrangements for the individual student with a mild learning problem. (In short, special education policies for the learning disabled involve us in the tension and arguments that exist between what is, what could be, and what ought to be.) When we look at arrangements made to accommodate today's almost two-million classified LD students (United States Office of Special Education, 1987), we must understand that these arrangements are not neutral or logical consequences of research but rather efforts to institutionalize a social process. The latter point is of major concern here.

Earlier intense debates on special education have focused on those children classified as mildly or educable mentally retarded (EMR). Learning disability is actually the newest key category in special education, and we are now confronted with a major controversy regarding it related to the questions raised above.

The purpose here is to provide a brief introduction to the "foundations of education," but mainly to show the new direction this field has taken—and relate it to special education. This new direction, the root or "radical perspective," can help us to better understand the relationship of educational practices to the culture at large. After explaining the intent as well as the means of applying this new perspective, an example will be shown of its use with special education.

Foundations of Education and the New Method

Many professionals involved in psychology and learning disabilities know very little, if anything, about the work from a field known as the "foundations of education." The foundations of education field subsumes the areas of sociology, philosophy, history, economics, and anthropology of education in addition to curriculum development and teaching methodology. For further clarification, these subdisciplines, listed above, are in many American universities located within a foundations department of a college of education. The ideas from the foundations field find expression in such professional journals as *Educational Studies, Educational Theory, Journal of Curriculum Studies, Harvard Educational Review, Journal of Education,* etc. The foundations field ties together, in a sense, the humanities with social science and actual educational practice, and when seen in this light, we are actually dealing with what is known as educational theory.

Inasmuch as the foundations of education relate to culture, knowledge of foundations work can offer greater insight into educational problems. In this way we are provided with a wider vision of schooling. This is especially true since a relatively recent outlook in the foundations field has pointed to a new direction for the study of schooling.

Earlier work in foundations, as in other fields, followed basically a functional oriented paradigm which—according to a liberal writer—stresses:

the positive . . . essential functions of schooling in an increasingly complex and meritocratic society. Schools teach cognitive skills and cosmopolitan values in attitudes; they represent an essentially rational way of sorting and selecting talent in a society that more and more demands competence and expertise for the effective performance of occupational roles. (Hurn, 1978, p. 53)

The functional research paradigm underlies both the liberal and conservative social philosophies. The liberals believe that education is the means to reforming and improving society, and that this is a slow but beneficial process. They also believe much public (or governmental) spending should go into doing this (Gill, 1980). The conservatives, on the other hand, view education as the means to preserve existing social arrangements, but want as little government funding as possible spent in support of free public education (Brann, 1979).

It is the "radical paradigm" which "sees schools as serving the interests of elites, as reinforcing existing inequalities, and as producing attitudes that foster acceptance of this status quo" (Hurn, 1978, p. 44). This radical perspective, therefore, presents another view of the history and practice of education. The cornerstone of this radical critique is generally considered to be a book from England edited by Michael F. D. Young (1971) entitled *Knowledge and Control: New Directions for the Sociology of Education*.

The "new" sociology of education differed from the earlier sociological "functionalism" in that it did not justify existing social doctrine and practices. Knowledge had generally been viewed as being neutral, while the enterprise of education was usually often seen only as a benevolent service provided by society and the means for upward social mobility. Schooling is scrutinized differently now. Knowledge came to be viewed as a possible ideological tool to perpetuate existing cultural institutions and social relationships. When seen this way, the use of certain knowledge constitutes a "formal curriculum" which can mask a "hidden curriculum" (Giroux, 1981; Harris, 1979).

Shortly after the publication of *Knowledge and Control*, books by other new sociologists of education (Karabel & Halsey, 1977; Levitas, 1974; Sarup, 1978), radical philosophers of education

(Apple, 1979; Harris, 1979), radical economists of education (Bowles & Gintis, 1976; Sharp, 1980; Willis, 1977), and also from a radical anthropologist of education (Giroux, 1981) appeared. These volumes directly or indirectly built upon the new radical educational theory, and produced a serious, extensive body of modern literature about educational processes and cultural transmission. At the core of this new line of thought is the relationship of ideology plus social philosophy to the politico-economic system and the role played by education within it. In some of the more recent of these publications, there is criticism about a straightforward conception whereby the means of economic production, conservative curricula and/or teaching methods yield a corresponding reproduction of consciousness. The most sophisticated radical thought on education now also considers resistance theory (Giroux, 1983a, 1983b) in addition to the straightforward reproduction notion of consciousness.

All radical analysis focuses on the underlying *cultural* elements of educational processes. As such, culture is the background from which certain schooling configurations can be studied. The problem, however, is that too much so in the past the dialectical or interactive relationship between the cultural ground and educational figures has been ignored, which must naturally yield a false dichotomy. The same has been said, in various ways, about psychological theories and practices as they do not often enough relate to social realities (Fromm, 1955; Nahem, 1981; among many others).

For clarification, radical analysis is somewhat related in method to "dialectical psychology" (Buss, 1979; Riegel, 1979) and psychological interactionism (Endler & Magnusson, 1976; Pervin & Lewis, 1978; Sigmon, 1984a, 1984b) because of its stress on development and reciprocal environmental presses. Until very recently, manuscripts written from the radical perspective have had difficulty gaining acceptance in conventional psychology and education journals because the method was viewed as foreign. Conclusions drawn from a radical analysis have often gone against the grain of current practice, which threatened the status quo, and it was really only quite recently that those concerned with special education issues have turned to it seriously, and then only in small numbers.

Foundations for Radical Analysis of Special Education

Because culture entails active antagonistic relations, power struggles take place within that affect the implementation of education. These struggles pit, in combination, various social class, ideological, gender, racial, religious, and ethnic groupings against each other. For example, it took a relatively long time in the history of the United States before mass free public compulsory schooling was established. The reason it took so long to pass compulsory schooling law was due not only to racist factors, but also to social class conflict because of "the refusal of well-to-do citizens to pay taxes for the education of the poor" (Rippa, 1980, p. 70). The affluent eventually grew to believe that some education for the masses was in their best interests, but the real impetus for compulsory schooling was that schools were assigned the task of "Americanizing" great waves of Eastern and Southern European immigrants around the year 1900 (Hoffman, 1974).

There has really been very little deliberate radical analysis of special education done to date. Work by Shapiro (1980) and Tomlinson (1982) were among the first. An article by Shapiro, which is clearly a radical analysis of special education, appeared in a journal whose major audience is philosophers of education, while a more lengthy radical critique of special education by a sociologist of education was brought out in book format in the U.K. (Tomlinson)—neither have been widely disseminated within the American special education community. Tomlinson's thesis is that special educational curriculum—as with any type of education—is related to knowledge and power. Shapiro's "crossover" article is quite important because he is a radical philosopher of education concerned with problems in special education; he helps us to clearly see the connection of education to culture and how special education ties in.

> Education, as a part of the cultural "superstructure," is fundamentally a dependent institution. Nevertheless, it would be wrong to exclude it entirely from the process of social change. In reflecting the wider ideology, it contains the parameters of choice, the possibilities of change, and the definitions of reality that shape the demands, expectations, and perceptions of

individuals. In this respect, education becomes, at times, the focus for the expression of tensions and conflicts arising out of our wider social experience. The attempt at reform, in special education, or in other areas of the field, becomes the attempt to resolve issues arising not simply out of education itself, but out of the broader social domain. (p. 223)

Shapiro, in essence, was not optimistic about worthwhile change in education, regular or special, unless society, the superstructure, changes. This is the basic orthodox radical position.

Although Shapiro (1980) is correct regarding the powerful influence of the existing social superstructure on (special) educational problems, we cannot merely wait until a humane transformation of society occurs before we examine educational microprocesses. This was really the thrust of Young's (1971) work. We cannot ignore the seemingly smaller areas of (special) educational practices because they can have a significant ultimate social impact. For example, the formal current American special education population has increased by almost $2/3$ of a million in the nine years between 1977 and 1986 (U.S. Office of Special Education, 1987). The institutionalized cultural practice of placing tens of thousands of additional children into special education annually cannot be taken lightly.

Ramifications for the Mildly Learning Disabled

There are three basic models for educating the handicapped: special residential and day schools, special classes in regular schools, and partial special educational programming combined with regular classes which is known as "mainstreaming." It is best to meet all of an exceptional child's needs, but this must be done with as little stigmatization, labeling, and segregation as possible. (Obviously, the more handicapped the child, the more restrictive must be the educational setting.) Although most of today's four million-plus formally labeled "handicapped" children in America (U.S. Dept. of Education, 1987) have only a "mild impairment" (Comptroller General of the United States, 1981), this group is nonetheless subject to special segregation through all the models other than residential. Yet, evidence continues to accumulate indicating that these mildly handicapped youngsters are, more often than not, "resisters" (Giroux, 1983a, 1983b; Sigmon, 1985) and underachievers (Epps, McGue, & Ysseldyke, 1982; Ysseldyke, Algozzine, Shinn, & McGue, 1982). American special education is not a conspiracy, nor was it originally conceived as a massive means of child control, but the latter is what it has become in many respects (Sigmon, 1985). Only through research that incorporates a foundations of education analysis will this social arrangement be illuminated and will solutions to change it be identified.

Chapter 4

Reducing the Number of Students Identified as Learning Disabled: A Question of Practice, Philosophy, or Policy?*

Lynn M. Gelzheiser

When children fail to meet standards for achievement and behavior set by a classroom teacher, they may be identified as learning disabled. Recently, because of rising identification rates and evidence of overidentification, it has been suggested that those who fail to meet expectations be accommodated by modifying classroom instruction. The pertinence of such a suggestion may not be recognized, because of the medical model of disability held by most educators. Accommodation to difference is consistent with a minority model of disability. Efforts to reduce the number of students identified as learning disabled would be more successful if they were advocated within a minority view of disability.

One's model of disability is a concept which shapes how disability is seen. A model of disability enhances the importance of certain factors related to a handicapping condition and conceals the importance of other factors. The way that a handicapped child is treated is determined by the way that professionals, family, and community conceptualize disability (Gliedman & Roth, 1980).

Efforts to change special education practice must take into account the power of concepts and beliefs about disability. In-

---

*This chapter first appeared in *Exceptional Children* (1987), Vol. 54, No. 2, pp. 145–150. Copyright © 1987 The Council for Exceptional Children.

novative practice is often not adopted because it conflicts with the belief system of those asked to change (Rogers & Shoemaker, 1971). For example, Graden, Casey and Bonstrom (1985) introduced a prereferral consulting model in six schools. Graden et al. encountered resistance in certain schools, which they attributed to beliefs about traditional testing practice and treatment. Also, innovation in schools may be subverted until it is consistent with traditional practice and routine (Sarason, 1971).

The identification of students as learning disabled is one aspect of special education where appropriate practice is debated and innovations have been recommended. The debate can be summarized simply: Should an increasingly greater number of students be identified as learning disabled or should mainstream classrooms be modified to accommodate greater variability in learning rate among students, and in particular, to accommodate those children so far from meeting expectations for progress that the discrepancy is troublesome?

These two ways of dealing with students who do not meet classroom expectations, identification and accommodation, are each logically consistent with a different view of disability. In a medical model of disability, disability is localized in a child. Disability explains school failure; school failure can be ameliorated by treating the disabled child. Because the cause of school failure is believed to inhere in the handicapped child, it is appropriate to assign these children to a separate education system. Because they are not "normal," it is assumed that handicapped students require specialized education from specially trained experts. Within the confines of a medical model, accommodation is not a logical way to deal with exceptional students, because it does not provide the specialized treatment required by the students' problems.

As dictated by P. L. 94-142, special education practice reflects a medical model of disability (Gliedman & Roth, 1980): Identification procedures locate disabilities in children, and remediation is provided to disabled students. A medical model characterizes the way that practitioners account for school failure and would appear to encourage the identification of students who fail as disabled. Teachers explain most instances of school failure by attributing problems to children (Croll & Moses, 1985). Referred students are assessed in isolation from the classroom environment, as if it is assumed that factors in the child are sufficient to explain failure (Smith, 1982). Of course, when information is gathered only about the child, the cause of school failure can then only be ascribed to the child, and it will often seem logical to identify the student as disabled.

Recently, the number of students identified as learning disabled has increased dramatically, in spite of declining school enrollments (U.S. Department of Education, 1984). Coincident with increased identification is some overidentification, or identification of students who fail to meet eligibility criteria specified in state or federal regulations. Perhaps as few as half of the students presently identified as learning disabled meet common eligibility criteria (Shepard, Smith, & Vojir, 1983).

Concern over overidentification and increased identification of students as learning disabled has prompted recommendations that classroom instruction be modified to accommodate a wider range of individual differences (Chalfant, 1984; Gerber & Semmel, 1984; Ysseldyke, 1983). A number of studies indicate that practices which facilitate modification of classroom instruction do reduce identification rate (Cantrell & Cantrell, 1976; Chalfant, Pysh, & Moultrie, 1979; Ritter, 1978; Ysseldyke & Thurlow, 1984) and can even increase the rate of decertification of previously identified students (Wang, Peverly, & Randolph, 1984).

Unfortunately, these innovations are illogical if one conceptualizes disability according to a medical model. To the extent that practitioners have adopted a medical model of disability, we can anticipate that their beliefs about disability may preclude or subvert the accommodation of exceptional students. To increase the likelihood that innovation will be genuine and widely adopted, efforts to encourage teachers to accommodate exceptional students must occur along with deliberate effort to ensure that teachers conceptualize disability in a manner consistent with accommodation. The purposes of this chapter are to review a variety of ways to accommodate within regular classrooms those children who fail to meet classroom standards and to explicate a view of disability consistent with these recommendations.

Ways of Accommodating Exceptional Students

Heller, Holtzman, and Messick (1982) specified identification procedures which emphasize examination of school context using a two-phase model. Aspects of the learning environment that may contribute to school failure are assessed by evaluating (a) the curriculum's effectiveness with students of similar ethnic, linguistic, and socioeconomic background; (b) the student's exposure to the curriculum; (c) the student's achievement relative to what was taught; and (d) the effect of a series of systematic educational interventions tried in the regular classroom environment. After identifying aspects of the learning environment which do not suit the child, efforts are made to make the environment appropriate. If the child continues to perform outside the limits of tolerance once the environment has been made more accommodating, then the child is assessed to determine eligibility for special education.

Ysseldyke and Thurlow (1984) proposed a similar process which they termed a modified norm-referenced model of assessment. To make the environment accommodate the child, instruction is evaluated and modified with increased time on task and careful monitoring of the relationship between instruction and student progress. Testing to establish eligibility for special education occurs only after classroom interventions have failed. Preliminary data collected about this model indicated fewer referrals to special education than had occurred previously.

Chalfant et al. (1979) instituted teacher assistance teams as a mechanism for teaching mainstream teachers how to adapt instruction and make classroom environments more accommodating. Select groups of classroom teachers serve at a building level and respond to requests from other teachers for help in altering instruction for particular hard to teach students. Chalfant et al. found that districts using teacher assistance teams identified few referred students relative to national averages, presumably because classroom teachers, with assistance, learned to accommodate a greater range of students.

Consultant models also provide assistance in serving a diverse range of students in the mainstream. Personnel who would traditionally deliver special services to individual children in a segregated setting, such as resource room teachers, language therapists, or school psychologists, instead serve to advise teachers (Cantrell & Cantrell, 1976; Frassinelli, Superior, & Meyers, 1983; Meyers, 1973). Consultation may assist the teacher in meeting the needs of an individual child or in developing a generally more adaptive teaching style (Meyers, 1973). Use of resource room teachers or school psychologists as consultants resulted in fewer referrals to special education (Cantrell & Cantrell, 1976; Graden et al., 1985, Ritter, 1978). In all cases, it was felt that referrals declined because teachers had become more able to cope with individual differences in the classroom.

Certain mainstreaming programs stress pluralistic or individualized goals for all students in a regular classroom. Some effective mainstreaming programs use individualized instruction in the mainstream classroom in the form of cooperative learning teams (Slavin, 1984), an adaptive learning environments model (ALEM) (Wang et al., 1984), or computer-assisted instruction (Trifiletti, Frith, & Armstrong, 1984). Teachers find these individualized formats manageable, and student achievement equals or is greater than that found with traditional models of group instruction supplemented by resource room assistance as needed.

Disability as a Social Construction

Each of the programs just reviewed stresses changing or "treating" the environment as well as the child experiencing school failure. Implicit in these programs is the assumption that school failure or disability occurs because of the way the individual *and* the learning environment interact. For this reason, these programs are logically consistent with a model of disability as a social construction.

According to this view, educational handicaps are social constructions. Their definitions reflect an agreement to dichotomize continuous variables such as aptitude or achievement into categories of normal and deviant. Because of their arbitrary nature, handicapping conditions can be defined in any way that a group agrees to define them. The American Association on Mental Deficiency periodically revises its definition of mental retardation (Grossman, 1973; Heber, 1959). States vary as to whether they include adaptive behavior in their definitions of mental retardation (Bickel, 1982) and employ different definitions, criteria, and formulae in identifying learning disabled students (Chalfant, 1984). Some have suggested that multidisciplinary teams have idiosyncratic definitions of learning disabilities, such as students referred by teachers (Ysseldyke & Thurlow, 1984) or children needing extra help (Smith, 1982).

Eligibility criteria are altered to meet the needs of the group who identifies. For example, for fiscal and political reasons, over a four year period the Social Security Administration classified as nondisabled 490,000 individuals previously identified as disabled, and then subsequently reclassified 200,000 of them as disabled once again (Pear, 1985).

Disability is constructed in two related but distinct ways. First, disabilities are created by social organizations like schools. This is most obviously true for learning disabilities (Geschwind, 1984) and mild mental retardation (Sarason & Doris, 1979). Detection of these conditions occurs in school, not prior to school entry. Most often, the individual is not perceived as disabled after schooling has been completed (Edgerton, 1979; Horn, O'Donnell, & Vitulano, 1983). In schools, uniform standards for achievement and uniform methods of instruction serve to create a group viewed as deviant. Deviance, however, is the result of both individual differences in learning and behavior, *and* the expectations for uniform performance held by educators. The process of the social construction of handicapping conditions in classrooms has been described using participant-observer techniques (Lazarus, 1985).

According to a social construction model of disability, the perception of a learning disability is dependent upon the uniform expectations of a traditional classroom. If a traditional classroom were converted to one with individualized goals, fewer students should be viewed as deviant or identified as learning disabled. As predicted by a social construction model, Wang et al. (1984) found that adopting an adaptive curriculum led to an unusually high rate of decertification of students identified as mildly handicapped. Similarly, Rosenholtz and Rosenholtz (1981) found that teachers perceived fewer students as achieving below average when performance standards were multiple, rather than uniform.

Disability is also constructed in the stereotyping that occurs once an individual is viewed as disabled. Assumptions about disability give it meaning. Often, it is assumed that a handicapping condition has a unique set of characteristics, all of which can logically be ascribed to the child. The disability becomes the child's most salient feature, to the extent that "disability can change the meaning of behavior" (Bogdan & Kugelmass, 1984, p. 186). Expectations for performance are based on assumptions about the handicap, rather than knowledge of the individual.

When disability is conceptualized as a social construction, individual differences take on the meaning of a disability because of the context in which an individual functions and the assumptions that others make about disability. Responsibility for school failure does not rest with the child or with educational handicaps. Rather, failure is produced by the transaction that occurs because of the child's nature and the school's structure (Sarason & Doris, 1979). According to this view, the purpose of assessment is to determine the nature of the problem transaction between the child and the instructional context. After describing the child's performance and classroom variables, remediation is directed towards both the child and the classroom. Efforts to modify classroom instruction for students whose performance is discrepant are logically consistent with the assumptions of disability as a social construction.

A Minority Model of Disability

Expanding on disability as a social construction, Gliedman and Roth (1980) suggest that handicapping conditions are best conceptualized through a minority model. A minority model highlights the element of discrimination in the social construction of disability, stressing that those perceived as different may be stigmatized, segregated, or oppressed.

An environment designed to meet only the needs of the majority will necessarily handicap some individuals. A uniform manner and pace for instruction ensures that some students will fall further and further behind, and can result in students being stigmatized and segregated from the classroom. Instruction can only be nondiscriminatory if it is individualized for all students and if pluralistic goals are set for achievement. Rather than requiring all students to meet a norm, a minority model emphasizes that students have the right to be different and that schools must tolerate diversity.

A minority model suggests that political action is a necessary part of the "treatment" of disability. If disability is constructed by an environment designed around the needs of those perceived as typical, services provided to individual students do little to alter that construction. In order to eliminate discriminatory treatment for students who fail in school, the way that schools are structured and instruction is provided must change.

A minority model suggests that policy should deliver service in the form of support for classroom teachers, in addition to providing service to individual children. Such support would be allocated on the basis of classroom needs, rather than on the basis of the number of identified students (Gerber & Semmel, 1984). Of course, this is not a change in special education policy. To effect substantive change in special education, policy concerning the organization of classrooms must be changed. According to a minority model of disability, special education policy and education policy are not separable.

Conclusions

Within the confines of a medical model of disability, seeing a need to alter classroom instruction because certain children fail is like seeing that the emperor has no clothes. Such insight can only occur if the viewer rejects a set of powerful assumptions validated by authorities and held by society at large.

Accommodating hard to teach students in the regular classroom rather than identifying them as learning disabled is a revolutionary suggestion. It requires that disability, identification, and remediation be conceptualized in ways counter to prevailing notions. With innovations designed to facilitate accommodation, the responsibility for school failure is transferred from disability to a social process. The focus of remediation is shifted from a child alone to a child in context; because policy plays a major role in defining school context, policy too becomes a target for change. Practices stressing accommodation of exceptional students in the mainstream are consistent with a minority model of disability and should be advocated within the logical framework of this model.

Chapter 5

Impediments to Implementing National Policy Change for Mildly Handicapped Students*

*George J. Hagerty and
Marty Abramson*

This chapter describes the current public policy environment and the impact of that environment on efforts to refine the system for serving mildly handicapped students. The authors discuss the accelerated growth in the numbers of mildly handicapped children, which has prompted educational decision makers to seek more effective methods of assessment, identification, and instruction. Specific areas requiring attention and response are detailed, including revisions in the service delivery system, the preparation of personnel, the administration of program and funding structures, and the management and use of existing national and state data bases.

For the American educational community, the 1980s have been a period of fervent reexamination. This national inquiry has been an unrestricted enterprise, distinguished by the intensity of debate, the range of instructional and social/political issues addressed, and the universal composition of the groups currently attracted to the cause of quality schooling.

The fundamental propositions and dimensions of the current debate about the status and direction of American education are

---

*This chapter first appeared in substantial form within *Exceptional Children* (1987), Vol. 53, No. 4, pp. 315–323. Copyright © 1987 The Council for Exceptional Children.

incorporated in the spate of national reports and manifestos generated by both public and private groups. The findings and recommendations originating from the majority of these reports promote reforms that are clearly designed to benefit and strengthen the provision of general education for a future of economic and scientific survival. Yet, the guidance offered by each group captures the similarities in need and remediation which coincidentally exist within regular and special education. These include improvement in:

- The establishment of clear educational goals in the local, state, and federal sectors.
- The level of measurable, meaningful student performance.
- The competence and training of current practitioners and new teachers.
- The curricular content and instruction available to all students at all levels of education.
- The accountability of school systems and the investment of the public in education.
- The management, leadership, and fiscal support of educational systems.

While considerable uniformity exists about the type of general changes needed, specific and, at times, far-reaching change is difficult to detect. This is particularly true where independent and dual systems of education exist, such as "regular" and "special," each with its own pattern of funding, instruction, and administration; with distinct professional jargon and affiliation; and with differing modes of personnel preparation. Such a dual system perpetuates inefficiency and unnecessary competition in the delivery of educational services to all students (Algozzine, Salvia, & Ysseldyke, 1983; Hersh & Walker, 1983; Pugach & Lilly, 1984; Stainback & Stainback, 1984). This dichotomy in the structure of school systems poses a particular challenge to improving the education of children characterized as mildly handicapped.

Problems in Serving the Mildly Handicapped

Mildly handicapped students are a heterogeneous group whose shared characteristic is their inability to fully benefit from the existing regular education system. Traditionally, these students have included learners in the categories of specific learning disabilities (SLD), mentally retarded (MR), speech or language impaired (SI), and seriously emotionally disturbed (SED). Clearly, the mildly handicapped classification covers a population of students exhibiting an extensive range of learning, communication, and/or socialization problems (Abramson et al., 1981; Chalfant, 1984; Stainback & Stainback, 1984).

As the severity of these students' deficits is not sufficient to warrant total immersion in the special education system, mildly handicapped students are frequently the responsibility of both regular and special education. The preferred method of educating mildly handicapped students is presently based on a "pull-out" strategy, despite an increasing volume of research on instructional effectiveness to the contrary (Chalfant, 1984; Hersh & Walker, 1983; Wang & Reynolds, 1985). In effect, for students to receive the services in "one system" they must be removed for a period of time from the "other system." This split-scheduling approach for providing services to handicapped children is neither administratively nor instructionally supportable when measured against legal requirements (U.S. Government, 1984), effective schools research (Chalfant, 1984; Hersh & Walker, 1984), or fiscal considerations (Kakalik et al., 1981).

Those researchers and educational decision makers most intrigued with and involved in the conceptual mapping of our nation's schools are investigating the use of less restrictive mechanisms for serving mildly handicapped students, particularly models that allow for the total integration of mildly handicapped students in the regular classroom (Sontag, Hagerty, & Button, 1983; U.S. Department of Education, 1985).

The need for timely, if not immediate, action cannot be understated if we consider the data available to us.

Growth and Identification of the Mildly Handicapped Student Population

While the total number of handicapped children served across the nation has increased slightly over the past several years (to approximately 4,377,254 in 1984–85), there has been a rapid acceleration in the identification of children within the mildly handicapped population (predominantly in the learning disabled category). The child count for all handicapping conditions expanded by 668,665 students from 1976 to 1985. This increase can be attributed to national, state, and local child find efforts, improvements in the availability of services to the overall handicapped population, and increasing state and local fiscal commitments to handicapped learners.

During this reporting period, however, the numbers of some mildly handicapped categories, particularly the specific learning disabled (SLD), expanded by over 1,000,000 students. Since 1976, this population alone has grown from a small, rather clearly defined population of 797,213 to its 1985 count of 1,845,928.

Despite a moderate reduction in the number of children identified as mentally retarded (MR) and slight increases in the child count categories for the seriously emotionally disturbed and speech or language impaired, the specific learning disabilities count alone has assured that the generic "mildly handicapped" grouping has accounted for the greatest proportion of increase in the total child count over the past eight years (Gerber, 1984; U.S. Department of Education, 1984, 1985). That the growth in the number of children identified as SLD has literally exploded can be highlighted by the fact that the percentage of all handicapped children classified as SLD in California has grown from 22.4% in 1976–77 to 54.5% in 1982–83. In New York State, the percentage of change was similarly extraordinary, 14.4% in 1976–77 to 44.1% in 1982–83 (Gerber, 1984). In fact, national special education data show that in every year since school year 1977–78 the increase in the number of children identified as specific learning disabled has exceeded the yearly child count increase for all other handicapping conditions combined (U.S. Department of Education, 1984).

Interestingly, difficulties associated with unchecked increases in the SLD population have been recognized for many years. Despite this recognition, very little has been attempted or accomplished in verifying that all of these students are appropriately identified and in need of special education services. In fact, certain states have taken a more prominent role in dealing with this situation than has the federal government. This condition is quite alarming in view of the fact that this is a national concern affecting the resources and services available to all students.

Given that the U.S. Department of Education's Annual Report to Congress indicates (a) that mildly handicapped students comprise over 90% of the handicapped population and (b) that an extremely high percentage of these children receive services "mainly in the regular classroom" (e.g., SLD–98%; SI–100%), improvements in instructional effectiveness found in regular education environments should logically yield significant benefits in the academic performance and socialization of mildly handicapped students.

Reviewing the history and development of the program administration and instructional interventions used for serving mildly handicapped students, it looks like regular education support systems have been supplanted by special education services. The creation of an alternative instructional environment for the placement of hard-to-teach students is a seductive notion indeed. Additionally, confusion over the appropriateness of regular versus special education interventions may well be attributable to the relative "softness" of such categories as learning disabled, educable mentally retarded, and emotionally disturbed, and the difficulty in clearly distinguishing students with these impairments from traditionally "remedial populations," such as the culturally deprived, economically disadvantaged, socially maladjusted (or virtually any other category of hard-to-teach student).

Certainly, the fears expressed on a 1981 General Accounting Office (GAO) report, specifically related to the identification of learning disabled students, ring true today:

> Congressional fears that a disproportionate share of funds might be allocated to the learning disabilities category (the magnitude of which is not clearly known or understood) seem to have been realized with the lifting of the 2 percent cap on the number of learning disabled children who can be counted for Federal funding purposes. Little is known about who is being served in this category. These children may include those with mild learning problems, slow learners, and/or children who formerly would have been retarded. (GAO, 1981)

The Colorado study of perceptual-communicative disorders presents data further damaging to the notion that we currently use evaluation and measurement procedures sufficiently accurate to identify and categorize mildly handicapped students. The study concludes:

> The single most important finding is that more than half the children do not meet either statistical or valid clinical criteria for the identification of perceptual and communicative disorders. (Shepard & Smith, 1981)

The problem of identifying specific categories of mildly handicapped children, for example, the learning disabled or the emotionally disturbed, is further exacerbated by variations among states in terminology, definitions, and the establishment of criteria such as behavioral characteristics, test scores, capacity and achievement discrepancies, and so forth (Chalfant, 1984; Pugach & Lilly, 1984; Shepard, 1983; Stainback & Stainback, 1984). Although the federal definitions for the various mildly handicapped categories are rather specific, the regulations are sufficiently flexible that state and local educational agencies continue to experience substantial difficulty in formulating operational definitions for any one of the categories.

This is not to say that the sophistication necessary for decision making is not available at the present time. For example, the recent work of Wilson and Reynolds (1984) demonstrates one approach to creating a pool of students who exhibit a severe discrepancy and who may have, or may not have, a specific learning disability depending upon further qualifying features of an SLD. Yet, while the capacity exists to further define the nature of this handicapping category, the social, political, and educational consequences of doing so have not made this approach viable for identifying the population. Thus, it is not just the "softness" of the categories that is at issue, but also the failure to make needed policy and program decisions to prevent the dilution of special education treatment.

Fiscal Concerns

As the mildly handicapped population expands in number and diversity, issues of cost evolving from the identification, placement, and specialized instruction process required for these students is gaining particular attention. Table 1 shows comparative placement costs for various categories of handicapping condition.

Table 1
Comparative Placement Cost by Category
of Handicapping Condition

Type of Class	Learning Disabled TC	AC	Educable Mentally Retarded TC	AC	Emotionally Disturbed TC	AC	Speech Impaired TC	AC
Regular class plus indirect service	2552	902	3113	1463	3147	1497	2477	827
Regular class plus itinerant instructor	4456	2806	3884	2234	7946	6296	2360	710
Regular class plus part-time special class	4714	3064	3874	2224	6904	5254	4025	2375
Special class plus part-time regular class	4011	2361	4058	2408	5417	3767	3500	1850
Full-time special class	4432	2782	3265	1615	5750	4100	5439	3789

Note: TC = total cost in dollars; AC = added cost in dollars. From *The Cost of Special Education* by J. S. Kakalik, W. S. Furry, M. A. Thomas, and M. F. Carney, 1981, Santa Monica: The Rand Corporation. This study was conducted under contract number 300–79–0753 for the U.S. Department of Education. Adapted by permission.

During the 1977–78 school year, the "added cost" of special education (i.e., those costs above the cost of regular education) was calculated to be $7 billion. With a 37% growth rate in national educational expenditures over the next three years, the 1980–81 "added cost" was estimated to be over $10 billion (Kakalik et al., 1981). Although no "added cost" calculations for 1983–84 are presently available, an extension of the Rand study's 1980–81 estimate (Kakalik et al., 1981) would yield a projected expenditure of approximately $11.8 billion. This figure assumes that the per pupil cost of both regular education and special education increased by a moderate 5 to 7% over the past three years (U.S. Department of Education, 1984).

Based upon existing data, it is projected that in school year 1983–84, the total cost of providing instructional services to only two of the less "resource intensive" populations (i.e., LD and SED) exceeded $7.2 billion nationally (U.S. Department of Education, 1984).

While the nature and severity of a child's exceptionality are presumed to dictate the appropriate educational placement(s) and delivery of instructional and related services (GAO, 1981), the data elicited from the Rand study (Kakalik et al., 1981) reveal the cost-effectiveness of using "less restrictive" or "increasingly integrated" instructional settings for serving mildly handicapped students.

With the exception of isolated local and state level studies (GAO, 1981), more recent data on expenditures across the range of special education service delivery models are not available. The U.S. Office of Special Education and Rehabilitative Services has recently funded Decision Resources, Inc. of Washington, DC, to conduct a comprehensive study of the financing of special education, which should provide a detailed accounting of the way state and local education agencies support and deliver special education and related services to existing categories of handicapped students.

Adequacy of Programs

Fiscal concern is heightened by the realization that differences in educational placement for mildly handicapped children are not necessarily indicative of differences in instruction (Pugach & Lilly, 1984; Sontag, Hagerty, & Button, 1983; Stainback & Stainback, 1984). In essence, there is some question as to what constitutes the treatment in special education. A recent Task Force on Special Education evaluation found that programs for mildly handicapped children did not differ substantially from compensatory education programs (Kennedy, 1982). More troubling are the findings of the Colorado investigation of identification and education systems administered for children with perceptual-communicative disorders (PCD). This study reported that:

> On (the) average between 30% and 35% of the time (in PCD classrooms) is spent on repetition and drill on basic skills and between 15% and 18% of time is spent in one-to-one tutoring with regular classroom work. Therefore, roughly half of the

special instructional time for PCD pupils is spent directly on academic work. (Shepard & Smith, 1981)

Of equal concern are the findings of educational effectiveness studies (Bloomer, Bates, Brown, & Norlander, 1982; Glass, 1982) which raise compelling questions as to the benefits of current special education intervention strategies for mildly handicapped students. For example, in a study of children identified as learning disabled, Bloomer and colleagues found that 40 to 65% of the students (depending on subject matter) did not realize the expected benefits from special education.

Due to the difficulty in identifying a homogeneous population exhibiting recognizable, common features, and the multiple reasons for which students are identified as handicapped, it can be difficult to judge the adequacy of programs in relation to a student's perceived needs, actual needs, and outcomes. Moreover, the interaction of a possible treatment with the host of other educational and noneducational variables makes it virtually impossible to determine if special education as a treatment is effective or which special education treatment for particular students is effective. Thus, without the possibility of refutation, and only the slimmest support, the continuation of special education, in all its forms, is assured. Adequacy, while definable as a legal process, is indeterminable as a product or set of outcomes.

The calls for special education reform, for the re-integration and transfer of a large portion of mildly handicapped students into the domain of regular education, as well as parallel public demands for improvement in teacher performance, educational accountability, academic standards, and school environments have for the most part gone unanswered. With our apparent national consensus for educational change, what can possibly stand in the way of reform? The answers may well be reflected in a Biblical adage applicable to public policy: "The spirit is willing, but the flesh is weak."

Impediments to Policy Change in Special Education

In the final section of this chapter we explore selected issues to discover the obstacles to proactive policy change in serving mildly handicapped students. Such impediments, whether merely blemishes on the surface or more deeply rooted and insidious defects in the process of making and administering educational policy, must be addressed and overcome before meaningful, system-wide refinements occur in our schools.

Deficiencies in the Existing Data Base

Calls for changes in the service delivery system for mildly handicapped students have been stimulated largely by the findings of social scientists (Gerber, 1984; Glass, 1983; Pugach & Lilly, 1984; Shepard, 1983; Stainback & Stainback, 1984; Wang & Reynolds, 1984). While data available at the federal and state levels serve the general, immediate needs of program administrators, legislative staffers, budget/finance officers, and auditors, currently available information is inadequate for public decision making.

While aggregate, categorical data submitted by states to the federal government have a beguiling quality, it is clear that such information has little value beyond mandated reporting requirements. Inadequate instructions, non-uniform standards and collection procedures, and missing data all contribute to the inadequacy of such information for program administration and resource management. Yet, due to the lack of availability of alternate information sources, these data are used to justify expenditures of funds and decisions for program selections, priorities, and general reporting functions. It is only necessary to examine identical data elements from two or more states to begin to understand the invalidity of aggregated, categorical data.

Apart from the deficiencies in the data base, an increasing number of studies suggest that issues such as instructional effectiveness, appropriateness, and availability of services are not dealt with comprehensively in either a national or statewide data base. Some would suggest that these elements are the most critical and necessary indicators for decisions about policy and the translation of policy into programs. In order to make clear decisions among numerous policy alternatives, educational decision makers will require future-oriented service delivery information, particularly data that address the duration and extensiveness of services, the personnel used to provide the various services and their professional preparation, and the effects of instruction (i.e., comprehensive school exit data).

Existing Program and Funding Structures

Despite weaknesses in the measurement and identification processes used for special education, programming for special populations and the funding to support it has been almost exclusively categorical in nature (Shepard, 1983; Shepard & Smith, 1981; Stainback & Stainback, 1984; U.S. Department of Education, 1984, 1985; Wang & Reynolds, 1984). Efforts to re-orient special education funding to the instruction and related services actually needed or provided (versus the present per-child allocation method) have generally been opposed by the special education establishment and advocacy groups because of fears that consideration of a new "resource distribution" system could jeopardize a number of hard-earned educational rights, including financial support, procedural safeguards, and appropriate, individualized services. The natural instinct to "hold on to what has been won" serves as a major impediment to reforms that the educational community (including parents) recognizes as advantageous for a significant population of special students. Special education is especially prone to this "no change" reflex because it has been a mere decade since the passage of P. L. 94–142, The Education for All Handicapped Children Act (1975), and memories of deregulation efforts during the early years of the Reagan Administration are still fresh.

Prudence is essential, especially if policy makers determine that the existing system of categorical labels, funding, and programming is not the most efficacious means of serving students presently identified as mildly handicapped. In spite of requirements regarding placement and instruction in the least restrictive environment (LRE), it appears that in some states the practice of establishing eligibility on the basis of handicapping categories is complicated by the use of categorical models for determining eligible (i.e., fundable) special education services. In one state, for example, eligible services for handicapped children included related services, transitional support services, resource rooms, special classes and schools, and home instruction, but did not allow for the support of full time specialized instruction provided by the regular classroom teacher (Wang & Reynolds, 1984).

Fears of the over-identification of "hard-to-teach" students, particularly the mildly handicapped, have precipitated a host of frequently regressive administrative, diagnostic, and programmatic controls. Concern about a future of spiraling special education costs has been met with renewed calls for containment remedies such as funding and child count caps for certain categories of handicapped students and revisions in identification and special education placement criteria. In practice, these efforts have proven only to solve the immediate administrative problem of reducing child counts in certain categories. Such restrictive measures (e.g., categorical capping) will not resolve issues of inadequate instruction for hard-to-teach children exhibiting learning, communication, emotional, and/or socialization deficits.

Personnel Preparation

The vast majority of programs training special education and related service personnel to work in schools are categorical in nature (Pugach & Lilly, 1984; Stainback & Stainback, 1984). This categorical preparation is influenced by, and frequently influences, the categorical models which most states maintain for purposes of certification. Although the existing systems of personnel preparation have already received considerable attention, it is important to address several critical issues relevant to the educational change process.

A significant factor in determining effective versus less effective school environments is the degree of staff interaction. As has been pointed out elsewhere:

> Four classes of interaction appear crucial (in successful schools): discussion of classroom practice, mutual observation and critique, shared efforts to design and prepare curriculum, and shared participation in the business of instructional improvement. (Little, 1982)

These basics of collegiality serve as the foundation for effective instruction. The existing regular education/special education dichotomy imposes restrictions on the level of interaction that can logically be realized in our schools. Unfortunately, the separate instructional system currently in place is perpetuated not only by administrative convenience, but also by a system of professional preparation and certification that further institutionalizes program and staff segregation.

Reforms toward more integrated classroom models for serving mildly handicapped children and youth must be paralleled (if not preceded) by changes in the structure of training programs and certification requirements (Hagerty, Behrens, & Abramson, 1983). Such revisions will demand the cooperation and collective energies of college and university personnel, state and local educational agencies, legislators, and advocates. Efforts to implement comprehensive systems of personnel development (CSPD), to ensure the effective implementation of new regular classroom interventions for mildly handicapped students, will demand that states direct increasing attention to (a) the traditional regular education community (e.g., principals and general education teachers), and (b) a new cadre of specially trained regular educators.

Of course, revisions in the structure of colleges and departments of education, as well as refinements in state certification requirements, will not be undertaken without corresponding changes in legislation, prevailing instructional models, and professional/programmatic incentives. For example, it is unthinkable that universities will commence a wholesale restructuring of their teacher education programs (i.e., from categorical to unified preparation) without significant modifications in general certification standards, and changes in the distribution and targeting of federal and state training funds. However, challenges to the categorical status quo for preparing teachers and related service providers must ensure that the unique needs of severely handicapped populations are recognized and addressed. In essence, efforts to improve services for mildly handicapped students should in no way jeopardize the educational rights, protections, and special education programs that have benefited the most severely involved children and youth.

The Service Delivery System

We conclude this chapter by examining some fundamental barriers to policy change found in the extant service delivery system for mildly handicapped students. As noted, the identification, placement, and instructional system in which mildly handicapped students are served is in reality a dual system. In attempting to cull out those students who possess "handicaps" (for special education) from students who exhibit learning problems (for placement in regular education), state and local education agencies have invested considerable time, funds, and energy into establishing intricate assessment models, criteria for identification, and standards for placement and instruction.

The components of a legally and administratively compliant service delivery system are now substantially in place in the 16,000 local education agencies and intermediate units across the country (U.S. Department of Education, 1984, 1985). Moves toward reforming the existing educational system to more efficiently serve mildly handicapped students and "hard-to-teach" populations will undoubtedly meet considerable local resistance. This reaction will not result from any ill feelings toward students with learning problems, but will be the natural response of educators, parents, advocates, and bureaucrats to the seeming onslaught of everchanging policies, directives, and standards emanating from agencies other than the local school system.

Conclusion

Revisions in the structure of the current educational system undoubtedly will create initial anxiety, confusion, and dysfunction as educators wrestle with the inherent administrative and instructional problems associated with developing and operating a reformed (i.e., merged) program for serving children now labeled mildly handicapped.

While the flaws in the existing system are readily apparent to local educational agencies (LEAs), designs for change in the educational structure must be contemplated and implemented in a way that creates a "receptive spirit" among those who are in the trenches on a daily basis. While calls for a change in the system by which we educate mildly handicapped students are filtering up from the local level to state and federal decision makers, those who actually provide the services are wary of "reform" since they recognize that the rules by which funds are distributed and programs administered have been traditionally (i.e., since the 1960s) in the hands of legislators and administrators located in state and federal agencies.

Despite an increasing emphasis at the federal and state level on local control of educational decision making and programming, LEA administrators, practitioners, and board members will be circumspect about calls for change. Correct or not, the perceptions and memories of local personnel have been molded by the scars of attempts to meet the standards of legislated initiatives with inadequate preparation and resources.

Evoking the active support and participation of "grassroots" populations (e.g., LEA personnel, advocates, parents) will demand a coordinated effort by education officials (from all levels), legislators, advocates, related service professionals, teacher educators, material developers, and book publishers (among others) to clearly define deficiencies and needs and to collectively establish a logical agenda and a reasonable timetable for change.

Part II

Progress

Overview

Scott B. Sigmon

With this second part, the focus moves primarily on to the future. Specifically, what should be special education's guiding direction in regards to theory and practice? Theoretically, the factors that could affect the learning environment are explored in greater measure. Thus, we move away from intrapsychic notions about the disabled learner—at least when discussing the so-called mild education handicap—to the interaction of the learner with the environment. Perhaps what sets apart these writers is the degree to which they believe the social environment outside the school should be changed. Nevertheless, it could be said safely that the authors in this second part—and the whole book, actually—agree about: the need for better instruction in most schools, an enthusiastic attitude about individual learning potential, and a school setting in which students are properly prepared to learn.

There is no point in designating a low achiever as mildly educationally handicapped unless the student has first been prepared to learn. That is, a proper educational foundation must be in place. What constitutes a proper foundation? Not only are solid basic skills required, but training in learning strategies as well. The pupil must be familiar with the demands of the school environment. There must be a give-and-take between the student and the school. We cannot assume that a student comes to school with even a rudimentary knowledge of learning strategies or institutional survival skills. Thus, we should not take the stance that the pupil must adjust or else suffer negative consequences—without first receiving the benefit of being shown how to learn, within the school itself.

Too many things about education and schooling are naively taken for granted. We must ensure that: (a) children learn how to study (learning strategies); (b) they learn the social expectations of school (rules of behavior); (c) students receive a solid foundation in basic academic skills through competent instruction (the three Rs); and (d) the pupil's affective needs are met (the child is made to feel a part of the group and that he or she has self-worth regardless of actual performance on tests of any kind). Only when these four essential criteria have been met can we state that we have humanely attempted to teach a child.

Chapter 6

Toward a Radical Methodology for Rational Discourse on Special Education*

Scott B. Sigmon

A new, formalized but flexible, qualitative methodology known as "radical socioeducational analysis" (RSA) is proposed for the study of special education—which has not often been a subject of the new radical perspectives on education that have developed over the last twenty or so years. Radical refers here to an appeal to roots or basic elements. The methodology is essentially interdisciplinary, dialectical and interactionistic. Philosophical foundations for RSA are discussed. The purposes are to help gain insight into the relationship between special education and cultural transmission, to make special education more humane and to encourage additional rational discourse for the most sensible future policy.

Overview

The history and contemporary practice of American schooling have been portrayed by liberals as a slow but steady progression toward democracy and equality, and by conservatives as a slow but steady regression toward mediocrity and incompetence. Where these agree is in their failure to connect the history and

---

*This chapter is based upon chapter 2 of S.B. Sigmon's *Radical Socioeducational Analysis* (1985; New York: Irvington Publishers), and contains also a few small passages from S.B. Sigmon's *Radical Analysis of Special Education: Focus on Historical Development and Learning Disabilities* (1987; London, New York, & Philadelphia: The Falmer Press/Taylor & Francis).

practice of schooling consistently with larger structures of power, social class, ideology, etc. With the radical educational viewpoint developed over approximately the last two decades, we have been presented with another perspective on the history and practice of education which attempts to explain through radical analysis the roots of cultural transmission. These radical perspectives have enabled a fresh look both at the problem of education and the possibilities for change.

With very few exceptions (e.g., Carrier, 1983; Shapiro, 1980; Sigmon, 1983), special education has not enjoyed the fresh insights to be gained from this radical analysis. Special education, as a sub-field of education, warrants in-depth study from the radical perspective. Nevertheless, Shapiro (1980), like other orthodox radical educational critics, indirectly discouraged comprehensive radical analysis of special education because he saw its problems as merely mirroring those within the general education system at large. My position is that there are problems within our society and education as a whole, but that we must work to improve special education and clarify its role in a democratic nation while attempting simultaneously to change society. Neither should be neglected. It is only sensible to think that special education, like all other education, is rooted in larger structures of power, ideology, etc. For special education to be fundamentally understood both historically and currently, in order to develop a sound basis for future policy, it too needs a radical analysis.

In essence then, this work calls for interpretive and historical study of special education. The method is qualitative while the methodology in which this radical perspective will proceed is what here will be called "radical socioeducational analysis" (RSA). RSA is an interactive-interdisciplinary way of looking at the social conditions which impinge upon schooling or education and which in turn impact upon the social facts of life. (There is an important difference between education and schooling, as the latter is made up only of a certain variable percentage of the former.) RSA as a methodology is not based upon truly unique thought on the part of the author, although the term RSA probably is original. Rather, RSA is a synthesis arrived at from previous radical thinkers.

Often in the past both radical (e.g., Giroux, 1981) and non-radical (e.g., Hurn, 1978) alike would tend to describe the radical paradigm in basically negative terms; i.e., what it is opposed to and what it is not, such as Giroux's (1981) description of the non-radical functionalist paradigm below:

> a perspective that gave priority to questions of efficiency, management and prediction, educational research surrendered its capacity to question and challenge the basic imperatives of the dominant society to a functionalist ideology fueled by the politically conservative principles of social harmony and normative consensus. Within the functionalist perspective there was little room for educators to raise questions concerning the relationship between critical concepts such as ideology, power, and class struggle and their relationship to the process of schooling. (p.5)

If the radical position is to be faulted it should not be for being negativistic, but rather for being too idealistic about the extent to which the human condition can be improved. Moreover, RSA incorporates the credo from critical social theory so well expressed by Buss (1979):

> Critical theory attempts to go beyond the facts, beyond mere appearances, and penetrates to the underlying values and theoretical assumptions of a position. That theory which leads to greater human emancipation is the one to be endorsed according to critical theory. (p. 20)

Toward a Radical Socioeducational Paradigm

Giarelli (1982) noted that despite disagreement in the methods and conclusions of radical educational critics, there are strong commonalities in their work. On this basis, it could be said—using Kuhn's (1962) argument from his important work entitled *The Structure of Scientific Revolutions*—that this field of thought lacks a unifying paradigm. More recently, however (cf. Kuhn's "Postscript-1969" in the second edition of *Structures*, 1970), "Kuhn has elaborated further on his concept of paradigms, and has proposed identifying them according to sociological criteria." Thus, "A paradigm governs. . . not a subject matter but rather a group of practitioners" (Buss, 1979, p.1). Therefore, when seen in this light, it can easily be argued that a fundamental radical paradigm does exist. What remains to be done, though, is to further elaborate an actual, more identifiable, substantial—albeit flexible and qualitative—radical methodology for education, and to apply it to areas of schooling heretofore rarely examined or in important areas requiring further examination.

RSA is thought of as a combination of previous radical educational methodology (e.g., Giroux, 1981; Sarup, 1978; Sharp, 1980; Young, 1971; etc.), and is open-ended as it fills gaps which exist in the literature, because it goes beyond any particular discipline. Many radical thinkers restricted themselves too dogmatically to particular schools of thought (e.g., neo-Marxism) or only to certain areas of study (e.g., curriculum). RSA combines and relies upon work from certain fields because they have broken new methodological ground while examining schooling, society, or the social sciences. These fields of thought are radical philosophy of education, critical social theory, "new" sociology of education, neo-Marxist critiques of schooling, and dialectical (Buss, 1979; Riegel, 1979) or interactional psychology (Endler & Magnusson, 1976; Pervin & Lewis, 1978; Sigmon, 1984a & 1984b). Recent radical philosophy of education and the new sociology of education are especially interested in cultural transmission via the school experience on the student. Critical social theory from the 1920s— acknowledging here the myth that "it has a unified theory of society"—is mainly concerned about the relationship of fact with interpretation and has had a significant influence on new sociologists who study schooling. Dialectical-interactional psychology examines not only traditional intrapsychic factors (psychoanalytic force one), behavioristic external presses (force two), and humanistic introspective as well as global feelings for humanity (third force); but attempts to tie them together in an open system fashion while being sensitive to changes from within and without (producing a fourth force psychology). Further, knowledge and experiences gained while working in schools serve as an especially vital *in vivo* research tool as well.

Knowledge and its history, that is, how any particular body of thought comes to be called knowledge, is essential to radical analysis. Giroux (1981, see especially p. 82) discusses how theory and facts are the subjective and objective dimensions of knowledge. The dialectical notion of knowledge is that it is not something necessarily objective, just "out there." "It cannot be divorced from traditions, cultural and political, that give it meaning and/or dissolve it into objecthood" (Giroux, 1981, p. 19). Marx used history as a sociological tool. By the same token, history is a vehicle on which a socioeducational analysis moves. Again quoting Giroux: "For we must turn to history in order to understand the traditions that have shaped our individual biographies and intersubjective relationships with other human beings" (1981, p. 57). Giroux also discusses the "suppression of historical consciousness in the social sphere and the loss of interest in history in the sphere of schooling in the United States at the present time" (1981, p. 40) as being an impediment to change. An RSA can accommodate this problem in praxis.

A radical socioeducational analysis (RSA) would be a useful method of inquiry for special education as well as other areas of education concerned with *how external social forces exert pressure on schools and how the schools are forced to react.* RSA is a term used to designate a model for the complex study of schooling. It is an interactive, reciprocal or dialectical way of viewing not only institutions and society but also how persons or groups are forced to operate within a school environment while keeping in mind the links between economic factors and cultural institutions. Additionally, it remains open to information from all fields of human endeavor, especially the social sciences and the humanities. RSA, like conventional methods of inquiry, is for studying what is; but also, it is the study of why and what could be and how. This is to deny any claim of being value-free. Humans are a product of their total experiences which in turn shape their values. An honest, intelligent appraisal is the goal of an RSA. Thus, as radical here means an appeal to "roots" or "basic elements," a radical socioeducational analysis focuses on the roots or basic elements underlying educational processes.

RSA is an attitude, mainly a method, but also methodology. It is attitude in the sense that any method of inquiry holds certain implications about how the world is viewed. It is primarily method in that a chosen path is followed to deal with facts and hypotheses. And, RSA is to some lesser extent methodology because to do a radical socioeducational analysis well, knowledge of other research procedures is required. In this line of thought an effort is made to avoid the trap of empiricism whereby the method is thought to be value-free and completely objective, a feat which is not actually possible when studying social systems or even individuals. Multidimensional social factors impinge upon the individual which cannot be completely "held constant" or "factored out." The method chosen obviously says something about the researcher doing an inquiry. Any method chosen either has ideological biases, or at the very least connotations denoting the researcher's orientation toward the world. The use of the RSA method makes one very important philosophic point: A well-rounded interpretive inquiry is sought.

I believe that the universe is an ultimate unity but that change is constant. The changes taking place give the impression of contradiction. Hence, science searches for regular laws of nature to help establish order in what appears to be a chaotic universe. These laws have more and more been uncovered, but even they require revision due to evolution. By being able to apply certain laws of nature, we as atomic-age humans have advanced in creating some comforts, but have also greatly spoiled our environment. Nevertheless, modern science and its positive by-products—convenience, material comforts, extraordinary machines to make life easier, etc.—create the feeling that all or most all problems can be solved or that anything can ultimately be learned. The scientific method used in the physical sciences is much less sensible when studying people, as we then become both subject and object. Further, when making an inquiry about a person, an institution, a society, or even a concept, dialectical thinking is far more appropriate than the traditional (quantitative) empirical mode of thought, as the former is dynamic rather than static. Change, which is inevitable, is the basis of the dialectic. Buss (1979), as he describes what he calls the "dialectical paradigm," articulates these last two points well:

> the reciprocal, interactive relationship between the person and reality such that each may serve as both subject and object. . . . the idea that the subject-object relation is two-dimensional, rather than one dimensional. . . .which accommodates the structure of both Person Constructs Reality and Reality Constructs Person. (p. 8)

There is no way that a methodology used to study people can be said to be truly realistic if delimiting parameters are set up, either by a single academic discipline's narrow frame of reference, or even worse, when the approach borrowed from the physical sciences, "all things being equal," is used, as they never are with humans. Schooling is too complex a process to confine its study to certain habits of any particular professional area. If a valid picture of schooling is sought, it must be through the well focused lens of an interdisciplinary approach, so as not to deny any factual possibilities which various fields can offer. Any area from the social sciences can offer something useful for clarification purposes because schooling is a social process itself, while the humanities help maintain the proper ethical perspective. The study of the schooling process must be interdisciplinary or it would be a distortion of the truth, a mere biased slant comprising a tiny slice of reality.

Dialectic as Radical Methodology

For the ancient, "dialectic was understood by its users as pertaining exclusively to debate and reasoning" (Tolman, 1983, p. 321). In more modern times it was revived as a method of analysis for philosophers. When the nineteenth century philosopher Hegel formulated his dialectical method he recognized the importance of contradiction. He believed skepticism, negation and reason to be essential ingredients for understanding or arriving at truth. "To understand something dialectically it must be understood in terms of what qualities it both does and does not have, where the true essence of a thing is ultimately defined in terms of an endless set of relations" (Buss, 1979, p. 78). Hegel was opposed to the simplistic static notion of little autonomic facts which could form totalities for understanding, as well as the sequence "thesis, antithesis, synthesis," according to Buss (1979, p. 78), who directs us to Hegelian scholars to support these contentions:

> Fichte introduced into German philosophy the three-step of thesis, antithesis, and synthesis, using these three terms. Schelling took up this terminology; Hegel did not. He never once

used these three terms together to designate three stages in an argument or account in any of his books. And they do not help us understand his *Phenomenology*, his *Logic*, or his philosophy of history; they impede any open-minded comprehension of what he does by forcing it into a schema which was available to him and which he deliberately spurned. (Kaufmann, 1966, p. 154)

There has been a lot of loose talk about Hegel's dialectic being a movement from thesis to antithesis to synthesis. Not only do these concepts play an insignificant role in Hegel's philosophy, they are essentially static concepts and completely misrepresent what Hegel means by "dialectic." The dialectic . . . is essentially a dynamic and organic process. One "moment" of a dialectical process, when it is fully developed or understood, gives rise to its own negation; it is not mechanically confronted by an antithesis. (Bernstein, 1971, p.20)

Marx, a student of Hegelian thought, adapted Hegel's dialectic to his own work after turning it upside down. Freedom was a most important ideal to Hegel, but as "an idealist, he believed that freedom could be attained in the mind and this would of logical necessity correspond to the realization of freedom in reality" (Buss, 1979, p. 79). Marx, being a realist-materialist, naturally saw it the other way round. Marx is important, among many other reasons, for applying a philosophic methodology to his historical socio-economic studies (known then as political economy). The dialectic method, as per Tolman (1983), does have certain "essential ingredients": "movement from state (ignorance, uncertainty, error) to a qualitatively different state (knowledge, certainty, truth) by means of a process (conversation, debate, dialogue) that is characterized by opposition (contradiction, refutation, negation) and governed by an internal necessity (logic, deduction)" (p. 321).

Marx's use of dialectic, as well as his writings in general, were taken up by scholars in various fields such as sociology, economics, history, political science, etc. Also, even though Marx had virtually nothing to say about education (Pacheco, 1978) except in its relation to social class (and scantily even here), his influence has been felt in the areas of philosophy of education and sociology of education and at an increasing rate over the last twenty years or so.

Marx's ideas have been taken up by some contemporary psychologists as well. Though no specific allegiance to Marx is usually made by proponents of dialectical psychology—a growing influence found especially within the subspecialty of human development—it is becoming an important orientation. Whereas "dialectic is a method of seeking and sometimes arriving at the truth by reasoning" (Hall, 1967, p. 385) for philosophers, it is becoming more widely used by behavioral and social scientists to investigate social forces.

Perhaps the first psychologist to use the dialectic methodology was the Russian psychologist Lev Semyonovich Vygotsky who lived from 1896 to 1934. See, for example, Vygotsky's (1931/1978) work cited below.

> The concept of a historically based psychology is misunderstood by most researchers who study child development. For them, to study something historically means, by definition, to study some past event. Hence, they naively imagine an insurmountable barrier between historic study and study of present-day behavioral forms. *To study something historically means to study it in the process of change;* that is the dialectical method's basic demand. To encompass in research the process of a given thing's development in all its phases and changes—from birth to death—fundamentally means to discover its nature, its essence. (pp. 64–65)

> *The search for method becomes one of the most important problems of the entire enterprise of understanding the uniquely human forms of psychological activity. In this case, the method is simultaneously prerequisite and product, the tool and the result of the study.* (p. 65)

Only now are both Vygotsky and the dialectical method being taken seriously by Western psychologists.

Riegel (1979) utilized dialectical psychology to better understand human development. The following is how he viewed dialectical thought as a scholarly endeavor. "Dialectical thinking emphasizes the interdependence of form and content. In its narrow sense, this principle deals with the interrelationship between methods and results, in its most general sense, between subject and object" (p. 47). Also, below is Riegel's (1979) brilliant, most radical, theory of learning, although he did not refer to it as such. "Thinking, in a dialectical sense, is the process of transforming contradictory experience into momentary stable structures. These structures consolidate the contradictory evidence but do not by themselves represent thinking, they merely represent the products of thinking" (p. 45).

The underpinnings of RSA, both theoretical and practical, as a specific methodology are discussed below. It has been emphasized already that RSA has an integral historical component. This is because dialectical rather than traditional logic is used; and while the latter is a-historical, dialectical logic cannot be. This is explained nicely by Riegel (1979):

> Traditional logic, as well as traditional philosophy and science, have been exclusively concerned with nontemporal conditions. The concept of a nonchanging state of being, as originated in Eleatic philosophy, was thought to reflect the universal order of the cosmos. Traditional logic and mathematics are the remnants of the a-developmental and a-historical thinking of Eleatic philosophers. (pp. 177–178)

> The development of dialectical logic, especially by Hegel, has not been commonly accepted in natural sciences. . .and, most surprisingly, it has received even lesser attention in the behavioral and social sciences. Since. . .dialectical logic is the mode of thinking that alone can deal appropriately with change, development, and history, such a disregard is regrettable indeed. (pp. 178–179)

Stressed also has been that RSA is an accommodating, flexible methodology that does not ignore information that is potentially enlightening, regardless of its field of origin. Turning again to Riegel (1979):

> Dialectic logic represents an open system of thinking that can always be extended to incorporate the more restricted systems. Traditional logic aims at a single universal analysis. As a consequence it is inflexible and cannot apprehend itself; in particular, it cannot apprehend itself in the developmental and historical process. (p. 178)

Additionally, society is viewed here from Marx's "historical dialectic"—basically, "humankind and history are in tension yet in an
inescapable harmony" (Angeles, 1981, p. 62). The epistemic rationale is dialectical (rather than positivistic), and the underlying
theory is that of the Marx-Engels' "dialectical materialism," as explained below:

> 1. The theory that (a) social progress occurs through struggle,
> conflict, interaction, and opposition (in particular of economic
> classes), and (b) the development (or emergence) of one level
> of society from another does not happen gradually but by
> sudden and occasionally catastrophic jumps.
> 2. The type of thinking process which attempts (a) to perceive
> how all things are inexorably interrelated as a whole, and (b)
> to accept the absolute necessity of that interrelated whole
> (which is the essence of freedom), and (c) to accept the in-
> evitability of struggle, conflict, contradiction, change, and
> emergence of novelty in the universe. (Angeles, 1981, pp.
> 161–162)

Just as Karl Marx traced with his interactionistic dialectical
method the materialist progression of capitalism to better understand it as a phenomenon, this work, by analogy, calls for a fuller
comprehension of American special education's development,
through RSA, to more rationally direct its future. If this can be
done with some degree of success, it is believed that discourse
on special education can be more enlightening and humane. The
end result will be that it can be better known what special education should actually encompass in a free society.

Chapter 7

The Orthopedically Disabled Child: Psychological Implications with an Individual Basis*

Scott B. Sigmon

[The author believes that the "individual psychology" of Alfred Adler (1870–1937) and "field theory" associated with Kurt Lewin (1890–1947) are most efficacious theoretical positions in understanding orthopedically disabled children, as such youngsters have a remarkable range of individual differences, both in type of disability as well as level of adjustment. This chapter also deals with educational and social factors regarding the orthopedically disabled youngster. This is a model which can be used with any impaired, individual student. It must be kept in mind that an impairment is not necessarily a handicap. Therefore, impaired pupils should not automatically be placed into special education—they should first be allowed if at all possible to attend ordinary classes with any necessary supports.]

Overview

This chapter addresses the influence of environmental interaction on the development of orthopedically disabled (OD) children. The OD child is one who has a deformity that causes interference with the normal use of bones, muscles, or joints. Difficulties in movement and access to places create special adjustment needs.

*This chapter is here, with the exception of minor editorial changes, as it appeared when first published in *Individual Psychology: The Journal of Adlerian Theory, Research & Practice* (1986), Vol. 42, No. 2, pp. 274–278. Copyright © 1986 the University of Texas Press.

Parental attitude regarding independence is critical to the overall adjustment of the OD child. OD children often have problems due to overprotection and dependency. The more experiences parents can provide, the more likely it is that the OD child will succeed in school situations (Bradley, 1970). The style of childrearing has great effect on personality development.

The OD child, naturally, as all children do, compares oneself to others. However, the self-evaluation for someone with such condition reflects, in varying degrees, a less than perfect body image. Moreover, when viewed this way, fear of further injury may result producing a lack of confidence in addition to lowered self-esteem.

The educational program for OD children should have similar basic educational requirements as those for other children. Schooling for all exceptional children should be based on developing their strengths, rather than simply coping with their weaknesses. Wherever feasible and advantageous to the OD child, school placement should be within regular classes (also known as "mainstreaming"). Educational adaptations that may be necessary are: (a) rest periods during physical education time provided for non-disabled classmates, although "adaptive" physical education or physical therapy should be substituted; (b) ample space and adjustable or movable desks; (c) special transportation; and (d) special entry and exit considerations, such as (un)loading platforms for buses and door ramps. Specific adaptations—perhaps tape recorders for note taking for those who cannot write—are necessary depending on the particular case. OD children may be reluctant to try new things—such as musical instruments—and therefore, encouragement and support are advisable. OD children may sometimes seem to have limited social skills, but it is likely that such limitations are a result of a poorly conceived educational plan for these children, and are not imposed by the disability.

Research

The accumulated knowledge of psychology has provided much evidence that human personality and behavior are shaped not solely by either hereditary or environmental influences, but by a combination of the two. Kurt Lewin (1936) further developed this thesis with his "theory of topological space" or "field theory" which states that human behavior is a function of an individual's *interaction* with the environment. Lewin is of immense help because he stresses the examination of a person's "life space," as the additional problems orthopedically disabled children will confront actually involve access to places. Once the aspect of personal life space has been considered, then the psychology of such children as individuals can be more cogently explored.

The research says that children with physical disabilities, as a group, tend to have frequent and more severe psychological problems than others (Meyerson, 1971). This is because they are more frequently placed in novel psychological situations which often impose traumatic demands on them—especially when they attempt unrealistic tasks. However, there "is no such thing as a psychology of disability" per se; instead, problems arise "as a result of the reduced mobility associated with their disability" (Livingston, Korn, & McAlees, 1982, p. 735). More precisely, "there appears to be little evidence that a specific [physical] disability is associated with a specific personality" (Diller, 1972, pp. 611–612). It is believed that the following research confirms Adler's thesis concerning the inferiority feeling and compensation. Mussen and Newman (1958) designed a study to discover what factors are significantly related to children's general adjustment to physical defects. Basically, they found that adjustment may involve acceptance or recognition of disability. Thus, the well adjusted OD child—who accepts disability—recognizes that more help may be needed from others than is needed by intact children. Hence, one will accept and react positively toward this dependency rather than suppress it. Others are of similar opinion. Livingston et al. (1982) wrote that "personal adjustment involves . . . accepting the real limits of a disability without feeling personally devaluated" (p.735). To assist in adjustment, Meyerson (1971) recommends an "education of the disabled person in specific social skills which will facilitate his acceptance as a person" (p.34).

Individual Psychology

Adler's (1907/1917) main contribution, concerning "organic inferiority" and "compensation," was the development of a technique which permits a clarification of the psychological dynamics in each individual case (Dreikurs, 1948). The "life-style" (a term first used in the psychological literature by Adler) is developed at a young age through the interpretation children make of the experiences and difficulties that confront them. A disability—even a severe handicap—is only one, although often an important personality determinant. It is not what the child has—in hereditary endowment and environmental experience—but what is done with it that is the essential determinant. Ultimately, the individual alone determines what significance the influential forces from within and without have (Dreikurs, 1948).

Adler's ideas on the psychology of deficiency are ideal in explaining either positive or negative consequences for development, especially for the OD child. Inferiority can refer to any objective inadequacy in function or status, but it does not necessarily produce an "inferiority feeling." On the other hand, an inferiority feeling may exist without any objective inferiority. The personality development of the OD child is often more complicated than that of the physically intact child as there is an objective organ inferiority in addition to functional inferiorities. Inferiority feelings are based on correct or incorrect assumptions of one's social inferiority and are primarily determined in early childhood. Personality is not determined by an inferiority, but by the reaction of the individual to the inferiority (Dreikurs, 1948). "Feelings of inferiority, arising from the sense of imperfection and incompletion" motivate "the individual to strive for a higher level of development and as such, are the cause of all improvement in life situation" (Wolman, 1973, p. 193). When a new plateau is reached, inferiority feelings recur, possibly causing more upward striving. If the perceived inferiority becomes exaggerated, development is thwarted, striving is greatly reduced or halted, and a psychopathological situation can develop. Only the inferiority feeling can stimulate a compensation on the part of the individual. With regard to actual biological inferiorities and organ deficiencies, there may be physical compensation without any awareness by the individual. The "inferiority complex" implies awareness but does not necessarily lead to any compensation, and this complex is therefore a deadlock for any further development.

Conclusions

There is an impressive range of individual differences in type and level of adjustment even for persons with identical physical handicaps. One may become dependent and despondent, while another becomes independent and mature—this is what Wright (1960) called "reconciling the expectation discrepancy." Lifestyle, courage, and social interest are most important factors determining social adjustment of individuals with orthopedic disabilities. Needed is a lessening of prejudice toward the orthopedically disabled, and an increase in ecologic public facilities (such as elevators and ramps) for them, in addition to specific studies geared to their particular needs. Unnecessary are false claims for a group psychology of orthopedically disabled children, despite their similar needs according to particular physical disabilities. Their psychologies are individual.

The orthopedically handicapped have, in many cases, actually been discussed in the modern literature from an individual psychology perspective—but in non-Adlerian terminology. This has been unfortunate because concepts such as inferiority feelings not only help us to better understand the OD child's individual psyche in relation to environmental interaction, but knowledge of individual psychology allows us to better implement psychotherapeutic as well as educational interventions.

Chapter 8

Minority Overrepresentation:
A Case for Alternative Practices Prior to Referral*

Larry Maheady, Richard Towne,
Bob Algozzine, Jane Mercer,
and James Ysseldyke

Although the problem of minority overrepresentation in special education programs for the mildly handicapped has been widely recognized and documented, the factors responsible for such an overrepresentation remain the source of much controversy. The most popular explanation continues to be the presence of systematic bias in the assessment process, particularly with regard to intelligence testing. Unfortunately, attempts at isolating and controlling specific facets of this bias have been largely unsuccessful. Furthermore, preoccupation with this problem has detracted our attention from a much more pressing concern: the identification and provision of effective instructional services *prior* to referring minority students to special education. The purpose of this chapter is to describe alternative approaches to dealing with the overrepresentation problem. Specifically, we have highlighted the importance of using alternative instructional strategies prior to referral, and have described five practices that appear to hold promise in this area.

More minority children are served in special education programs for the mildly handicapped than would be expected based

*This chapter first appeared in *Learning Disability Quarterly* (1983), Vol. 6, No. 4, pp. 448–456. Copyright © 1983 the Council for Learning Disabilities.

solely on the proportion of minority students in the general school population. This *disproportion* or *overrepresentation* is neither a new nor an isolated phenomenon, and is especially true for black children (Dunn, 1968; Heller, Holtzman, & Messick, 1982). The 1978 Office for Civil Rights (OCR) biannual nationwide survey of students, for example, revealed that while only 16 percent of all elementary and secondary students in this country were black, approximately 38 percent of the students in classes for educable mentally retarded (EMR) students were black. More recently, Tucker (1980) noted a similar trend in programs for the learning disabled as a result of concern for overrepresentation in EMR classes. In his words:

> when it was no longer socially desirable to place black students in EMR classes, it became convenient to place them in the newly provided LD category. It took a year to make the changeover, but the resultant proportional differences were maintained. (p. 104)

Although overrepresentation is clearly occurring in special classes for mildly handicapped students, it is not so clear what causes this situation and what can be done to correct it. No single causative factor has been identified, yet the preponderance of literature in this area points to *test bias* as the major contributor to the overrepresentation problem (see Bailey & Harbin, 1980; Greenwood, Preston, & Harris, 1982b; Oakland, 1977; Williams, 1970, for a more complete discussion of this topic). Of particular concern to minority groups has been the process by which items are selected for inclusion in standardized tests, the standardization sample used in norming these measures, and the tests' validation process (Greenwood et al., 1982b). In general, it has been argued that traditional standardized tests (particularly IQ tests) rely heavily upon the values and experiences of the white, middle-class culture and, therefore, discriminate against persons from differing cultural backgrounds. Furthermore, critics have noted that normative samples, which traditionally include greater numbers of whites, systematically weigh performance levels in favor of the white, middle-class culture. In the face of these persuasive arguments, educators have spent a considerble amount of time attempting to rectify such test bias. Attempts have included: (a) developing "new" testing procedures (e.g., culture-fair and culture-free tests), (b) using adaptive behavior scales in conjunction with intelligence measures, (c) using criterion-referenced measures, and (d) interpreting results using local and/or special group norms (Bailey & Harbin, 1980). For the most part, these procedures have not significantly reduced overrepresentation (Bailey & Harbin, 1980; Reschly, 1979, 1980; Sattler, 1982; Tucker, 1980).

Given the complexity and long-standing nature of the minority overrepresentation problem, it is not surprising to find that attempts at ameliorating only one facet of the educational decision-making process (i.e., assessment) have not been successful. Indeed, even if truly nondiscriminatory assessment measures were developed, they would do little to reduce the systematic bias that has been documented to occur both prior to and following assessment (Ysseldyke & Algozzine, 1982). More importantly, systematic improvements in our ability to fairly assess minority children would be of little value without similar advances in our ability to effectively instruct these students.

Previous efforts to correct the overrepresentation problem by searching for *The* "fair" test or set of tests have been shortsighted. Indeed, such conceptual tunnel vision has seriously impeded our attempts at carefully evaluating other options at our disposal (e.g., improving the quality of regular education services *before* referring a child for special services). For example, compared to the number of articles about non-discriminatory assessment and test bias, there is a relative paucity of literature on effective alternative instructional strategies that can be used with minority students at risk for academic failure prior to referral. Similarly, very little has been written about alternative screening practices which do not result in disproportionate numbers of minority children being identified as needing special services.

The overrepresentation problem has been part of the agenda at the Office for Civil Rights for some time. Charged with the task of ensuring that local education agencies (LEAs) comply with mandates prohibiting discrimination against minority students, OCR's technical assistance division recently sought guidance from the National Research Council. As a result, the Council established the Panel on Selection and Placement of Students in Programs for the Mentally Retarded (1979) and charged it with a twofold mission:

(1) to determine the factors that account for disproportionate representation of minority students and males in special education programs, especially programs for mentally retarded students and (2) to identify placement criteria or practices that do not affect minority students and males disproportionately. (Heller et al., 1982, p. ix)

Following a period of study and debate, the panel proposed six "principles of responsibility" to guide LEA efforts to validly assess the educational needs of minority children and provide appropriate, high-quality services. The recommendations were consistent with existing laws and were already being practiced by some LEAs. Briefly, the panel's six principles asked participants in the educational decision-making process to engage in multiple educational interventions and note the effects of such strategies on a student experiencing academic failure in a regular classroom before referring him/her for special education assessment. Further, the panel recommended: (a) use of functional assessment procedures, (b) ongoing monitoring of the effectiveness of existing special education programs within LEAs, and (c) deemphasis on distinct categorical programming. By shifting attention from presumed deficiencies in the child to an analysis of contributing factors in the child's school environment, the panel was essentially recommending a radical change of current educational decision-making practices.

The purpose of this chapter is to identify and describe five instructional strategies that can be implemented prior to referring a student for assessment. Before describing each practice, however, some mention must be made of the empirical underpinnings of sound instruction. According to Rosenshine and Berliner (1978), most recent attempts at identifying "effective" instructional practices for use with traditionally low-achieving populations (e.g., minorities) have moved from a primary concern with teacher behaviors to a consideration of specific student variables. In particular, educational researchers have become increasingly concerned with determining if students are *directly* engaged in mastering basic academic skills and what kind of progress they are making towards the mastery of those skills. This critical examination has led to a concept known as "academic engaged time" (AET) (Rosenshine & Berliner, 1978). Essentially, AET refers to the amount of time a student spends engaged in academically relevant materials which are at a moderate difficulty level. It should not come as a surprise that a strong correlation has consistently been found between AET and student achievement gain. That is, in those programs where higher AET was reported, student achievement levels were higher, whereas achievement gain was negligible in programs with minimal amounts of AET (Marshall, 1976; Stallings & Kaskowitz, 1974).

The implications of these findings for educational personnel in charge of selecting alternative instructional practices for students at risk for academic failure are clear, i.e., whenever possible, programs should be chosen which maximize or lead to increased academic engaged time. To aid educational decision-makers in this selection process, researchers have suggested that a set of instructional procedures termed *direct instruction* provide the most effective format for increasing AET. Essentially, *direct instruction* refers to a set of teaching behaviors in which: (a) instructional materials are academically focused, (b) learning goals are clear to students, (c) time allocated for instruction is sufficient and continuous, (d) content coverage is extensive, (e) student performance is continuously monitored, (f) teacher questions are at an appropriate level so that many correct student responses occur, and (g) feedback to students is immediate and academically oriented (Rosenshine & Berliner, 1978; Stevens & Rosenshine, 1981). Each of the five practices selected by our project reflects, to varying degrees, the characteristics inherent in a direct instructional approach.

Instruction may be organized in many ways for the purpose of increasing the amount of time students spend actively engaged in the material being presented. Of interest in our research were practices that met the broad, general criteria listed in Table 1. A review of recent literature (including government documents, final reports and published articles) as well as information provided by OCR personnel and other practicing professionals led to five alternative instructional practices believed to effectively improve the academic performance of minority students at risk for special educational referral. The practices included: DISTAR, Exemplary Center for Reading Instruction, precision teaching, classroom-wide peer tutoring and the Adaptive Learning Environments Model.

Table 1
Global Criteria for Selection of Alternative Practices
for Instruction, Referral, and Assessment
of Low-Achieving Minority Students

1. Alternative educational strategies must conform to the legal requirements of Public Law 94-142 and Section 504 of the Rehabilitation Act.

2. Alternative educational strategies must be consistent with the applicable principles enumerated by the *Panel on Selection and Placement of Students in Programs for the Mentally Retarded.*

3. Alternative educational strategies must be *feasible* in terms of program effectiveness, practicality and replicability (based upon professional opinions).

4. Alternative educational strategies must be currently implemented in target sites representative of those available in public school systems.

5. Alternative educational strategies and/or assessment practices must be representative of at least one type of practice as outlined by the Office for Civil Rights.

DISTAR

Perhaps the most widely known direct instructional approach is published by Science Research Associates under the trade name DISTAR. DISTAR programs grew out of the combined work of Wesley Becker at the University of Kansas on the systematic use of reinforcement procedures in the classroom and Siegfried Engelmann's work in the Bereiter-Engelmann (1966) preschool programs for disadvantaged children (Becker & Carnine, 1980; Engelmann, 1971). In general, these programs emphasized the use of small-group instruction by teachers and aides following carefully sequenced lessons in reading, arithmetic, and language (Becker & Carnine, 1980).

Initial attempts at evaluating the effectiveness of DISTAR programs were undertaken as part of the United States Office of Education's (USOE) funded Follow-Through project. Essentially, Project Follow-Through represented a concerted effort on the part of the U.S. government to evaluate the effectiveness of a variety of educational approaches to the reduction of school failure among economically disadvantaged children (Becker & Carnine, 1980). Data from this massive project were collected by Stanford Research Institute, analyzed by Abt Associates, and eventually published by the latter organization (Abt Associates, 1976, 1977). Although the publication of these data has resulted in considerable debate (see House, Glass, McLean, & Walker, 1978, for a critique of the Follow-Through evaluations), the general findings appeared to indicate that the DISTAR program did result in substantial positive effects. Additional support for DISTAR programs can be found in the special education literature. For example, a recent review by Gersten (1982) concluded that a number of experimental studies have shown that,

> Direct instruction reading and language programs consistently produce higher academic gains than traditional approaches in both mainstreamed and self-contained classes, and across a range of handicapping conditions. (pp. 19–20)

Finally, further support for DISTAR programs came from recent field-site visits, undertaken as part of our project. For example, in one large urban district with a substantial proportion of minority youngsters (i.e., Hispanic, black, and Asian), a primary objective stated that by the end of second grade, students with continuous participation in DISTAR programs since entering kindergarten would, on the average, be performing at or above the national average. LEA data indicated that at grade two the objective was indeed attained in all subject areas, i.e., reading, math and language. In addition to improving basic academic performance, LEA personnel reported that student referral rates from DISTAR classrooms to special education programs were approximately one-half the rate of those from traditional classrooms.

Exemplary Center for Reading Instruction

The Exemplary Center for Reading Instruction (ECRI) was funded in the mid-1960s by the United States Office of Education. Since that time, ECRI has functioned as a Joint Dissemination Review Panel (JDRP) approved developer-demonstration project to instruct teachers on how to use classroom time more effectively and efficiently. ECRI focuses primarily upon individualized instruction techniques and positive reinforcement. More specifically, teachers are taught how to: (a) elicit correct responses from nonresponding pupils, (b) establish mastery levels of responses with performance and rate as criteria, (c) provide time for supervised practice, (d) correlate language arts activities to facilitate accurate responding, (e) use effective management and monitoring systems, and (f) diagnose and intervene immediately when errors or no responses occur (ECRI, JDRP Report No. 74–78, 1981).

Essentially, ECRI is a total language arts instructional program that provides instruction simultaneously in reading, oral language, spelling, comprehension, and other activities in a structured, systematic pattern that ensures mastery. ECRI students learn to read each word, spell it, write it, understand its meaning, and use it in a sentence as they encounter it in reading exercises. ECRI also shares many of the characteristics of the DISTAR programs, i.e., small-group instruction, controlled practice, group choral responding, mastery learning, and rapid student response rates. The primary difference between the two programs lies in the content covered. Whereas DISTAR provides specific lessons in commercially packaged formats, ECRI procedures can be readily adapted to existing basal series.

The original ECRI project was validated over a three-year period (1971–1974) with more than 700 pupils in four Utah school districts. First graders were reading at a 3.8 grade level; second graders averaged the 95th to 99th percentile; clinic pupils averaged four months' gain per month; Title I pupils averaged 1.4 to 3.2 years' gain per year (ECRI, JDRP Report No. 74–78, 1981). Additional support for ECRI comes from a more recent investigation (Bayman, 1979) in which it was found that ECRI programs significantly improved the standard reading test performance of Navajo students in three elementary schools. With the exception of one group, every class of fourth through seventh graders using ECRI met and/or exceeded expected growth levels. Linn (1980), an elementary principal in a large urban school district, composed primarily of economically disadvantaged minority students, also reported that students enrolled in ECRI classrooms for five years all scored above grade level in total reading. Finally, Reid (undated) found that two schools with long previous histories of low reading scores (one school contained 60 percent Ute Indians, the other was comprised of over 65 percent black and Hispanic students) raised their yearly achievement levels above neighboring, non-minority middle-class school districts after only three years of ECRI instruction.

Precision Teaching

Unlike the previously described practices, precision teaching is *not* necessarily a method of instruction. Instead, it is a way to plan, use, and analyze any teaching technique or instructional method. More specifically, precision teaching is a set of measurement procedures that *guide* educational decision-makers in making better instructional decisions (Beck, 1979). Precision teaching requires the *direct* and *daily* measurement of student academic performance. Data are typically collected through one-minute timings in which students attempt to complete as many items as possible from individualized worksheets (e.g., completions of math problems, oral reading of vocabulary words). Daily accuracy and error rates are calculated (by the students if possible) and graphed on standard acceleration charts. An evaluation of students' performance charts provides classroom teachers with formative evaluation data allowing them to make data-based educational decisions. For example, if student performance data show increasing daily accuracy rates with concurrent decreases in errors in basic math computation skills, the teacher can conclude that the child is making adequate progress toward the specified instructional objective. Therefore, current instructional practices should be continued. If, on the other hand, daily performance data reveal: (a) no improvements and/or decreases in ongoing accuracy rates, or (b) escalating error rates, existing instructional practices must be modified.

Precision teaching provides the classroom teacher with: (a) a precise means of describing academic behavior, (b) a unique recording and charting procedure, (c) a set of techniques for interpreting and applying decision rules from charted data, and (d) a bank of practice sheets designed to complement and reinforce the classroom teacher's current curriculum objectives (Beck, 1979).

On two occasions the Precision Teaching Project of Great Falls, Montana, has demonstrated before the U.S. Office of Education the efficacy of its model. In 1975, as a special education-oriented program, precision teaching was validated and approved for national dissemination. In order to collect longitudinal data on the project's effects, the Precision Teaching Project conducted a follow-up study on special education students identified and remediated three years earlier. The investigation revealed minimal washout effects as measured by standardized achievement tests, classroom performance, and teacher judgments. Within the past four years, precision teaching has received validation and approval for teaching basic academic skills in regular elementary classrooms (Beck, 1979).

Although precision teaching per se is not a method of teaching, it shares many of the characteristics of both DISTAR and ECRI. First, all three practices emphasize the necessity of direct measurement of student performance. That is, student progress is evaluated in terms of how well students perform *within* their curricular materials. Second, precision teaching, DISTAR and ECRI stress the necessity of frequent, intense practice sessions in which students perform at high accuracy rates. Third, all three practices have established performance standards that students must reach before proceeding to more complex tasks. In the case of DISTAR and ECRI, mastery learning is stressed, whereas precision teaching emphasizes accuracy and speed with high performance standards (Beck, 1983).

Class-Wide Peer Tutoring

A fourth, alternative instructional practice identified by the current project is class-wide peer tutoring. This practice is an outgrowth of the work of Charles Greenwood and his colleagues at Juniper Gardens Children's Project in Kansas City, Kansas. Like precision teaching, class-wide peer tutoring is not a unique method of instruction, nor does it require a prescribed curriculum such as DISTAR. Instead, class-wide peer tutoring can be best described as an alternative instructional activity that can be effectively implemented across a broad range of settings, academic skills, and instructional materials.

One of the primary purposes of class-wide peer tutoring is to increase the amount of time low-achieving students spend directly practicing appropriate academic responses (e.g., reading orally, spelling, and/or completing math problems), or in the words of Rosenshine and Berliner (1978), to *increase their academic engaged time*. To accomplish this, the Juniper Gardens staff (Delquadri, Whorton, Elliott, Greenwood, & Hall, 1981) devised a program whereby entire classrooms are divided into tutoring dyads. The tutoring pairs alternate tutor and tutee roles for ten minutes each on a daily basis. Tutors are required to: (a) monitor ongoing tutee responses, (b) identify and correct errors, and (c) give points for correct performance. The teacher monitors the class-wide process, awards bonus points to tutors for "good" tutoring, and, if needed, answers tutees' questions (Greenwood et al., 1982a). Additional programmatic features include: (a) weekly competing teams, (b) public posting of game charts, (c) a modeling error correct procedure, and (d) weekly teacher assessment of individual student progress (Greenwood et al., 1982a).

Class-wide peer tutoring shares many of the characteristics previously outlined for DISTAR, ECRI, and precision teaching. That is, an emphasis upon direct measurement of academic competence (i.e., student accuracy and error rates), a need to increase student engaged practice time, and a specific set of performance standards (Beck, 1983). It appears that facets of all four practices could be used interchangeably in a variety of instructional combinations. For example, class-wide peer tutoring can be easily integrated into existing DISTAR programs to provide students with additional opportunities to practice their daily lessons. Similarly, daily precision teaching timings may be carried out during peer tutoring sessions. This would be especially beneficial for subjects who must be timed on an individual basis (e.g., oral reading). It should be noted, however, that class-wide peer tutoring will only be effective if implemented within a framework of good teaching practices (e.g., appropriate placement within instructional materials and adequate sequencing of learning tasks).

The effectiveness of class-wide peer tutoring as an alternative instructional strategy for use with low-achieving, minority students has been described elsewhere (Greenwood et al., 1982a). Briefly, these data revealed significant increases in academic engaged time and student academic performance while class-wide peer tutoring was in effect. Based on preliminary data from a recent investigation, Greenwood et al. (1982a) are attempting to link increments in students' daily response rates to demonstrated changes on standardized achievement measures.

Adaptive Learning Environments Model

The Adaptive Learning Environments Model (ALEM), developed by Margaret Wang and her colleagues at the University of Pittsburgh's Learning Research and Development Center, is the product of more than a decade of educational research (Wang, 1981). Presently, the ALEM model is being implemented in 136 school districts across 28 states. In essence, ALEM, which is based on a systems approach to program development, consists of three basic elements and five major program components. Major program components include: (a) a highly structured and hierarchically organized prescriptive curriculum, (b) an instructional -learning management system designed to maximize the use of available classroom time and resources, (c) a family participation program aimed at increasing communication between school and home, (d) a multi-age grouping and instructional-teaming classroom organizational support system, and (e) a systematic staff development program (Reynolds & Wang, 1983).

Like DISTAR, the Adaptive Learning Environments Model places a clear emphasis on the necessity of a tightly structured, hierarchically sequenced curriculum. Similarly, the ALEM shares the concerns of DISTAR, ECRI, precision-teaching and class-wide peer tutoring for maximizing student engaged time through better management of teacher time and resources. Finally, like the previously described practices, the ALEM recognizes the necessity of grouping students according to their *instructional* needs rather than by age and/or grade level.

Although the Adaptive Learning Environments Model has much in common with the instructional alternatives discussed previously, several differences do exist. For example, unlike the other more "direct" instructional programs, the ALEM incorporates a more open-ended exploratory learning component. This facet of the model is designed to promote students' processes of inquiry, as well as social and personal development (Wang, 1981). Unlike DISTAR, ECRI, or class-wide peer tutoring, the ALEM does not appear to place as much emphasis on the role of extrinsic reinforcement in developing and maintaining student response rates. Finally, the ALEM differs somewhat from the previously outlined practices by containing systematic procedures for determining the degree to which it is being effectively implemented. With the exception of DISTAR, few systematic attempts have been made to describe the other programs as independent variables.

Data regarding the effectiveness of the ALEM have focused on a number of variables including: (a) student achievement in basic skills, (b) classroom process effects (e.g., students' time on task), (c) degree of program implementation, (d) attitudinal and social outcomes, and (e) cost effectiveness. According to Wang (1981), results from research on ALEM's impact on student achievement in basic skills and on their social behavior have shown consistent positive trends. For example, analyses of standardized achievement test results of a number of classrooms in the national Follow-Through program revealed that ALEM students scored above both the estimated population norms for students from low-income families and national norms established by the standardized tests (Wang, 1981). In addition, Wang (1981) noted that from a fiscal perspective, the ALEM has generally been shown to be cost effective.

Summary and Conclusions

The problem of minority overrepresentation in special education programs for the mildly handicapped has been clearly recognized and documented. What remains unclear, however, is what causes this problem and how it should be addressed. As suggested in this chapter, most individuals familiar with the over-representation issue have affixed blame to systematic bias in the standardized testing process. Subsequently, attempts at reducing minority overrepresentation have resulted in unending endeavors to find *The* fair test or set of tests. It is our contention that this search has not been overly successful. Furthermore, we believe that the pursuit of quality in testing has diverted our attention away from a much more pressing concern, that is, the provision of quality instructional services *prior* to referral for special education.

The purpose of this chapter was to describe alternative approaches to dealing with the overrepresentation problem. In so doing, we have highlighted the importance of using alternative instructional strategies prior to referral, and have described five practices that appear to hold promise in this area. The practices share many characteristics, and, to varying degrees, all five reflect components of the direct instructional models frequently cited in the "effective schools" literature (Bickel, 1983; Rosenshine & Berliner, 1978; Stevens & Rosenshine, 1981). It should not be inferred, however, that choosing any one of these models will result in an immediate solution to the overrepresentation problem. Nor should it be construed that changes in just one facet of the educational decision-making process (i.e., what and how to teach) will, in and of itself, dramatically affect the numbers of minority students being placed in special programs. However, we do believe that the use of these practices *in conjunction with* systematic improvements at the screening, assessment, and placement phases of the educational decision-making process will contribute much to improving the quality of educational services for *all* children.

Chapter 9

A Vygotskian Perspective on Assessment in Reading*

Peter H. Johnston

Current methods of assessment in reading are deeply entrenched in the structure of educational practice and social values. Thus it is easy to take as immutable some of the major premises supporting the status quo. In this chapter I propose to examine reading assessment from an alternative perspective, that of the Russian psychologist, Vygotsky. The chapter deals with Vygotsky's emphasis on process-oriented, dynamic methods of assessment. It deals with the implications of some of the major elements of Activity Theory, particularly goals, motives and contexts. Although activity theory has been substantially developed since his work, its beginnings are clearly attributable to Vygotsky. Finally, the chapter addresses issues in the interpretation of performance.

In line with Vygotsky's emphasis on younger children, the focus of the chapter is on assessment in the early years of reading development. It is argued that serious application of Vygotsky's notions to assessment in reading would require substantial revision of current assumptions in both assessment and teacher training.

Process-Oriented, Dynamic Methods of Assessment

Process versus Product

Vygotsky's emphasis on assessing cognitive processes rather than mere products of these processes was at least as strong as

---

*This chapter first appeared in *Reading-Canada-Lecture* (1986), Vol. 4, No. 2, pp. 82–92.

our current penchant for the reverse. Criticism of product-oriented approaches permeates his writing. Currently, reading assessment in North America deals mainly with selective products of reading, and consists of group-administered, multiple-choice, pencil-and-paper tests. Even in individual assessment of reading performance we tend to employ product-oriented assessment instruments such as the *Woodcock Reading Mastery Test* (Woodcock, 1973), the *Peabody Individual Achievement Test* (Dunn & Markwardt, 1970), or the *Wide Range Achievement Test* (Jastak, Bijou, & Jastak, 1965). This state of affairs has come about through historical accident. Particularly, the normative, competitive focus of society, and the press for accountability have been instrumental in this outcome. The major motivation for assessment has always been accountability (Resnick, 1982), and tests have been developed to satisfy this concern rather than to examine the status of specific children's learning and causes for their failure. Tests developed for other purposes have simply been modifications of the same form. Even in individual assessments, we worry particularly about good normative comparisons. This state of affairs has been maintained by some questionable assumptions about the costs and benefits of different approaches to assessment, such as the dubious belief that group assessment is both effective and more efficient than individualized assessment (Johnston, 1984). It is important to recognize these factors before discussing the implications of work which arises from the context of a philosophy which is radically different from that surrounding research and practice in North America.

An "item" in current assessment is something which produces an outcome which is correct or incorrect. From a Vygotskian perspective this outcome is of relatively little importance, since it could have resulted from a number of alternative processes. It is the phenotype of the behavior, whereas Vygotsky was concerned with the genotype. A student's score on a reading test can be achieved by diverse combinations of item successes and failures. Similarly, the item successes and failures can be produced by a wide variety of reasoning and reading processes.

If we were to take Vygotsky's work seriously and become more concerned with assessment of processes, we would be less inclined to administer group tests, and we would either seriously question the need for accountability information before we administer such tests or at least be less inclined to claim that the information was useful for instructional purposes. Further, we would be more inclined to invest the extra effort to do individual assessments of children's performance since these are more likely to supply the process information which is relevant for instruction.

In keeping with Vygotsky's research methods, this would promote tracing the development of processes rather than a mere description of behavior. Also it would involve the observation of development with training or setting up conditions which force otherwise automated processes into the open for observation. Error/miscue analysis in reading is not unlike this latter method. When the task is at the point of difficulty at which the learner's automatic processing breaks down (an error, or a word which must be worked out), processes come into the open.

In addition, Vygotsky introduced obstacles or difficulties into the task in order to make normal problem-solving methods inadequate. Interventions of this nature can provide useful data. For example, an adult reader's oral reading errors often were roughly synonymous, even if up to the point of producing the error, yet there was insufficent context to produce such synonyms. One hypothesis was that he was a "deep dyslexic" (Coltheart, Patterson, & Marshall, 1980) who had difficulty accessing the phonological representation of a word. A second hypothesis was that his word attack strategy was to continuously use several lines of text ahead of that currently being orally expressed. To test the latter, he was asked to read while he uncovered only one word at a time. This produced an entirely different pattern of errors and quality of reading (Johnston, 1985), enabling evaluation of the different possible processing explanations.

In general, Vygotsky considered qualitative data based on rigorous, detailed observations to be at least as "hard" a data source as any other. In contrast, we consider teachers' observations to be "subjective" and hence unacceptable data sources. "Subjective" has two meanings according to Scriven (1972). The first is qualitative, and means unrigorous, a matter of opinion, and probably biased. The second, quantitative meaning, refers to the fact that the observations were made by a single individual. Often we incorrectly equate the two meanings (Crooks, 1982). A reasonable implication might be that teachers be trained to be sensitive observers of children's reading behaviors rather than passive receivers of numbers from other sources.

The Relationship between Teaching and Testing

In current standardized approaches to reading assessment, we have gone to some lengths to separate teaching and testing, both functionally and contextually. This has the overall effect of keeping the classroom teacher dependent on an external authority for information about his or her charges, of usurping ownership of the assessment data, and of undermining faith in teacher assessments.

For Vygotsky, teaching and testing were closely related. Indeed, assessment was an integral part of teaching. Particularly in the early stages of reading development, much learning involves social interaction which is external and observable. The use of "big books" in a "shared book experience" (Holdaway, 1979) is an approach to reading instruction which is very closely aligned with Vygotsky's views on the internalization of social learning. At the same time, the children's learning about books, print, and other reading-related issues is external and available for the teacher's observation in a natural, stress-free situation. Prediction, and other comprehension-related processes can thus be readily assessed at this stage of development without the "accountability" focus evident in the basal reader approach to comprehension in which children, having read a story, are grilled with questions. The same can be true in later years when using such methods as the reciprocal questioning techniques suggested by Palincsar (1982) and her colleagues (Brown, Palincsar, & Armbruster, 1984).

Vygotsky described an aspect of assessment of mental functioning which he calls the "zone of proximal development." This zone is described as:

> the distance between the actual developmental level as determined by independent problem solving and the level of potential development as determined through problem solving under adult guidance or in collaboration with more capable peers. (Vygotsky, 1978, p.86)

A plausible interpretation of the zone of proximal development in reading assessment relates to the extent to which a given strategy is used independently, or with varying degrees of instructional assistance. The zone arises as a consequence of Vygotsky's notion of internalization which is concerned with the development in the individual of the ability to perform socially-formulated, goal-directed actions with the help of mediating elements. For example, a teacher prompting a stalled reader might prompt with any of the following:

> No prompt.
> What can you do now?
> How could you figure that out?
> Do you know any words like that?
> What letter does it start with? What word would make sense there?
> The word is. . . . (terminal prompt)

These prompts are organized here from the most general to the most specific. If the most general probe initiates an appropriate response, then that element is comfortably within the reader's zone. If only a terminal prompt restarts the reading process, then the problem is not within the reader's zone. This interpretation poses the word as the problem requiring solution rather than the text. The comprehension aspect may be similarly developed at the paragraph or text level.

In summary, Vygotsky's quest for information about processes and their development was more oriented toward informal assessment procedures than formal ones. He stressed the importance of structuring situations to provide maximum opportunity for the learner to engage in diverse activities that could be observed in naturalistic situations, not just rigidly controlled. This approach runs counter to most current assessment practices in North America.

A Beginning Solution

Analysis of children's oral reading errors is quite well-aligned with a Vygotskian approach to developmental research. Such analyses force the deautomation of the processes which may have become automated through frequent use ("fossilized," in Vygotsky's terms), so that their use and development may be examined. Clay

(1979) described an assessment procedure which is closely aligned with Vygotsky's general approach to research and his model of development. The assessment procedure begins with the child reading a given text while the teacher keeps "running records" of the performance. Interpretation of performance is specifically in terms of the strategies and knowledge which the reader brings to bear on the text, and the flexibility with which these are used. For example, the teacher records every attempt which a reader makes at decoding a problem word. This allows the teacher to examine the order and manner in which various strategies are used in the decoding process. For example, the record

$$\frac{\text{he/he/li/he/hevely}}{\text{heavily}} \Big|\ \text{SC}$$

can be interpreted as a misreading of the word "heavily" as "hevely" after initial attempts of he/he/li/he after which the reader self-corrects the error.

An important aspect which sets Clay's running record apart from most assessment is the departure from standardized administration procedures. It is permissible for a teacher to intervene during the reading performance to restart a stalled reader (after allowing opportunity for the child to perform without support). At the same time, provision is made for the nature of the intervention to be recorded. For example, the teacher might prompt with "Try that (sentence) again" which is recorded TTA. Systematic use of this type of prompt allows the teacher to gain substantial insight into the reader's zone of proximal development. Particularly important is the fact that records can be made during regular instructional sessions, under identical conditions to those to which the assessor wishes to generalize. Running records provide the opportunity to do this by taking regular records which can be referred back to. This practice allows performance to be evaluated in the context of past performance.

Similarly, Clay's (1979) *Concepts About Print* (CAP) test is aligned with a Vygotskian approach to assessment and to learning and development. This test examines the manner in which young students in the early stages of reading development handle print. The approach is somewhat naturalistic in that it is basically a shared reading of a book in which the examiner asks the reader to take partial responsibility for the reading, and then introduces obstacles into the problem by facing the child with errors to be detected. Furthermore, the examiner starts out the test with "I am going to read you this book, but I would like you to help me." This enlists cooperation, which helps align the child's goals with those of the teacher. This goal alignment is very important from a Vygotskian perspective.

Both of these assessment devices, running records and the CAP test, are distinguished from almost all others by the position of tester and testee, who sit alongside each other rather than in opposition to one another. This seems like a small point, but I think that it is indicative of a much larger difference in orientation, particularly in the power structures involved. The assessor's (teacher's) role is that of an advocate rather than that of an adversary.

Some Issues

Focusing on the reading process changes the way in which concepts of validity are applied to assessment. Some traditional concepts no longer apply and different issues are foregrounded. The major difference between current (particularly group-based) methods of assessment and the individual, informal approaches to assessment is the conflict in the concern for internal versus external validity. Vygotsky would probably have been reluctant to trade external validity for any amount of internal validity. As will be discussed later in this chapter, the context of performance was considered crucial.

Always in assessing cognitive activity (such as reading processes), we attempt to infer hypothetical constructs from observable behavior. In process assessment, we attempt to infer the strategies and hypotheses which a reader uses while proceeding through a text. An example of an inferred strategy would be the interpretation of a reader's rereading of a line of text. This could be caused by a loss of place, or by a strategic rereading of a section of text to verify an interpretation, or to correct a perceived error, or to figure out a word. Each of these interpretations of the mental processes represents an inferable, instructionally-relevant construct. Thus, construct validity is a particularly important type of validity for process measures of reading.

Obtaining evidence of construct validity has been one of the biggest weaknesses of current testing procedures. Correlations between different tests have been used as the main form of evidence for construct validity. Such correlations may be of limited relevance to assessments of the reading process. A much more powerful (though currently little used) form of evidence is provided by training studies. If a construct can be identified and modified predictably by training, then substantial support can be gained for the validity of the construct. For example, a student who is hypothesized not to be predicting might be taught to do so through the use of cloze and related activities. Changes would be expected in the nature of the student's oral reading errors.

Reliability also applies differently in a number of ways to individual process-oriented tests of reading than it does to standardized, product-oriented group tests. First, since the comparisons to be made are usually within–subject, one looks for consistency in strategy use in a similar context. One of the prime determiners of context in reading is text difficulty, usually defined by error rate. Thus, strategy use of a given error rate in a specific situation of text seems to be an appropriate indicator of internal consistency. Note, however, that the objects of the reliability estimate are the learner and the assessor, rather than the texts used (parallel forms). That is, performance variability is not attributed to error in the test instrument, but rather to the process of recording, and to the performance of the reader. Thus, a second form of reliability that becomes important is the extent to which two assessors produce the same record of behaviors (interobserver reliability). In Clay's running records, this is simply a matter of obtaining a match between two observers' records of the same reading sample.

Another level of reliability relates to the subsequent interpretation of the running records in terms of the underlying constructs. This can be estimated in terms of both repeated interpretations by the same assessor and interassessor agreement. Furthermore, reliability refers to the replicability of the interpretation of performance from the same reader on different texts. Thus, the burden of decision quality is shifted from the test to the teachers, an important issue in terms of teacher selection and training.

The relationship between reliability and validity would also suggest some changes in interpretation. Currently, reliability is thought of as producing a ceiling for validity. However, with running records, the task is externally valid in that it is exactly the task to which performance is to be generalized. Variability in performance, rather than being attributed to unreliability in the test, is attributed either to the reader or to unreliability in the recorder. From this perspective, a different response to the same item from the child on different occasions is more likely interpreted as telling us something about the child rather than about the test.

The place of the experimenter/assessor is also important. As Vygotsky noted by quoting Koehler, "Investigations of intellectual capacity, . . . necessarily test the experimenter as well as the subject" (Vygotsky, 1962, p. 37). This is a difficult problem. Teacher-student interaction is demanded during assessment, and since the teacher's prompting is determined by theory and situation, it cannot be standardized. As Wertsch (1979b) points out, "The issue is not simply one of whether or not the adult is providing strategic assistance—it is also an issue of what type of other-regulation is being used" (p. 19). Attempts to deal with these issues would necessarily involve instructional resource allocations which em-phasize extensive training of teachers rather than purchasing of better tests. In other words, it would involve considering the teacher as the instrument to be developed rather than the task.

Goals, Motives, and Context

Vygotsky's colleagues and students have developed some of his notions in an extensive theory of activity. Most notable in this development has been the work of Leont'ev. His activity theory has considerable implications for assessment in reading. The general structure of the theory allows for three major levels of analysis: activities, actions, and operations.

The major distinguishing element of activities is motive, the object which impels activity and toward which the goal is directed. The second level, that of actions, is distinguished by the goal, the representative of the result of an action. The third and lowest level, that of operations, is distinguished by the conditions under which the goal-directed behaviors are carried out. They represent an action's technical composition which can be formalized and externalized. In order to take a Vygotskian approach to assessment, then, we need to relate to assessment the concepts of motives, goals, the context of the performance, and the importance of unity and coherence between the levels of behavior.

The notion of a goal and goal-directedness play an important part in the theory of activity. In the West, psychologists have tended to be concerned with the characteristics common to different forms of behavior, regardless of goal. In the assessment of reading, this is particularly the case. For example, in the interpretation of oral reading errors, we argue about the goodness or badness of meaning-preserving errors, but unless we know the reader's goal, and the context of the performance, we have no basis for the argument. In instruction we have always stressed the need for children to have a purpose (goal) in their reading but not so in the case of assessment (except, perhaps in the recent *Metropolitan Achievement Tests* [Prescott, Balow, Hogan, & Farr, 1985]). Indeed, in general, we ignore the fact that our assessment activities often create sets of goals which are so artificial that the performance provides little information about the normal psychological processes involved in reading.

In reading assessment generally, we have paid little or no attention to the role of motivation, even though we have occasional studies which highlight the magnitude of its influence (e.g., Lahey, McNees, & Brown, 1973). The lack of attention to motivation is also evident both in the causal sense and in the sense of consequence. That is, not only have we ignored the individual's motivation in the assessment situation, but we have ignored the frequently negative effects of assessment procedures on the short and long term motivation of students. Vygotsky, on the other hand, was concerned about these issues. His concern for the general motivational side effects of classroom practices may be noted in his quoting Tolstoy's comments about teaching children literary language: "We have to admit that we attempted several times to do this, and always met with an invincible distaste on the part of the children, which shows that we were on the wrong track" (Vygotsky, 1962, p.83).

The lack of concern over motive is directly related to our lack of research on the esthetic aspects of reading. We often talk about books which we "couldn't put down." Similarly, many of us often have to read text which is intensely boring. On the latter, one can get to the bottom of the page, even the end of an article, and be unable to recall more than "it was about reading." It is these latter texts which are used for reading tests. Note that with running records, one can simply choose to record only when the child is reading involving texts. Indeed, unless the individual is absorbed in the reading task, or at least has the goal of learning, any prompts used by the assessor can create dependencies. If survival or ego-defense are the goals for the student, then he/she can become motivated more by the social cues than by the text cues.

Another feature of activity theory which must be considered is the emphasis on viewing behavior as an integrated whole. In general, writers from the "Vygotsky school" talk about the "flow of cognitive activity" (Wertsch, 1979a, p. 99). Vygotsky (1962) provided an analogy useful for understanding assessment methods which fragment the process being observed. He noted that such a method:

> analyses complex psychological wholes into elements. It may be compared to the chemical analysis of water into hydrogen and oxygen, neither of which possesses the properties of the whole and each of which possesses properties not present in the whole. This type of analysis leads us, moreover, into serious errors by ignoring the unitary nature of the process under study. (p. 3–4)

Again, current assessment practices in reading are guilty, in many ways, of fragmenting the process which they are to assess. This may partly be a result of the failure to attend to the goals and motives which form the warp of the behavioral cloth. For example, current assessment in reading still frequently involves children decoding isolated elements, including nonsense syllables. These non-words require the suspension of the normal word recognition process, especially the semantic search aspect. The most frequent errors children make on such nonsense syllable tests are real words (e.g., Walmsley, 1978-79). That is, they are actively trying to make the stimulus fit their notions about the goals of reading.

Recall that context is also crucial to activity theory. It is context which dictates the set of behaviors, or operations, which will be used to attain a goal. Thus, activity theory emphasizes the role of social context: "the human individual's activity is a system in the system of social relations. It does not exist without these relations" (Leont'ev, 1979, p.46). Vygotsky, too, argued strongly against the decontextualization of speech activity for study. His feeling was that without the context of the performance, one could not understand the causal pattern of behaviors. We can assume that he would argue the same for the study of reading.

The failure of assessments to take into account the communicative context of the assessment is well-illustrated by a study by Harste and Burke (1979) who showed that the extent and quality of childrens' free recalls of text were influenced by their knowledge that the listener had or had not read the text previously. Recalls were quite abbreviated when the reader knew that the listener had already read the text.

This importance of context is not particularly congruent with current approaches to assessment in reading. While current assessment practitioners concede that context can affect performance (to a lesser extent), the solution is seen as the reduction and control of the context. The "standardized" context is presumed to be equal, and equally appropriate for all learners. However, the "same" social context is interpreted differently by different individuals.

Awareness of the verbal interactions during reading prior to and during assessment have both been shown to be important in determining reading performance. McNaughton (1981) has shown that the instructional interaction which the reader normally functions under, particularly the time allowed by the teacher before assisting children, affects performance in other contexts such as assessment situations. Similarly, others (McGill-Franzen & McDermott, 1978; Mehan, 1978) have shown that the assessor's prompting behaviors can change during an individual testing session, and that the reader's behavior changes with it. The resulting diagnosis is thus seen as being "negotiated" between reader and assessor.

The importance of the relationship between context, motive, and goal, comes to the fore when one considers the teacher prompts given in a dynamic assessment situation. These are help-giving behaviors, and can have unfortunate consequences in certain situations. For example, Allington (1980) and McNaughton (1981) have both noted the negative dependency-producing effects of aspects of help-giving, such as terminal feedback, in reading groups. Yet we find McConkie, Tavakoli, Wolverton, and Zola (1983) noting that adult illiterates working one-to-one with a computer actively reduce dependency on these supports.

Holt (1964) suggests that for many students, classroom goals involve an ego-defense motive more than anything to do with learning. Ames (1983) has provided a framework within which to interpret this problem. Normative and competitive contexts tend to produce different goal structures from those produced in cooperative or individual settings. Nicholls (1983) similarly notes the goal structure difference between task-involving and ego-involving situations. We might thus expect different performances on tests in different contexts. Task-involving, individual settings are most likely to produce unambiguously learning-directed systems (Johnston & Winograd, 1985). Failure to assess in such circumstances may produce changes in the measured zone of proximal development since independent performance may cease more quickly than necessary. Learners suffering from "passive failure" tend to lack persistence in the face of failure (Johnston & Winograd, 1985). Paris, Lipson, and Wixson (1983) have noted the need for both "skill and will" to be present for the successful completion of learning tasks.

Interpretation of Test Performance

In terms of interpretation of performance, contrary to most current practice which is aimed at detecting weaknesses, Vygotsky (1979) stressed that one should look for the positive:

> If we wanted to characterize in one general principle the basic requirement the problem of development poses for modern research, we would say that this requirement is that one must study the positive aspects of the child's behavior. . . . Up to the present, all psychological methods applied to the investigation of the normal and abnormal child's behavior, despite all the great variation and differences that exist among them, have one feature in common: negative characterization of the child. All these methods tell us about what the child does not have or what is lacking in the child compared with the adult. In the

abnormal child these deficiencies are specified in terms of the
normal child. We are always confronted with a negative picture of the child. (p.149)

This is still equally, and unfortunately, true of assessment in
reading, with few exceptions (e.g., Clay, 1979).

Vygotsky claimed that any analyses of children's mental
processes must be based on knowledge of the earlier stages of
development experienced by the child. This focuses on self-
referenced assessment procedures rather than on norm-referencing
which forms the basis of most current test interpretations. This
is also quite counter to most current assessment approaches which
are one-shot product-oriented measures rather than continuous,
or at least regular, analyses of processes. Perhaps such an orientation would also make changes in the definition of reading difficulty,
defining it in terms of low progress rather than an absolute level
of performance. It might also get us thinking about assessment
of comprehension skills, such as prediction, in different terms. For
example, when teaching the use of prediction in reading comprehension, often the predictions do not come quickly. However,
if teachers were to ask prediction questions while students were
reading, a good indication of development toward automation of
the prediction process would be changes in the students' speed
of response to such questions.

Vygotsky's research methods were aimed at tracing the development of behaviors. Mere descriptions of behaviors were
insufficient, since causal explanation was his goal. The causal-
developmental analysis is frequently not a part of reading assessment. We are likely, for example, to generate a diagnosis from,
say, the *Stanford Diagnostic Reading Test* (Karlson, Madden, &
Gardner, 1976) that a child is poor at inferencing. We have no idea
from the assessment why performance was low on inferencing
items. Indeed, often test publishers are quite explicit, even cavalier,
about this failing. For example, consider the following excerpt from
the manual of a popular test:

test results. . .should be viewed as tentative until substantiated
by additional information. . . . Accept the test results as a
challenge to your ingenuity in finding out why the class or

individual pupils obtained certain scores. (Nurss & McGauvrin, 1976, p. 16)

As a further example, we find a child who is far behind in reading, diagnose basic sight word deficiency and try to drill sight words, without looking further. Frequently such children actively avoid reading and thus never practice the sight words or anything else. Thus a Vygotskian might shift the diagnostic interpretation to the level of motive.

Vygotsky lamented the analog of the processes of plant growth in thinking on child development. Thus, he rejected the readiness notion that development was prerequisite to learning. Vygotsky was much more aligned with Clay's (1979) early reading behaviors notion, in which an attempt is made to describe the reading-related conceptual and strategic development of the child. Vygotsky also did not think of development as a smooth continuous unfolding, again contrary to the plant growth analogy. Rather, he stressed the occurrence of qualitative shifts producing revolutionary changes in the patterns of behavior. The type of shift to which he refers might be exemplified by the sudden shift in some children from fluent reading to disfluent reading with fewer errors following the realization that reading involves exact matches between print and speech.

Along with the rejection of development being driven by brain maturation, Vygotskians further subordinated "hardware" interpretations of assessment by stressing the effect of development on the brain: "We no longer can approach brain (psychophysiological) mechanisms in any way other than as the product of the development of objective activity" (Leont'ev, cited in Zinchenko & Gordon, 1979, p. 125). Thus Vygotskians would be less likely than current diagnosticians to diagnose children's reading failure in terms of neurological disorders as primary causes.

The whole process of diagnosis might be worth studying from a Vygotskian perspective as a higher mental process. This might entail an historical analysis of the nature of diagnostic efforts and perceived educational needs and practices. It might also involve an analysis of the factors which teachers take into account when performing reading diagnoses. Work along these lines has been proceeding in several quarters. Dweck and Bempechat (1983) have noted differences in the processes used by different teachers in their analysis of children's performance. Similarly, Rohrkemper and Brophy (1983) have noted the kinds of behaviors and interpretational processes which influence the diagnostic process.

Vygotsky and other Russian scholars emphasize the volitional element of behavior as the factor which differentiates between man and beast. This concern over voluntary control may be important for assessment. It suggests that an important consideration in the assessment of reading is the extent to which children choose to involve themselves in reading behavior. I have often thought that reading programs might best be evaluated by providing children with diverse, attractive options for things to do, including lots of good, well-displayed books. The collective amount of time spent by children reading the books would tell us a lot more about the programs than we currently concern ourselves with. Incidentally, if such a test were accepted, it might not be such a problem if teachers "taught to the test."

Concluding Comment

In presenting my opinion of how Vygotsky might have viewed assessment in reading, I have stressed the large differences between his theoretical and methodological orientations and those underlying reading assessment in North America. There are several cautions which need to be observed. First, most of our assessment is not driven by a theory of cognitive development at all. Rather, it is driven by pragmatic concerns of management and accountability. These are societal concerns and have taken priority. It may be that the options which Vygotsky might have supported would be unacceptable in our society with its present priorities. The public is constantly suspicious of teachers, and it can be assumed that activity theory applies equally well to teachers' behavior as to students' behavior. Teachers' motives and goals are thus important, especially when one talks of making them more responsible for assessment and less accountable in the socially-accepted sense. Indeed, this is particularly so when the teaching context is under change with respect to attempts by legislative bodies to modify teachers' goal structures. Resultant competitive environments could make substantial changes to individualized assessment by changing teachers' goal structures. A case might be made that Vygotsky's methods might be less appropriate in a culture such as this.

On the other hand, to make suggestions about how to improve the assessment methods which we already have using Vygotsky's ideas may be rather like suggesting a new and better toothpaste for smokers. Perhaps the better way to remove the yellow might be to stop smoking. Perhaps the whole educational enterprise needs evaluation and possibly radical reform. At the very least, I think that we should strongly consider turning over much more of the assessment responsibility and expertise to the classroom teacher with informal approaches, thus putting testing back in teaching. I imagine that Vygotsky would have heartily approved of a statement made by Easley and Zwoyer (1975):

> If you both listen to children and accept their answers not as things to just be judged right or wrong but as pieces of information which may reveal what the child is thinking you will have taken a giant step toward becoming a master teacher rather than merely a disseminator of information. (p. 25)

Chapter 10

The Use of Non-normative Procedures in the Assessment of Handicapped Children: Rationale and Guidelines*

Steven A. Carlson

Educational assessment is best conceived of as a three stage process. Each stage of the process meets a different purpose and requires the use of different data collection procedures. The place of both normative and non-normative procedures in the evaluation process are discussed in the light of important legal requirements and ethical practices.

The process of psychoeducational assessment has long been an integral part of the delivery of special education services. Few would disagree on the need to determine who should be afforded special services and what the nature of those services should be. Recently, a confluence of research has led to the conclusion that psychoeducational assessment may be more defensible conceptually than it is in practice. It has been demonstrated that large numbers of children are misclassified (Shepard, Smith, & Vojir, 1983), that assessors often use technically inadequate tests (Thurlow & Ysseldyke, 1979), that decision makers may have little understanding of essential principles of measurement (Bennett & Shepherd, 1982), that incorrect assessment procedures are often used (Salvia & Ysseldyke, 1981), and that there may be little

---

*This chapter first appeared in *The [NJ] Learning Consultant Journal* (1985), Vol. 6, pp. 35–42.

correspondence between the data collected and the educational decisions which ostensibly are based upon those data (Algozzine & Ysseldyke, 1980). What is noteworthy about the research into assessment practices over the last decade is the consistency of findings about the inadequacy of current practice even though different questions are addressed and different research methodologies are used. This body of research has led to a serious re-examination of the assessment and decision making process within special education and to proposals for major changes in the practice of assessment within the State of New Jersey (Burstein, 1985) as well as throughout the United States.

One of the more important findings to emerge from this body of research is that the focus of assessment tends to be on identification rather than on treatment. Furthermore, the data collected for purposes of identification are usually normative and are rarely cross-validated with other, non-normative information. As a result, students are commonly assigned a label and placed in a special education program without consideration of information which might have been obtained from other sources and which might be more representative of a student's actual functioning even though this information is readily available (Wesson, King, & Deno, 1984).

Once this pool of normative data has been used to determine eligibility for special education, it is commonly extended to make decisions about the child's program of studies (Thurlow & Ysseldyke, 1979). There is, apparently, confusion over the appropriate mix of normative and non-normative data, the value and limitations of each, and the place in the assessment process where normative and non-normative information each make their greatest contributions.

The Value of Assessment Procedures

There is no particular assessment procedure or device which, in an absolute sense, is of more value than others. The value of a procedure or device is determined by the degree to which it yields accurate information relevant to a decision which must be made. This point is important because, not uncommonly, there is a perception that standardized, normative tests are a superior means of information collection. Some school districts have gone so far as to require standard test batteries and to de-emphasize any data not drawn directly from normative tests.

The perception that these practices are more appropriate and yield more believable and relevant data is false for at least two reasons. First, normative tests vary in quality. A poor normative test might yield false or misleading information where some other procedure would be more accurate. Secondly, normative tests have primary value for only one type of decision and their value to the assessment team tails off sharply as other important decisions must be reached. The requirement that various procedures for assessment be used (normative testing being a single procedure regardless of the number of tests administered) was incorporated into the Rules and Regulations for Public Law 94–142 (U.S. Office of Education, 1977). Since that time, attempts have been made to provide guidance regarding the strengths and weaknesses of particular procedures (Eaves & McLaughlin, 1977) and to encourage the use of multimethod assessment (Bennett, 1983; Salvia & Ysseldyke, 1981).

Determining How to Proceed

Since a multimethod assessment process is both a legal and ethical requirement, assessors are left with the need to determine what procedures to use, when in the process they should be used, and whether they are of sufficient quality to yield believable information. A set of steps adapted from Salvia and Ysseldyke (1981) provide a structured means for determining what procedures to use and when they should be used.

Clarify the Problem

First, it is important to clarify the nature of the child's problem. The referral problem should be carefully defined and assessment should be limited to the referral problem and closely related areas. There are two reasons for limiting the focus of the evaluation. If unnecessary information is collected, valuable time which could be more profitably used is wasted. Second, unnecessary information may lead to the perception of a problem where a problem does not exist. It is not uncommon to find IEP goals and objectives that were drawn from data totally unrelated to the referral problem and in areas about which no teacher has expressed concern.

Determine the Nature of the Decision

The second step is to determine the type of decision to be made. This step is critical because different types of decisions require different types of information and, therefore, different assessment procedures. Screening decisions are comparative and confirm or refute the existence of a problem. Such decisions require some means of comparing a target student to his or her peers and yield information about the relative performance of the target child within the norm group. Since the concern at this level of decision making is to confirm and quantify a problem, shallow samplings of behavior are adequate. Normative tests are generally used and are often the best available procedure if appropriate scores such as percentiles or standard scores are used as the unit of analysis (Bennett, 1982).

A second and more important type of decision relates to the characteristics of both instruction and the instructional program which a child should receive. This information is best obtained from thorough behavior samples obtained from diagnostic or criterion-referenced tests, from trial teaching, from analysis of work samples, from structured interviews, and from carefully preplanned observation of the target student, teacher(s), and peers. Due to their construction, normative tests are of little value at this level of decision making. In order to make valid instructional decisions, a thorough knowledge of specific skill deficiencies, as well as the nature of present and prior instruction, is necessary. Normative tests are designed to serve neither of these functions. They are, therefore, legally inappropriate for use in instructional decision making. Such tests may be used to determine areas for further assessment but should not be used for this purpose themselves.

A third type of decision relates to the student's progress once a program of studies has been initiated. Several sophisticated procedures for determining student progress are available to the teacher or child study team. The use of direct and daily measurement is relatively easy and is highly sensitive to small changes in student learning (Deno, Marston, & Mirkin, 1982; Deno, Marston, Shinn, & Tindal, 1983; Howell, Kaplan, & O'Connell, 1979). Continuous collection of work samples throughout the course of instruction allows evaluators to examine qualitative changes in a child's work. The use of criterion–referenced instructional and management systems will yield specific information about pupil progress on specific objectives. Not uncommonly, student progress is determined by pre- and post-testing with norm referenced tests. Norm referenced tests are not designed to measure small increments of growth and may actually indicate no progress or negative progress when the student has learned a great deal (Eaton & Lovitt, 1972).

Determine the Behaviors to be Sampled

Once the type of decision to be made is known, the assessor must determine the specific behaviors to be sampled. For example, two children might have been referred for reading problems. One child had been taught using a meaning centered reading approach while the other has been taught using a tightly structured phonetic approach. At the screening level the first child must be assessed with a normative measure which assigns no penalty for meaningful substitutions. The second child must be assessed using a normative test which treats meaningful substitutions as an error. The primary focus of the first test should be comprehension while the focus of the second should be on specific decoding skills. At the instructional planning level, the first child might be asked to engage in repeated readings of a particular passage while the second might be asked to read increasingly difficult passages a single time. In both cases errors would be recorded but similar reading behaviors would be interpreted differently. Assessment procedures must be selected only after a careful determination of the specific behaviors of interest. This, among other reasons, is why a standard test battery given to all children is a clear indication of a dysfunctional evaluation system. The test can only be properly selected after the critical behaviors have been determined. The critical behaviors will be unique to the individual or to the curriculum within which the child is experiencing difficulty.

Evaluate Potential Measures or Procedures

After the problem, the decision type, and the specific behaviors of concern are known, the examiner must evaluate the quality of potential measures or procedures. The technical adequacy of formal tests should be carefully considered and informal procedures should be carefully designed. Guidelines for evaluating some formal assessment instruments and for constructing informal assessment procedures will be discussed later.

Cross-Validate Findings

The assessment should be designed in such a way that behaviors of concern are evaluated using more than a single procedure. For example, if normative data indicate memory problems, the team should ask parents and teachers in a formal interview to comment on any memory problem which they have observed. The child might be asked if he or she forgets, and, if so, why. All of these pieces of evidence, formal and informal, might be consistent and confirm the existence of a problem. A second possibility is that the child states he/she only tries to remember things that are interesting or fun. This simple response by the child might lead to a very different interpretation of the nature of the problem as well as to a very different set of suggestions for problem resolution.

Teams are often confused and concerned when obtained data is contradictory. If contradictions appear in the data base through this process of cross-validation, they may be more indicative of the technical limitations of the procedures used than of a true problem. A deficit large enough to constitute a handicap should be pervasive and evident in all relevant aspects of a child's functioning. Assuming that different assessment procedures were selected to look at specific common behaviors, a true problem should nearly always be evident across procedures.

Evaluating Assessment Procedures

Bennett (1983) has provided a classification scheme for, and a fine discussion of, the advantages and limitations of different assessment procedures. Since standards for normative tests and testing are commonly known, they will not be dealt with here nor will the important measurement issues related to informal assessment. The reader is referred to Bennett for a discussion of these important issues. Suffice it to say that issues of reliability and validity are critical in the selection of any assessment procedure and that the nature of the normative sample, whether it is a formal norm group or a teacher's comparative judgment of children based upon experience, is important if any comparisons are to be made. In order to select or design procedures which yield better and more accurate information, the examiner must understand those practices and qualitative characteristics of instruments which are important. The subsequent discussion is intended to provide such information. The thoughtful selection of procedures, the use of multiple methods, and the cross-validation of information will serve to minimize errors of measurement or judgment.

Diagnostic and Criterion–Referenced Tests

A diagnostic test is designed to indicate the nature of specific errors which a child makes. A criterion–referenced test, while designed for a similar purpose, also provides an absolute standard or criterion against which the child's performance can be compared. Generally speaking, a diagnostic test will provide little or no guidance as to the adequacy of performance and a criterion-referenced test, while possibly less useful than a diagnostic test for determining error patterns, may do both well. One of these test types should be used for every area of deficit to be assessed.

When selecting a diagnostic or criterion–referenced test there should be a careful analysis of the specific behaviors measured. The best tests will have a table of specifications or chart which lists specific behaviors and the test items which assess them. This allows the examiner to evaluate the sufficiency of the test and to easily interpret the meaning of student failure on any given item. The examiner should carefully compare the objectives on this chart or table to objectives on the scope and sequence chart from the child's present curriculum. Skills which have not yet been taught should be noted and the test should include items measuring the vast majority of skills covered in past instruction. Although there is disagreement over the optimal number of items necessary to assess each objective, there should be no fewer than three, and five to seven would be far better. Not uncommonly, tests will bill themselves as diagnostic while sampling only a smattering of objectives with one or two items each. The wise examiner will ignore the publisher's characterization of the test and make his or her own judgments.

The test items themselves should be unambiguous, should sample only the skill being assessed, and should be linguistically appropriate for the child to be tested. This latter consideration is particularly important if the child is suspected of having problems with language. Items should contain no irrelevant clues or information unless the ability to discern what is relevant is the skill being measured. There should be no evidence of clues within the test which might provide help for later items. The sequencing of items should be sensible and closely related to the item sequencing within the curriculum itself.

In the case of criterion–referenced tests, the criterion levels should be validated. This simply means that children who are considered proficient in the target skill should have been shown to be able to pass the test. Again, buyer beware. Although criterion levels are provided, they may have been neither established using appropriate means nor properly validated. If criterion levels are not supplied, Howell and Kaplan (1980) suggest a procedure which allows them to be established rather easily.

The assessor may choose not to use commercially available program–level tests for a number of reasons. Informal inventories can accomplish the same goal of skill level assessment, provide the examiner with a greater degree of flexibility, and, since they are constructed with a specific instructional curriculum in mind, often may have greater content validity. Two texts provide detailed information on how this may be done (Howell & Kaplan, 1980; Zigmond, Vallecorsa, & Silverman, 1983).

Permanent Product Analysis

The analysis of permanent products provides what may be the richest and least utilized source of assessment information available (Bachor, 1979). Errors in reading, writing, mathematics, etc. are often systematic and therefore repeated. For an error to be repeated consistently the child must have learned some faulty procedure or must be laboring under some fallacious belief. If these faulty procedures or beliefs can be discovered, corrective actions may be quite apparent.

There are two ways that information may be drawn from permanent products. The first is through critical analysis. Ashlock (1976) provides exercises designed to familiarize the assessor with common error patterns in mathematics. Zigmond et al. (1983) demonstrate the process of error analysis in several academic areas. If the assessor is unable to determine the reasoning behind an error, the student should be asked to explain his or her logic by orally describing the thought process which was followed. It may be necessary to demonstrate this to the child first. Ashlock maintains that nearly half of all mathematics errors are systematic and may be determined through analysis and interview. The non-systematic errors are those which should be of particular concern. Non-systematic errors indicate failure to learn rather than correct learning of incorrect procedures. Generally, non-systematic errors will be free of repeated patterns and will be inexplicable to the child.

Interviewing

Interviewing should be of central importance in any assessment. Interviews with parents, with teachers, and with the child provide an opportunity to cross-validate data obtained through testing and to gain insights and information available in no other way. The responsibility of the examiner is to elicit the necessary information rather than to expect that the party being interviewed knows what information is important. This means that the interview must be carefully planned in advance. It is helpful to have completed testing and to have previously reviewed all results to identify patterns of concern. The examiner should then think of situations common to the classroom, playground, or home that would require particular behaviors or abilities of concern.

For example, test results indicate problems with visual perception. The examiner could ask the classroom teacher how the child performs when aligning numbers in columns, or ask the parent to describe any hobby the child might have which requires fine perceptions such as threading a needle, building a model, or identifying mint marks on old coins. Yet another student appears to have problems in long term memory. It might be interesting to ask the student how, as quarterback of the football team, he can remember where ten teammates are on the field in each of thirty different plays. A similar question posed to the coach might indicate that such learning came only with difficulty, that there was a technique which was used which might be of help later, or that there was no difficulty at all, that the problem is one of interest and motivation rather than capacity.

In addition to the cross-validation of test results, the interview should be used to gather specific information. The teacher should be asked questions about instructional techniques which have been tried, for how long they were tried, which were effective, and what his or her expectations for performance are. The primary responsibility of the child study team is not to make an eligibility decision but to explicitly state what must be learned and how instruction should be delivered. Any question designed to yield this information would be helpful. Specific, targeted questions tend to elicit helpful information. Open ended, general questions tend to waste everyone's time and to yield little of value.

Parents should be asked specific questions about effective reinforcers, about factors influencing performance such as amount of sleep, conflicts, and values which might affect the process of schooling. The student shoud be asked questions which deal with attribution of the problem, with motivation, with personality conflicts, and with personal difficulties. This should all be in addition to questions designed to cross–validate previous findings.

Observation

Observation, like interviewing, is often unplanned and, therefore, unproductive. Observation provides an opportunity to see the child in his or her natural school environment. Many children find their way into special education not due to a true handicap, but due to a mismatch of teacher and pupil (Algozzine, 1979). The purpose of observation is, therefore, to determine whether instructional and environmental factors are at the heart of the problem rather than some characteristic of the student.

Observation, like interviewing, should be planned in advance. The observer should have prepared a recording form and a list of questions to be answered by the observation. These questions should be specific, substantive, and directly related to prior information or to variables known to influence student learning or behavior. There is little probability that an unstructured visit will lead to the quality of information easily obtained by a structured observation. The teacher's understanding and use of instructional principles such as feedback, reinforcement, pacing, allocated versus engaged time, and modeling should be carefully noted. Whether the teacher uses different and appropriate techniques at the levels of early acquisition, mastery and maintenance may be a crucial piece of information in unraveling the problem. The teacher's level of expectation, tolerance for individual differences, and rapport with the students should be observed. The instructional materials, their relevance, and the demands they make upon the learner are important factors as well. The student should be watched in order to determine level of motivation, compliance, work strategies, and peer interactions. Finally, it must be understood that a single observation may yield highly unreliable information. An effort should be made to observe for a short time on several occasions rather than a single time.

Summary

Mounting evidence indicates that school assessment teams make very poor decisions regarding eligibility and instructional programs for handicapped youngsters. This may be due to over reliance on norm referenced tests and to their use for purposes for which they are unsuited. Normative tests are only rough screening measures but are valuable for confirming the existence and magnitude of a problem. Non-normative and informal assessment procedures are not only legitimate but are the only tools suitable for making most instructional decisions.

Not uncommonly, assessors maintain that such procedures would be helpful but that they can't be used due to restrictions on time. This argument is valid only if non-normative procedures are viewed as an additional requirement. In fact, these procedures should replace rather than augment many of the normative tests commonly administered. When this is done, the amount of time necessary for student evaluation is much the same. Such a change in approach is not only required by the legal necessity to use different evaluation methods, but is supported by research, and underscored by the team's specific responsibility to determine what should be taught and how it should be taught.

Chapter 11

Setting Demand Variables: A Major Factor in Program Planning for the LD Adolescent*

Jean B. Schumaker and Donald D. Deshler

[The purpose of this chapter is to present results of studies conducted at the University of Kansas Institute for Research in Learning Disabilities (KU-IRLD) for the purpose of characterizing the setting demands in secondary and post-secondary settings. Additionally, KU-IRLD results on the characteristics of LD adolescents are matched to the identified setting demands. Finally, information will be provided on the effects of teaching LD adolescents specific learning strategies to enable them to cope with some of these setting demands.]

Remedial interventions for mildly handicapped adolescents have traditionally focused on specific learning characteristics manifested by the students. These students' deficiencies have most often been measured with psychometric aptitude or achievement tests which typically reveal areas of strength or weakness in different academic skill areas (such as reading, mathematics, or written expression) or areas assumed to be related to successful school achievement (such as visual memory, digit span, or block design). Explanations of why students are failing in school are, in turn, provided in terms of students' difficulties in responding to items on these instruments.

---

*This chapter first appeared in *Topics in Language Disorders* (1984), Vol. 4, No. 2, pp. 22–40. Copyright © 1984 Aspen Systems Corporation.

Remedial interventions designed on the above-mentioned model may be limited in their power to impact performances of handicapped adolescents in natural settings for several reasons. First, most formal test instruments typically used with mildly handicapped adolescents do not assess the broad array of skills needed to successfully cope with the curricular demands of the secondary school. Some of the critical skills seldom assessed by these instruments are note taking, critical listening, independent study habits, and test taking. Consequently, resultant intervention plans are often limited in scope and appropriateness. Second, the academic failure experienced by mildly handicapped adolescents is best understood by analyzing numerous factors such as teacher behaviors, curriculum expectations, response requirements, and social expectations. In short, an understanding of the learning characteristics of the student alone will fail to provide sufficient understanding of factors related to and precipitating academic failure.

The importance of analyzing factors beyond student variables has been shown by Schlick, Gall, and Riegel (1981), who have demonstrated how basic curriculum requirements vary greatly across grade level and subject areas. This variance in nonstudent variables underscores the importance of considering the demands of the setting as much as the deficits of the youngster in making intervention decisions. The probability of designing interventions that allow handicapped adolescents to cope with the demands of secondary schools is increased only to the extent that assessment practices measure both student and nonstudent variables.

The importance of taking a variety of factors into account in planning intervention programs has been discussed recently in the literature. Brown (1982) has proposed the use of a tetrahedral model (adopted from Jenkins, 1979) as an organizational framework for exploring questions about why learning may or may not occur. Brown suggests that the following factors must be considered when designing a plan for learning: (a) the nature of the materials to be learned (text structure, logic of content, and available cues); (b) the criterial tasks or the end point for which the learner is preparing (generalized rule use, verbatim recall vs. gist, and following instructions); (c) activities engaged in by students (the strategies, rules, procedures, or macrorules used for making learning an effective process); and (d) general characteristics of the learner (prior experience, background knowledge, abilities, and interests). Thus this model includes student attributes as only one of several components to explain why learning difficulties may exist.

Schumaker, Alley, Warner, and Deshler (1980), in designing a research paradigm for the University of Kansas Institute for Research in Learning Disabilities (KU-IRLD), have discussed the value of a comprehensive model for designing interventions for handicapped adolescents. They proposed that the behavior of learning disabled (LD) adolescents can best be described by using Lewin's (1935) model, which views behavior as a function of the interaction between the characteristics of learner variables and environmental variables. Lewin's formulation is $B = f(PE)$, where B = behavior, P = person, and E = environment. This model has proved productive in designing interventions that have facilitated the LD student's ability to meet the expectations of the secondary school setting. The major intervention model that has been developed and field tested at the KU-IRLD has been based on a *learning strategies* approach. Learning strategies, as defined by Alley and Deshler (1979), are "techniques, principles, or rules that will facilitate the acquisition, manipulation, integration, storage and retrieval of information across situations and settings" (p. 13).

An underlying instructional goal associated with the learning strategies approach is to teach students "how to learn" so that they can better cope with the demands of the mainstream academic setting. Thus LD adolescents are taught both task-specific and general control strategies to enhance their ability to meet academic demands. Basic to implementing this intervention approach has been the necessity of not just analyzing specific deficiencies that characterize the LD adolescent as a learner, but also analyzing the demands of the setting in which the student is ultimately expected to be successfully integrated.

Setting Demand Research

Studies identifying mainstream classroom demands for the secondary and post-secondary school LD student seem to fall into two general groups. In the first group of studies, the investigators asked teachers to divulge, in some way, their preferences and expectations and/or asked students to describe the demands they perceived to be present in their mainstream courses. Some investigators used survey instruments; others used interviews or asked the teachers to evaluate samples of student work or student performance data. Still others used a combination of these techniques. In the second group of studies, teachers and students were actually observed in mainstream classrooms, and classroom tasks were analyzed to shed light on the demands that are actually present in these settings. The group of investigations can be further broken down into two categories of studies: those related to secondary school settings and those related to post-secondary school settings.

Studies Related to Secondary School Settings and Teachers' Perceptions

In one of the earliest studies involving the assessment of teacher expectations, Link (1980) surveyed 133 elementary and secondary school teachers and administrators. Eighty-nine (67%) of the respondents were employed in secondary school settings. Link asked them to rate on a 7-point Likert scale each of 24 academic skills. He also asked them to rank, using a weighted scale, those items that were rated 6 or 7 on the Likert scale. According to the educators in Link's study, the top 10 skills (those that were rated as most essential for adequate performance in a classroom) were: "following oral and written directions, skimming reading selections, locating information in a textbook, recalling information for tests, turning in assignments on time, locating answers to questions, taking notes from lectures, participating in discussions, making logical deductions, and studying for tests" (p. 23).

The majority of the skills identified in the Link study can be classified as "study" skills, that is, skills outside the normal basic skills curricula (reading, mathematics, spelling) or content course curricula delivered in schools. Few schools provide courses in these skills, and even fewer special education programs cover these skills. When the educators were asked to rank the skills, again the majority of the top 10 skills could be classified as study skills. In this list, reading at grade level and expressing ideas clearly through writing were among noteworthy replacements of study skills on the other list. Unfortunately, since the elementary educators' responses were not separated from the secondary educators' responses, it remains unclear what the top 10 skills would be for secondary schools.

In a study in which only secondary school educators were involved, Knowlton and Schlick (in prep.) collected expectations for LD students mainstreamed in regular classes from 17 junior high school teachers and 10 senior high school teachers using the Critical Incident Technique (Flanagan, 1962). The resultant 476 critical incidents reflecting teacher expectations were organized by a panel of judges into 5 categories and 48 subcategories. The 5 categories of behaviors expected of LD secondary students were independent work habits, socialization skills, communication skills, study skills, and subject matter skills. Subcategories under independent work habits included such behaviors as bringing appropriate materials to class, completing homework assignments, budgeting time, requesting assistance, accepting help, and working independently. Socialization skills included displaying respect for authority, following classroom rules, accepting criticism, and working as a team member. Examples of communication skills identified by the teachers were speaking clearly, making oral reports, participating in discussions, and explaining reasons for one's actions. Study skills included note taking, using the library and reference materials, writing compositions and reports, test taking, and copying. Finally, subject matter skills included such behaviors as reading, mathematics, art, science, and physical education skills.

Knowlton (1983), in a later study, had 100 secondary school teachers provide weighted rankings for each of the five general expectation categories identified in the Knowlton and Schlick (in prep.) study. The teachers also rated the importance of each of the 48 subcategories using 7-point Likert scales. Knowlton analyzed differences in the rankings and ratings, comparing teachers' target student population (junior high vs. senior high) and subject matter taught (academic vs. nonacademic).

With regard to the ranking of the five general expectation categories, there were no significant differences related to the teachers' target populations. Independent work habits were ranked first in importance, socialization skills were second, communication skills were third, study skills were fourth, and subject matter skills were fifth. The teachers of academic and nonacademic subjects had the same general categories as described above in first and second place; however, teachers of academic subjects ranked study skills in third place, whereas teachers of nonacademic subjects ranked study skills last. Communication and subject matter skills were given higher importance rankings by teachers of nonacademic subjects than by teachers of academic subjects.

With regard to the rating of the 48 subcategories, only one significant difference was related to the target population of the teachers. Junior high teachers rated copying as significantly more important than did senior high teachers. Two skills were rated as more important by teachers of academic subjects than teachers of nonacademic subjects: completing homework and other assignments, and reading. Nine skills were significantly more important for the teachers of nonacademic subjects: being on time to class, remaining on task, serving as a helper, working beyond normal expectations, showing respect for property, offering help to others, working as a team member, conducting oneself appropriately in class, and performing shop tasks.

These results indicate that teachers at the secondary level place the highest value on independent work habits and socialization skills within the classroom environment. Teachers of nonacademic subjects see overt classroom behaviors such as classroom conduct as more important than do teachers of academic subjects.

Some other investigators have looked at the specific demands of the secondary school setting pertaining to one of the skills identified as important in the previously described studies: written expression. In an early study of the written language demands of secondary school settings, Moran (1980) asked teachers to report the relative frequency with which they assigned five categories of written work. The teachers rated papers on which students have to make a partial response (e.g., fill in the blank, spell a word, mark a correct answer) as the most frequently assigned written task (the mean rating on a 5-point scale was 4.13). Closely following this task in frequency was the task of taking notes from lectures or written materials or noting ideas for a paper ($M = 4.03$).

Papers requiring more than one sentence were less frequently required. Descriptive, narrative, and argumentative papers had mean ratings of 3.56, 3.06, and 1.76, respectively. Since the actual differences between two of the mean ratings are relatively minimal, it can be assumed that these two writing activities (short response, note taking) are emphasized about equally. According to these data, secondary school students rarely have to express new ideas, issues, and arguments in essay form.

In a later study in which teacher expectations for written language were identified, Moran and DeLoach (1982) had 35 high school teachers rank seven criteria used by teachers to evaluate the quality of written assignments. They also had the teachers rate samples of students' writing that had been artificially altered to include particular kinds of errors related to the seven criteria. The teachers' reports of their demands differed from the way they actually rated the papers. They reported that they considered sentence structure to be the most important criterion. Next most important in descending order were the topic sentence, correct inflections and number agreement, mechanics (e.g., punctuation, capitalization), spelling, sentence complexity, and sentence length.

In contrast, when the teachers actually rated the papers, versions in which spelling had been corrected were rated as the best versions. Those papers in which sentences had been lengthened were rated second best, followed by those in which sentence structure was corrected, and then by those in which sentences were made more complex, where the topic sentence was rewritten or inserted, where inflections and number agreement were corrected, and finally where mechanics were corrected. According to the actual ratings, students who can spell and write long, complete sentences will receive the highest grades on their papers. Unfortunately, Moran and DeLoach did not include overall organization and quality of content as criteria in their study, so it is unclear where these two criteria would rank among the others.

Two other studies involved the collection of teachers' responses with regard to required competencies at the secondary school level. In one of these studies, Carlson and Alley (1981) asked secondary school teachers to indicate what the competency cutoff points should be with regard to students' scores on five study skills: scanning, error monitoring, test taking, note taking from lectures, and recalling lecture information for a test. The teachers indicated that students must achieve scores ranging between 62 and 70% of the points available on each of the five skill tests in order to "pass" or to be judged as competent in the skill.

In the other study focusing on required competencies at the secondary school level, Meyen, Alley, Scannell, Harnden, and Miller (1982) asked special education teachers and regular class teachers to judge whether competency objectives designed for nonhandicapped students should be used for LD students. Parents of LD students were also asked whether they thought the same competencies applied to nonhandicapped students should be required of their LD children. The teachers and parents agreed that the objectives designed for nonhandicapped students held curricular validity for LD students.

The teachers and parents identified objectives related to practical reading skills (e.g., reading directions, interpreting warning signs and labels, and reading to complete applications for a social security card and jobs) as the most important skills. They also identified practical mathematics skills (e.g., figuring wages and deductions, comparison shopping, totaling a bill, and making change) as the most important competencies in mathematics.

Only two mathematics objectives out of 80 reading and mathematics objectives were identified as being unimportant for LD secondary school students. The only concession made by the teachers and parents with regard to the handicaps of LD students was to indicate that LD students should be tested 1 year later than nonhandicapped students with respect to certain competencies. With the recent emphasis on meeting minimal competency standards to receive a high school diploma (Pullin, 1980), the skills targeted for competency must be seriously considered as secondary school setting demands.

Observational Studies Related to Secondary School Settings

In one of the earliest observational studies of the demands of secondary settings sponsored by the KU-IRLD, Moran (1980) attempted to identify the oral language demands present in secondary school classrooms. She audiotaped class sessions and coded the verbal utterances of secondary school teachers in 12 categories. She found that the most prevalent type of teacher utterances were in the form of lectures (i.e., statements of fact). Those statements of the teacher that required no verbal response from the students were found to make up 75% of all the utterances, and 10% required a "yes" or "no" response. Thus only 15% of the teachers' utterances required an extended language response of the students. Most of these (11%) required the students to make statements of fact, draw inferences or conclusions, or state opinions. One might infer from these data that listening and note taking are emphasized demands of the secondary school setting.

These results were extended by two other studies. In the first, Skrtic (1980) observed and analyzed the interactions of secondary teachers and their students in regular classrooms. He found that regular classroom teachers required the same frequency of verbal responses from LD students as non-LD students.

In another study analyzing the interactions of regular classroom students, Powell, Suzuki, Atwater, Gorney-Krupsaw, and Morris (1981) replicated Skrtic's (1980) results. They found no differences between the interactions of teachers and LD students and teachers and non-LD students.

In still another study using the observational technique, Schumaker, Sheldon-Wildgen, and Sherman (1980) observed students and teachers in regular junior high classrooms and classified time-sample intervals according to the activity taking place. These researchers found that independent seatwork activities made up the largest portion (48% of the intervals) of the class period. The next most prevalent activity, comprising 18% of the intervals, was lecture by the teacher. Following these were discussion (11%), audiovisual activities (10%), group work (7%), oral reports (3%), and free time (3%). Discussion activities were used most frequently in the seventh grade (18% of the intervals), but they decreased in use in the eighth (11%) and ninth grades (3%).

Schumaker, Sheldon-Wildgen, & Sherman (1980) also found that students had few interactions with their teachers. Students spent about 1% of the class time intervals speaking with a teacher. In 50 hours of observations, teachers asked only 109 questions for students to answer (a rate of only 1 question every 28 minutes). Also during this time, there were only 27 instances of praise and

35 instances of criticism directed at the whole class or at the individual students targeted by the study (a rate of 1.2 instances of feedback per hour). These results underscore the findings of previously described studies that emphasized the importance of independent work habits (Knowlton, 1983) and note taking (Moran, 1980). Because seatwork and lecture activities comprise the great majority of class time, few opportunities for verbal responding are provided, and feedback from the teacher is minimal at the secondary school level.

Using a different approach to analyze the demands of the secondary school setting, V. Beals (personal communication, May 15, 1983) applied the Fry readability method (Fry, 1977) to determine the readability levels of the most widely used textbooks for required courses in secondary classrooms across the nation. The Fry readability scale has several levels; each level reflects that the majority of the people in a given grade can read that material. Thus, low 10th grade means that the material is written at a level which is readable by the majority of students who are beginning the 10th grade. The 17th grade plus level is for college graduates.

Beals found, for example, that the most widely used textbook for U.S. history (Todd & Curti, 1982) has a readability level of low 10th grade. The most widely used biology text (Otto, Towle, & Bradley, 1981) has a readability level of high 10th grade, and the most widely used government text (McClenaghan, 1979) has a readability level of 17th grade plus. These findings indicate that the academic demands of secondary schools are related to reading at these levels or proficiency in strategies for coping with materials written at these levels.

In summary, the results with regard to the demands of secondary mainstream education are revealing. Taken as a whole, the studies fill a previous void regarding the empirical identification of demands in the secondary school setting; however, the area has not been thoroughly covered. Certain lapses remain, and certain contradictions between teacher perceptions and teacher behaviors are evident. For example, there are few studies that directly measure the *actual* demands of the setting. Investigators must observe the demands within classrooms in a variety of ways to determine the most important demands with regard to passing and excelling in certain kinds of courses. Many questions remain in this regard. For example, what behaviors are actually used as a basis for grades? Do the actual demands of courses in which LD students enroll differ from the demands of courses in which they are not enrolled?

These are but a few of the questions that can be answered only through observational studies. Questions of this type become important in light of the fact that there is evidence showing that teachers' reports about their own behavior differ from their actual behavior (e.g., Moran & DeLoach, 1982).

Taking these weaknesses into account and realizing that many of the identified demands must be empirically validated, some agreement can be inferred across the studies reviewed here concerning some of the demands of the mainstream secondary school setting. For example, secondary school students must be able to:

- gain information from materials written at secondary levels (that is, they must either be able to read materials written at secondary readability levels *or* they must be competent in strategies for coping with such materials);
- work independently with little help and feedback from the teacher;
- complete homework and other assignments;
- gain information from auditorily presented stimuli such as lecture, discussion, audiovisual activities, and student reports (competence in note taking is often mentioned in the studies with regard to this demand);
- demonstrate their command of knowledge (studying and recalling information for tests, and taking tests with particular emphasis on objective-type questions were skills mentioned that pertain to this demand);
- participate in discussions (this can be viewed as one of the lesser demands in light of the few opportunities for participation that appear to be present in secondary classrooms; in addition, it is unclear whether actual grades are based on such participation);
- follow classroom rules (again it is unclear whether and to what extent grades are actually based on this demand);
- express themselves in writing (they must be able to write short answers and descriptive and narrative prose using relatively long sentences);
- spell words; and
- pass minimal competency examinations.

Studies Related to Postsecondary School Settings

In general, there are few studies available for review with regard to the demands present in postsecondary school settings; however, three studies conducted through KU-IRLD auspices yield a few hints with regard to these demands. Westendorf, Cape, and Skrtic (in prep.) studied the demands present in required courses in a large midwestern university. They interviewed professors and students and analyzed textbooks, syllabi, handouts, and tests. They determined which behaviors course grades are based on, and they inferred from these requirements, from their interviews, and from their analyses the skills that are needed in the postsecondary university setting. In the 11 course textbooks analyzed, the lowest readability level was 7th grade. Five of the textbooks were written at the 9th-10th grade level, and four were written at the 11th-12th grade level. The readability levels of handouts ranged from 7th to 12th grades. The tests that were analyzed ranged from 11th- to 16th-grade readability levels. Reading assignments ranged from 10 to 50 pages per class period.

Westendorf et al. (in prep.) found that course grades were largely based on written products. A few of the courses required attendance and class participation. Some language courses required oral examinations. For the most part, however, the course grades were based on tests, written assignments, and themes. All types of questions were included on the examinations, from objective-type questions (multiple-choice, true-false, fill-ins), to short–answer questions, to questions requiring long essays. Most of the course content was taught in a lecture format.

These results indicate that much the same demands that are present in secondary schools are also present at the university level. Because of these demands, emphasis is placed on competence in such skills as listening and note taking, working independently and completing assignments, gaining information from materials written at the secondary school level or above, writing themes and essays, and studying for and taking tests.

In another study focusing on the demands of postsecondary school life, Vetter (1983) surveyed 63 LD and 62 non-LD individuals who had been out of high school between 2 and 7 years. The LD young adults reported difficulties they were having in coping with certain setting demands in the postsecondary school environment, such as difficulty related to social and independent living skills. When asked to rate how happy they were with their social life, 31.8% of the LD individuals versus 17% of the non-LD individuals responded with ratings showing some dissatisfaction. A large percentage of the LD population (70.1%), as opposed to 45% of the non-LD respondents, reported that they were still living with their parents or relatives. More than twice as many non–LD young adults lived with friends as did the LD respondents.

On measures of leisure time activities, the non–LD group reported significantly higher participation than the LD group in reading, hobbies, and participation in sports activities. Finally, LD young adults encountered significantly more contacts with law enforcement authorities. Large differences were reported between the two groups on the number of times arrested (one time: LD, 19.3% vs. non-LD, 6.7%; two times: LD, 7.0% vs. non-LD, 1.7%; three times: LD, 3.5% vs. non-LD, 1.7%). Seventeen percent of the LD respondents reported actually being convicted of a crime versus 3.5% of the non-LD group. In a related area, 30.5% of the LD group reported having high-risk automobile insurance as opposed to 13.8% of the normal group.

The second major area of difficulty centered around learning effectiveness. For example, 46.4% of the LD group reported that they had difficulty in "knowing how to study" in postsecondary school training and education situations. Related to this was their response to the question about the area of their lives with which they were most dissatisfied (40.7% of the LD group vs. 16.7% of the non-LD group indicated the area to be "the way I learn"). These responses are particularly meaningful when considered in light of the types of future educational plans reported by the LD group including job training (11.4%), junior college (28.6%), and college (22.9%).

Although research on postsecondary school setting demands is limited, a partial profile of salient demand features may be drawn. Young LD adults must be able to:

• gain information from large volumes of materials written at relatively high readability levels (or they must be competent in strategies for coping with such materials);

- demonstrate their command of knowledge through acceptable performance on written tests, themes, and other written assignments; and
- increase their ability to make successful transitions to all phases of adult life including independent living skills and adherence to laws.

Relating the Characteristics of LD Adolescents to the Demands of Secondary and Postsecondary School Settings

Important information with regard to how well LD adolescents can be expected to meet the demands of secondary and postsecondary school settings can be found in a study including over 200 secondary LD students. Warner, Alley, Schumaker, Deshler, and Clark (1980) reported that the mean grade level of reading achievement achieved by seniors was 4-1. 4-1 refers to 4 1/10 grade levels; that is, a person receiving a certain score on a standardized achievement test is functioning like the majority of persons who have completed 4 1/10 years of elementary school. In this case, the average or mean score of the LD seniors is the same as the majority of students completing 4 1/10 years of school.

The students did not show substantial gains in reading achievement past their sophomore year ($M = 4$–6). In fact, mean levels decreased. These findings indicate that since LD students do not read at appropriate levels for the materials being used, they need to use more efficient strategies to cope with the heavy reading demands they are required to meet.

Unfortunately, LD adolescents appear to lack facility in using more efficient strategies. Carlson and Alley (1981), for example, found that LD adolescents could answer a mean of only 36% of the questions accurately when they were required to quickly scan reading materials. Their nonhandicapped peers answered a mean of 81% of the questions correctly. Schumaker, Deshler, Denton, Alley, Clark, and Warner (1982) showed that LD adolescents before training did not exhibit skills such as surveying a chapter before reading it. They also did not know how to obtain key information from a chapter in a short period of time.

Regarding independent work habits, LD adolescents appear to have greater difficulty than their nonhandicapped peers in working independently. Schumaker, Sheldon–Wildgen, and Sherman

(1980) found that LD junior high students spent about 7% less class time than their peers engaged in independent study behaviors. Deshler, Schumaker, Warner, Alley, and Clark (1980) found that non-LD students reported spending between 30 and 60 minutes on homework per night in contrast to LD students, who report spending an average of 15 to 30 minutes per night. Powell et al. (1981), Schumaker et al. (1980), and Skrtic (1980) found that LD students rarely requested help or feedback from a teacher. Thus LD students appear to work less independently than their peers, and they do not recruit needed help. Secondary school teachers of LD students report that more than 75% of the LD students in their resource rooms have difficulty in completing homework assignments (Whitaker, 1982).

With regard to gaining auditory information, LD students also appear to exhibit deficits. Schumaker, Sheldon-Wildgen, and Sherman (1980) showed that LD students attended to only 26% of teachers' statements of facts, whereas their non-LD peers attended to 54%. Carlson and Alley (1981) demonstrated that LD students (a) included an average of only 41% of key information from lectures in their notes while their high-achieving peers included an average of 79% of the information; (b) segregated only 40% of main ideas from details in their notes, whereas high-achieving students segregated 55%; and (c) answered only 64% of listening comprehension questions correctly, while high-achieving students answered 89% correctly. High–achieving students in this study were defined as students achieving above the 50th percentile on the most recently administered standardized group achievement test, having a cumulative grade point average of 2.5 or above (on a 4-point scale), and having no history of special education services.

LD students also seem to have difficulty demonstrating their command of knowledge. They know less about how to take and study for tests than their high-achieving peers (Carlson & Alley, 1981). Before training, LD students exhibit little or no facility in "study" routines, such as finding answers to study questions and memorizing them (Schumaker et al., 1982).

With regard to oral demonstration of a command of knowledge, LD students participate in discussions less often than their peers. They volunteer to participate less often (2% of the time vs. 6% of the time), and they provide about half as many appropriate answers as their peers (Schumaker, Sheldon-Wildgen, & Sherman, 1980).

The requirement of following classroom rules also presents problems for the LD adolescent. Schumaker, Sheldon-Wildgen, and Sherman (1980) found that LD students engaged in more classroom rule violation than normal students. As grade level increased, the LD students' rule violation behaviors increased relative to those of non-LD students. LD students exhibited rule violations in 9% more of the intervals than their non-LD peers in 7th grade, 17% more in 8th grade, and 26% more in 9th grade. When teachers left the classroom, LD students engaged in rule-violating behaviors during 92% of the intervals, whereas normal students did not exhibit a single rule-violating behavior.

Required writing is also difficult for LD adolescents. Warner, Alley, Schumaker, Deshler, and Clark (1980) found that LD adolescents do not achieve beyond a mean grade level performance of 4-8 on a standardized writing test while they are in high school (that is, the performance of LD adolescents is similar to that of persons who have completed 4 8/10 years of elementary school). Warner, Alley, Deshler, and Schumaker (1980) also found that the student's score on the standardized writing test was the factor that, by itself, best differentiated LD adolescents from other low-achieving students. That is, when the students' scores on the writing measure were entered into discriminant analyses, two-thirds of the LD and low-achieving students were correctly classified by the computer. No other single variable enabled the computer to be as accurate in classifying the students into the two groups (LD and low-achieving). Low-achieving students in this study were defined as those students having one or more Fs in required courses, achieving below the 33rd percentile on the most recently administered standardized group achievement test, and having no history of special education services.

In addition, Moran (1981) found that non-LD students wrote paragraphs that scored significantly higher than LD students' paragraphs with regard to conventions, spelling, mechanics, and mean morphemes per T-unit. A T-unit is "one main clause plus any subordinate clause or non-clausal structure that is attached to or embedded in it" (Hunt, 1970, p. 4). Related to their general deficits in writing, LD adolescents seem to have even greater difficulty with their spelling. When students' performance on spelling items was separated from the rest of their writing achievement performance, spelling was found to be as powerful a discriminator of learning disabilities as the whole writing score (Warner, in prep.). Replicating this, Moran (1981) found that spelling was the only formal feature of low-achieving students' writing that was significantly better than LD students' writing.

Additionally, the studies to date show that LD students have great difficulty passing minimal competency examinations. Meyen et al. (1982) found performance discrepancies between LD students and their non-handicapped peers on minimal competency examinations at all grade levels. In fact, at the 11th grade level, for only one item on the test did the percentage of LD students meeting the criterion level on that item equal the percentage of non-LD students meeting the criterion on that item. Carlson and Alley (1981) found that only 43% of the LD students in their study passed at least two of the five study skills competency tests, whereas 100% of the high–achieving students passed at least two tests. None of the LD students passed four or more tests, whereas 85% of the high-achieving students passed four or more.

Finally, LD adolescents appear to exhibit deficits in the social realm. Compared with their non-LD peers, they are less active in school and out-of-school social activities (Deshler, Schumaker, Alley, Warner, & Clark, 1981). Their social skill performances are also significantly below their non-LD peers' performances (Mathews, Whang, & Fawcett, 1982; Schumaker, Hazel, Sherman, & Sheldon, 1982) and similar to the performance of juvenile delinquents (Schumaker et al., 1982).

These results indicate that LD adolescents have difficulties in precisely those areas that are targeted as demands of secondary and postsecondary school settings. They read poorly and exhibit difficulty using strategies for accomplishing reading tasks. They exhibit poor independent work habits and rarely ask for help. They do not attend well to auditorily presented information, nor do they take adequate notes. They exhibit deficits in the area of demonstrating their command of knowledge either orally or in writing. Their spelling is poor. They exhibit more classroom rule-violating behaviors than their peers. The disparity between the demands of secondary and postsecondary school settings and the deficits exhibited by the secondary LD population are a major cause for concern since they are probably the major cause of failure for these students in these settings.

Strategies Research

In light of the characteristics exhibited by older LD populations and the broad array of setting demands that they must meet for successful performance in secondary and postsecondary school settings, the KU-IRLD has designed a number of instructional packages, each of which can be used for the training of a learning strategy or a group of related substrategies. The strategies have been divided into three groups: strategies for gaining information from written (e.g., textbooks, shop manuals) and oral materials (e.g., lectures, films); strategies for expressing information in permanent products (e.g., assignments, tests, reports); and strategies for storing information (e.g., for tests).

Each group consists of several task-specific learning strategies. Multipass is one example of a strategy that has been designed to teach students to gain information from written material. This is a strategy for studying textbook chapters, using three passes over the chapter to survey it, to obtain key information from it, and to study the key information. To enable LD adolescents to better cope with the heavy reliance on lecture formats in secondary school classrooms, the Listening/note-taking Strategy (LINKS) has been developed to teach the student to identify organizational cues, to note key words, and to organize the key words in a simplified outline form.

The Error-monitoring Strategy (COPS) is an example of a strategy that has been designed to allow students to successfully meet written expression requirements. The Error-monitoring Strategy can be used to detect and correct errors of capitalization, overall appearance, punctuation, and spelling in written work. The First-letter Mnemonic Strategy can be used to store (memorize) information for tests. This strategy involves the formation of different kinds of mnemonic devices to facilitate the recall of lists of information.

The strategies in the above-described groups have been designed to meet certain criteria. First, they have been developed to correspond to a high-frequency demand in the academic setting. Thus these strategies are seen basically as task-specific ones. Second, they have been designed to overcome some of the major learning and performance deficits manifested by LD students. For example, each strategy has been developed to allow students with reading levels as low as the fourth grade to successfully use it. Finally, each strategy has been designed to be taught in a structured, systematic fashion using a teaching methodology designed by Deshler, Alley, Warner, and Schumaker (1981), which consists of nine steps:

• Make the student aware of his or her current learning habit.
• Describe the new learning strategy.
• Model the strategy.
• Have the student verbally rehearse the strategy.
• Have the student practice the strategy with controlled materials.
• Give feedback.
• Have the student practice the strategy in grade–level materials.
• Give feedback.
• Test.

After skill mastery has been demonstrated, a three-phased generalization procedure is implemented including (a) an orientation phase in which students are made aware of different settings and contents in which strategies can be applied, (b) an activation phase in which students are given practice with the strategy in a variety of materials and contents (e.g., textbooks, theme topics, or lecture topics), and (c) a maintenance phase in which periodic probes are made to ensure continued use of the strategy.

Each of the strategies has gone through a series of development and research activities to validate the strategy intervention. These activities include behavioral specification of the strategy, pilot testing with a few students to determine efficacy of the strategy conceptualization and design, and field testing of the refined strategy with six or more students to determine the effect of strategy intervention on student performance. Multiple-baseline designs were used to demonstrate the effectiveness of the training.

The data from these studies (e.g., Schumaker et al., 1982) reveal that prior to training, LD students showed little evidence of using effective strategies to meet task demands. For example, they evidenced poor reading comprehension (scoring less than 50% on comprehension questions) and poor written expression skills (written products were poorly organized and contained many errors), and their lecture notes were nonexistent or incomprehensible. In 80 instances, 98% of LD adolescents successfully mastered the strategies at criterion levels and demonstrated successful application of the strategies to improve comprehension of materials written at both their ability level and their current grade level. For example, the use of the Visual Imagery Strategy and the Self-Questioning Strategy enabled 6 students to improve their reading comprehension scores on tests covering grade-level materials from 2% to 81.7% and 46% to 89.8%, respectively (Clark et al., in press).

Studies on the ability of LD adolescents to generalize these learning strategies, however, indicate that students do not use the strategies at mastery levels in the regular class setting unless they receive specific generalization instruction in the resource room setting. The amount and type of generalization activities required was found to vary across subjects (Schmidt, 1983).

The implication of this research is that LD adolescents can learn task-specific strategies that will increase their ability to cope with the broad array of secondary school setting demands. Recent KU-IRLD research has focused on training LD students to design and apply their own learning strategies. Such training includes the modification of existing task-specific strategies or the design of a new strategy. Nevertheless, the major goal of the instructional process after the student has learned a repertoire of task-specific learning strategies (approximately 3-5) is to shift much of the responsibility from the teacher to the student. The purpose of this shift is to have the *student* learn the process of analyzing the setting demands with which he or she needs to cope and to modify or design an appropriate strategy to facilitate his or her learning and performance in that setting.

Recent research by Ellis (1983) has shown that it is possible to teach LD students that strategies are a class of cognitive behaviors and to design new strategies to solve whatever problems they face.

KU-IRLD development and research efforts suggest that the education of LD adolescents is facilitated if they can be made aware of (a) their own strengths and weaknesses as learners, (b) basic task-specific strategies for gaining and expressing information, (c) procedures for analyzing setting and task requirements, and (d) procedures for designing strategies to facilitate their ability to cope with setting and task requirements. Such self-awareness is seen as essential to the ultimate development of self–regulation skills in LD students, including the ability to plan, monitor, orchestrate, and check their own learning and performance (Deshler, Warner, Schumaker, & Alley, 1983).

Given the large number of setting demands that were found to require competence in independent living and social skills, the KU-IRLD has developed a curriculum to teach generalizable social skills based on a general skills training approach to LD adolescents and young adults. General social skills can be used to respond to classes of social situations. For example, resisting peer pressure is a general skill that can be applied to the class of situations represented by this scenario: the individual is interacting with at least one other person who is pressuring the individual to do something that he or she does not want to do. Thus the individual who has integrated the general skill of resisting peer pressure into his or her repertoire can deal with unreasonable or unwelcome demands from others by applying the skill in the unique situation.

The social skills curriculum is composed of materials for the training of 30 general social skills. Results show that LD adolescents can effectively use the materials to learn specific social skills to criterion in controlled situations and have demonstrated effective use of the skills in the ongoing activities within the school setting (Hazel, Schumaker, Nolan, & Pederson, in prep.).

By definition, a major instructional goal of secondary schools is the delivery of content information. A student's ability to successfully benefit from a curriculum is, in part, contingent on the existing knowledge base or pool of prior knowledge that the student possesses. A prior knowledge base allows the student to better understand the significance of material, to select main points, and to disregard trivia.

Cognitive psychologists have recently underscored the power of prior knowledge (Brown, Campione, & Day, 1981), scripts (Schank, 1983; den Uyl & van Oostendorp, 1980), and schema (Spiro, 1980) in facilitating comprehension by the learner. Marshall and Glock (1978), in studying the relationship between prior knowledge and reading comprehension, have suggested that prior knowledge may more profoundly affect comprehension than manipulations in text structures. Kintsch, Kozminsky, Streby, McKoon, and Keena (1975) have argued that text difficulty may actually be a function of prior knowledge.

In essence, then, another demand of the secondary school setting not identified by research is the expectation for students to bring a general storehouse of information with them to the learning situation. LD individuals may find themselves in a perilous situation in this regard. First, because of their learning inefficiencies, they lack the necessary skills to master content at the same rate and with the same degree of effectiveness as their normal peers, and second, because of prolonged placement in resource rooms that usually emphasize skill development (vs. content acquisition), LD students are denied exposure to a large amount of content information. These factors may greatly inhibit the LD student's ability to benefit from experiences in the secondary school curriculum.

A major challenge facing those who work with older LD populations is to devise ways to study the nature of the content deficiencies faced by these individuals and the effects of these deficiencies on their learning. In addition, innovative interventions will be required to enrich those with deficient backgrounds.

Chapter 12

Learning Strategies:
An Instructional Alternative
for Low-Achieving Adolescents*

*Donald D. Deshler and
Jean B. Schumaker*

As mildly handicapped students move from elementary to secondary school, they are expected to deal with increased curricular demands. The University of Kansas Institute for Research in Learning Disabilities has designed and validated a set of task-specific learning strategies as an instructional alternative for these students. Learning strategies teach students "how to learn" so that they can more effectively cope with increased curriculum expectations.

The challenge inherent in designing interventions to overcome or lessen the effects of a learning disability is a significant one. This challenge often grows in magnitude as learning disabled (LD) students move into adolescence and are expected to cope with the rigorous demands of the secondary school. While a number of different instructional approaches for LD adolescents have been described in the literature (Deshler, Schumaker, Lenz, & Ellis, 1984; Deshler, Warner, Schumaker, & Alley, 1983; Deshler, Lowrey, & Alley, 1979), little, if any, data have been reported regarding their efficacy.

*This chapter first appeared in *Exceptional Children* (1986), Vol. 52, No. 6, pp. 583–590. Copyright © 1986 The Council for Exceptional Children.

Intervention Description and Rationale

One of the major research goals of the University of Kansas Institute for Research in Learning Disabilities (KU-IRLD) has been to address this void by designing and evaluating interventions for mildly handicapped adolescents (Meyen & Deshler, 1978). Given the broad range of academic deficits evidenced by older students (Deshler, Schumaker, Alley, Warner, & Clark, 1982) that result in their inability to cope with secondary school curriculum demands, KU-IRLD staff adopted a learning strategies approach as the core component of an intervention model which has been developed and validated through 8 years of programmatic research. This intervention model is called the Strategies Intervention Model (see Schumaker, Deshler, & Ellis, 1986, for a detailed description of this model). This approach has been designed to teach students how to learn rather than to teach students specific curriculum content. Learning strategies, as defined by Deshler and Schumaker (1984), are techniques, principles, or rules that enable a student to learn, to solve problems, and to complete tasks independently.

In short, instruction in the use of learning strategies is instruction on how to learn and how to perform tasks. For example, through a learning strategies approach, the instructional goal is to teach students strategies for summarizing and memorizing material that has to be learned for social studies tests, rather than teaching them actual social studies content. Thus, while learning to use summarization and memorization strategies to improve their comprehension and retention of social studies concepts, students also learn a skill that, theoretically, will help them acquire information in other subject areas. An ultimate goal of learning strategies instruction is to enable students to successfully analyze and solve novel problems that they encounter in both academic and non-academic environments. The overall intent of learning strategies instruction, therefore, is to teach students skills that will allow them not only to meet immediate requirements successfully, but also to generalize these skills to other situations and settings over time (Deshler & Schumaker, 1984).

Three major rationales underlie a learning strategies intervention approach for adolescents. First, the development and application of learning strategies or metacognitive skills is significantly related to age; that is, older students consistently are more proficient in the use of such behaviors (Armbruster, Echols, & Brown, 1984). Second, adolescents who "learn how to learn" in secondary schools will be in a much better position to learn new skills and to respond to rapidly changing information and conditions in the future (Deshler & Schumaker, 1984). Third, a learning strategies instruction approach requires students to accept major responsibility for their learning and progress (Wong, 1985). Such a commitment must be made by students if they are to truly become independent.

To operationalize this learning strategies instructional approach, a set of learning strategy instructional packets was designed and field-tested. Together, these instructional packets make up the Learning Strategies Curriculum (Schumaker, Deshler, Alley, & Warner, 1983). Each packet consists of the instructional materials and procedures needed by a teacher to train students in a given learning strategy. The Learning Strategies Curriculum is organized in three major strands that correspond to the major demands of the secondary curriculum.

The first strand includes strategies that help students acquire information from written materials. The Word Identification Strategy (Lenz, Schumaker, Deshler, & Beals, 1984) is aimed at the quick decoding of multisyllabled words. Three other strategies are aimed at increasing a student's reading comprehension. The Visual Imagery Strategy (Clark, Deshler, Schumaker, & Alley, 1984) is used to form a mental picture of events described in a passage. The Self-Questioning Strategy (Clark et al., 1984) is used to form questions about information that has not been provided by the author and to find the answers to those questions later in the passage. The Paraphrasing Strategy (Schumaker, Denton, & Deshler, 1984) is used to paraphrase the main idea and important details of each paragraph after it is read. The Interpreting Visual Aids Strategy (Lenz, Schumaker, & Deshler, in press) is used by students to gain information from pictures, diagrams, charts, tables, and maps. Finally, the Multipass Strategy (Schumaker, Deshler, Alley, & Denton, 1982) is used for attacking textbooks' chapters by using three passes over the chapter to survey it, to obtain key information from it, and to study the critical information.

The second strand in the Learning Strategy Curriculum includes strategies that enable students to identify and store important information. The Listening and Notetaking Strategy (Deshler,
Denton, & Schumaker, in press) enables students to identify
organizational cues in lectures, to note key words, and to organize
key words into outline form. The First-Letter Mnemonic Strategy
(Robbins, 1982) and the Paired-Associates Strategy (Bulgren &
Schumaker, in preparation) provide students with several options
for memorizing key information for tests.

The final strand of the Learning Strategies Curriculum includes
strategies for facilitating written expression and demonstration of
competence. Four strategies have been designed to enable students
to cope with the heavy written expression demands in secondary
schools. The Sentence Writing Strategy (Schumaker & Sheldon,
1985) provides students with a set of steps for using a variety of
formulas when writing sentences. The Paragraph Writing Strategy
(Schumaker, in preparation [a]) helps students organize and write
a cohesive paragraph. Likewise, the Theme Writing Strategy
(Schumaker, in preparation [b]) helps students organize and write
an integrated five-paragraph theme. The Error Monitoring Strategy
(Schumaker, Nolan, & Deshler, 1985) is used to detect and correct errors in written products. An Assignment Completion Strategy
(Whitaker, 1982) is used by students to schedule and organize
themselves to complete assignments on time. Finally, the Test
Taking Strategy (Hughes, 1985) enables students to effectively take
classroom tests.

The task-specific strategies comprising the Learning Strategies
Curriculum are not a comprehensive set of learning strategies required for school success by poor learners; rather, they are representative of the types of learning behaviors required by students
to respond successfully to curriculum demands. They have been
chosen and developed after carefully reviewing the literature on
the demands of secondary settings (Schumaker & Deshler, 1984).

Guiding Principles

Three factors have influenced the way in which learning
strategies have been designed for and taught to LD adolescents.

First, it has been important to recognize that most LD students bring a long history of failure with them to remedial situations (Alley & Deshler, 1979). The ramifications of this negative experience in learning have been carefully considered as instructional activities have been designed such that students can experience success throughout the learning process. Second, many LD adolescents display minimal motivation for participation in academic instruction because of interest in nonacademic and peer associations (Goodlad, 1984). Thus, methods of motivating students have been interwoven throughout the instructional process. Third, as LD students move through the secondary grades, they encounter significant time constraints. That is, the amount of instructional time available to acquire skills becomes more limited as a student gets older. Therefore, methods of enhancing the intensity of learning strategy instruction have had to be developed. In addition to these factors, the following instructional principles have guided our implementation of learning strategy interventions.

Match Instruction with Curriculum Demands

The first step in the learning strategy instructional process is to understand the types of curriculum demands that the student is failing to meet (e.g., taking notes or writing well-organized paragraphs). This information is used in determining what task-specific strategy(ies) should be taught to the student. By matching the learning strategy instruction to existing (or forecasted) curriculum demands, students acquire skills that will enable them to cope with immediate academic pressures as well as prepare them for future curriculum requirements. This approach to instructional decision making is different from the course of action traditionally followed in special education in which student deficits (rather than environmental demands) are assessed to determine remediation. While we are interested in the unique deficits evidenced by students, our major concern is to understand the demands in the criterion environment that students are not meeting so we can structure instruction to help them cope with those demands.

Use Structured Teaching Methodology

For learning strategies to be useful "tools" for older students, these strategies must be learned to an automatic, fluent level. For that reason, a teaching methodology that is based on sound learning principles has been developed (Deshler, Alley, Warner, & Schumaker, 1981; Deshler, Warner, Schumaker, & Alley, 1983). The purpose of the acquisition steps of the teaching methodology is to give students the knowledge, motivation and practice necessary to apply the learning strategy successfully to materials and tasks in the resource room settings.

To this end, the acquisition methodology includes the following steps. First, the student is tested to determine his or her current learning habits regarding a particular task. The student is informed of his or her strengths and weaknesses and commits himself or herself to learning a new strategy to remedy the weaknesses.

In the second step, the new strategy is described to the student. It is broken down into component steps, rationales for learning the strategy are given, the types of results students can expect to achieve are provided, and situations in which the strategy can be used are delineated. Also in the step, students write their own goals regarding how fast they will learn the new strategy.

In the third step, the new strategy is modeled for the student from start to finish by the teacher while "thinking aloud." Next, students are involved in subsequent demonstrations of the strategy.

In the fourth step, the student uses verbal rehearsal to learn to name all of the steps of the strategy in order.

In the fifth step, the student practices the new strategy to a specified criterion performance in controlled materials (i.e., materials that are reduced in complexity, length, and difficulty level).

In the sixth step, the student practices the skill to a mastery criterion (both accuracy and speed are emphasized) in materials and situations that closely approximate tasks encountered in regular classes. Reinforcement and corrective feedback are given after each practice attempt in both steps 5 and 6.

In the final step, the student receives a post-test to determine if performance has progressed to a point that allows him or her to cope with curriculum demands in the target area. Each of these steps is used in teaching all of the task-specific learning strategies in the Learning Strategies Curriculum.

Deliberately Promote Generalization

The acid test of an academic intervention applied to mainstreamed students is the degree to which the skill taught under controlled conditions (e.g., the resource room) is generalized across settings and maintained over time. Our research has built on the work of Haring, Lovitt, Eaton, and Hanson (1978) and Stokes and Baer (1977) who have stressed the importance of carefully programming instructional activities to ensure generalization. Specifically, after students have demonstrated mastery of a learning strategy in a resource room, research results have shown that it is necessary to take them through a set of generalization steps designed to broaden their understanding of the strategy and to increase their facility in approaching regular classroom assignments.

The first generalization phase, the orientation phase, involves making students aware of the variety of contexts (e.g., classes, job situations, home situations) within which the recently learned strategy can be applied. A discussion is held to identify cues that should tell the student when to use the strategy and to brainstorm ways in which the strategy can be adapted to meet the unique requirements of a variety of class situations.

The next phase of generalization is activation. The purpose of this phase is to provide students with ample opportunities to practice the strategy in a broad array of materials, situations, and settings. The goal of this phase is to increase the degree to which students can automatically apply the strategy to novel tasks regardless of the setting in which those tasks are encountered. Thus, in this phase, students are required to use the newly learned strategy outside of the resource room and to report back to the resource teacher regarding their success.

The final generalization phase is called maintenance. To ensure continued use of the strategy over time, periodic probes are conducted to determine whether the student continues to use the strategy at an acceptable proficiency level.

Central to the entire generalization process just described are regular cooperative planning efforts between the resource and regular classroom teacher. Regular communication is essential to determine the degree to which the newly acquired learning strategies are being used in the regular classroom. In addition, in such meetings, classroom teachers can be encouraged to cue students to use the strategy at the appropriate time.

Apply "Critical Teaching Behaviors"

For adolescents to gain maximum benefit in the shortest period from learning strategies instruction in the resource room, it is essential for the teacher to regularly apply "critical teaching behaviors" in his or her instruction. We have defined critical teaching behaviors as those behaviors of a teacher that enhance the intensity or quality of instruction in a classroom.

Obviously, there are a broad array of such behaviors that are central to good instruction. The following teacher behaviors appear to be critical to optimizing instructional gains through learning strategy instruction: providing appropriate positive and corrective feedback, using organizers throughout the instructional session, ensuring high levels of active academic responding, programming youth involvement in discussions, providing regular reviews of key instructional points and checks of comprehension, monitoring student performance, requiring mastery learning, communicating high expectations to students, communicating rationales for instructional activities, and facilitating independence. It is interesting to note that in a recently completed study, Kea, Deshler, and Schumaker (in preparation) found that many middle and secondary resource teachers fail to regularly use many of these behaviors.

Use Scope and Sequence in Teaching

Most low-achieving adolescents show deficits in several academic areas (Deshler et al., 1982). To teach these students enough learning strategies to become competitive in the secondary setting, it is important to carefully organize both the scope and sequence of learning strategy instruction over several years (e.g., grades 7 through 12).

Students benefit most if they master approximately three to four learning strategies per year. When a systematic sequence of instruction is planned for students over a span of several years, they are ensured of receiving sufficient instructional coverage (i.e., scope). Furthermore, teachers have repeatedly noted that a "snowballing" effect takes place; that is, each learning strategy seems to build on the previous ones learned in a synergistic fashion such that students become capable of success in mainstream courses after learning several strategies across the three strands.

Ensure that Teaching Decisions are Governed by Outcome Goals

A major goal associated with the learning strategies intervention approach is to make LD students independent learners and performers. While experiencing the day-to-day pressures of teaching these students, it is often easy to lose sight of this goal.

Students truly become independent learners and performers when they start to generate their own learning strategies independent of teacher assistance. Thus, during the instructional process, in addition to learning task-specific learning strategies, it is important for students to become aware of how they learn and how they can take control over much of their learning (Brown, 1980). To accomplish this, students are first required to master approximately five specific strategies from the Learning Strategies Curriculum. They are then taught an executive strategy (Ellis, 1985) that, in essence, enables them to analyze a novel problem or demand and to design their own learning strategy.

Maximize Student Involvement

If adolescents are expected to ultimately become independent learners and performers, it is critical that they feel a vested interest in their intervention program. The learning strategies approach to instruction endorses the notion students understand that they must actively participate in their learning to ultimately assume control of the learning situation (Reid & Hresko, 1981; Torgeson, 1977). This is accomplished through a variety of mechanisms such as having students regularly set goals and evaluate their progress (Seabaugh & Schumaker, 1981), take part in individualized education program conferences as an active participant (Van Reusen, 1985), and regularly obtain their commitment to learn specific strategies (Schumaker et al., 1983).

Maintain Realistic Point-of-view

It is important that educators keep this intervention approach in proper perspective. The complex nature of school failure does not lend itself to one intervention approach. It would be a major error to attribute the poor performance of some older students solely to learning strategy or metacognitive deficiencies. While some students may be strategy-deficient, the intervention of choice may lie in another, more important area (e.g., social skill training). Likewise, adolescents who are significantly deficient in key skill areas (e.g., reading at the primary reading level) require intervention programs with a different focus and intensity.

Furthermore, while our research has documented the effectiveness of learning strategy instruction, it has also shown us that interventions besides those included in the Learning Strategies Curriculum are required to markedly impact the overall academic success and life adjustment of adolescents. Included within the curriculum of the overall intervention model that has evolved through KU-IRLD research are Social Skill Strategies, Motivation Strategies, Transition Strategies, and Executive Strategies (Schumaker et al., 1986). While a description of these curriculum components and other components of the model is beyond the scope of this chapter, it is important to stress that the conditions of LD in adolescents are sufficiently complex and resistant to intervention that they require the application of a comprehensive intervention model.

Data Illustrating Effectiveness of Learning Strategies

The learning strategy interventions just described have been tested in a variety of ways to determine their effectiveness. Initially each strategy underwent a series of development and research activities to ensure soundness of design. Over the course of about 7 years, each of the strategies in the curriculum was tested through multiple-baseline design studies to determine how students responded to the strategy instruction (e.g., Clark et al., 1984; Schumaker et al., 1983). In most instances, before training, students demonstrated limited evidence of strategy use. For example, they evidenced poor reading strategies in such areas as paraphrasing, self-questioning, and identifying critical features of tests. Similarly, their performance in writing skills, such as error monitoring and paragraph organization, were extremely low.

In all of the studies to date, once training in a strategy had been implemented, the students showed marked gains. For example, once students learned the Paraphrasing Strategy, their reading comprehension went from 48% to 84% on passages written at their current grade level. Mastery of the Error Monitoring Strategy reduced the number of errors that they made in written materials from 1 in every 4 words to 1 in every 33 words. Similar results have been found with each of the other strategies. In each of these carefully controlled studies, only a few students have been unsuccessful in learning the strategies.

As a result of many replications of these phenomena, it has become apparent that handicapped adolescents can learn to use a variety of learning strategies. Current research on these learning strategy interventions has moved into a phase of broad scale adoption of the interventions by different educational agencies (e.g., individual schools, school districts, intermediate units, or entire states). The Learning Strategies Curriculum is currently being implemented by teachers in dozens of school districts throughout the country. Similar results are reported by the participants in these sites. It is important to note, however, that significant student gains seem highly correlated with the level of staff training. In essence, we have found that it is essential to provide the kind of careful staff development called for by Showers (1985). When this occurs, student progress follows. In its absence, often little change is noted. (See author note following conclusion section.)

Conclusion

While KU-IRLD staff members are encouraged by the kinds of gains students who are exposed to learning strategy interventions are making, many questions still remain to be addressed concerning this intervention approach. Among the key areas of investigation are the following: (a) determining what students benefit most/least from these interventions; (b) determining if and how students in upper elementary grades (4, 5, and 6) can benefit from these interventions to better prepare them to transition into secondary schools; (c) determining how to effectively and efficiently enable these students to acquire much of the prior knowledge that they lack in core curriculum areas; (d) determining the long-term impact of these interventions on the academic success and life adjustment of these students; and (e) determining the types of teaching practices that promote optimal success for students who have been taught learning strategies.

Since the data in this chapter clearly show student gains to be highly correlated with staff training, the KU-IRLD makes the Learning Strategies Curriculum available to those educational agencies who commit to a staff development program designed to make their staff proficient in the use of these materials. Information for this training can be obtained by contacting Coordinator of Training, KU-IRLD, University of Kansas, Lawrence, KS 66045.

Chapter 13

School Counseling Psychology: A Vehicle for Role Change Regarding Special Education

Scott B. Sigmon

The regular public school educational system has become too reliant upon special education for dealing with its own problems in general—i.e., funding sources and achievement levels—and nonconforming students in particular. The position taken here is that until systemic changes are made to the American schooling process, the individual school psychologist, and other school professionals, should never formally classify a student (as being educationally handicapped) or place a child into special education unless such pupil has received remedial instruction and/or counseling—exceptions are often the moderately and almost always the severely handicapped. In this light, a number of basic considerations regarding school counseling psychology are discussed. This chapter emphasizes that the school is a social arena in which the psychologist school practitioner must function. Greater awareness of the consequences of professional functioning and a change in role are sought for the school psychologist.

Many school psychologists have come to believe that the best way to help students with problems in school is by placing them in special education. The basis for such a belief is that there are too few good remedial programs available, and because they feel there is not enough time to do counseling or they lack the skill to do so effectively. It is surely difficult for the individual school practitioner to change a well established traditional system or even consult effectively with certain school personnel for a host of sociological reasons. However, there is something satisfying that

167

the school psychologist alone can do which is beneficial for students: Counseling. This writer views counseling not only as a positive "return to the basics" with new (short-term) methods, but as a productive form of intervention, either to prevent special placement or, if deemed absolutely necessary, to facilitate it—as the student already is known from the counseling situation. By stressing the counseling role for psychologists in the schools, there is a simultaneous reduction in testing time. The school psychologist must defer classifying students for whom sufficient remedial services or counseling have not been made available, and this is really the only viable option until systemic changes—i.e., better regular educational instruction, more appropriate curricula, and school staff more sympathetic to consultation—are made.

In this chapter, a number of "basic considerations" germane to school counseling psychology are pointed out. However, keep in mind that the primary goal of this piece is to help change the role of the school psychologist in regards to special education placement.

Basic Considerations

What is "School Counseling Psychology"?

It is important to define what is meant here by the term "school counseling psychology" (hereafter usually referred to only as counseling), as opposed to psychotherapy or guidance, and why. For our purposes, counseling resides at a midway point on the helping continuum between school guidance and psychotherapy done within a clinical setting. The distinctions are very important because their purposes are different, each requires a distinct set of skills, plus there are legal and ethical limitations as to where they can be performed and by whom. Tharinger (1985), in her chapter on counseling elementary students, wrote that "The term 'counseling' rather than therapy is used throughout. . . because it is the term used in PL 94–142, the Education for All Handicapped Children Act. However, a distinction between counseling and therapy with children is not made" (pp. 447–448).

Guidance is a "type of counseling in which an individual is assisted through the use of interviews and tests, in choosing educational and vocational careers which will offer. . . maximum satisfaction" (Wolman, 1973, p. 164). Thus, guidance is primarily school/career oriented in nature. By contrast, for the purposes herein, psychotherapy, in its most complex form, involves changing or reconstructing the patient's personality. It is for this reason many people are apprehensive over the issue of whether psychotherapy has a place in the schools. Freudians believe that the adult personality can change radically only as a result of "psychotherapy or the trauma of catastrophe" (Maddi, 1972, p. 253). In any event, the child's personality is more malleable than the adult's, so great care and competence are required when practicing child psychotherapy. Hence, reconstructive psychotherapy is a "form of therapeutic aid offered to individuals to help them understand and resolve their adjustment problems. A variety of diverse techniques are used including the giving of advice, mutual discussion, and administration and interpretation of tests" (Wolman, p. 82). Because of differing theoretical persuasion, there may be some disagreement about these three definitions. However, let us consider these as working definitions.

Who Should Counsel in the Schools?

The training of school personnel for doing counseling varies greatly, even amongst school psychologists, primarily depending upon the college or university attended—and at what educational level; e.g., master's vs. doctoral. "Direct intervention through individual counseling is familiar ground for many school psychologists, uncharted ground for others and a place unknown to still others" (Tharinger, 1985, p. 447). Some guidance counselors have received formal training in counseling, but it is my experience that many shy away from it because of a lack of skills, especially for group work. On the other hand, some school social workers, especially those with the (clinical MSW degree) may be extremely proficient in doing psychological counseling, perhaps even more so than many nondoctoral school psychologists, and may serve as good resource persons in the schools for consultation on doing effective counseling.

Often times, despite the large number of psychological evaluations and many other duties that are required, another role expectation of the school psychologist is counseling. Hence, the psychologist working in the schools must have, at least, minimal skill in doing counseling. Competence and self-confidence are developed with practice, especially when success is seen. Shaffer (1985) wrote that "it is difficult to be dogmatic about what constitutes adequate qualifications for counseling, and how to acquire them" (p. 394). Therefore, if one did not receive much clinical experience while attending a formal college or university program, there are steps that can and should be taken to enhance one's skills. Reading about counseling is helpful, and professional associations often sponsor workshops. Moreover, there are clinical training programs offered by many different therapeutic groups, of various theoretical persuasion, for which the school psychologist, even at the subdoctoral level, is eligible, and often encouraged, to enroll. Sometimes the employing public school system will pay for such useful training, or at least a part of it. Yet, the most practical avenue is to seek supervision or advice on case handling from local school district colleagues, or your supervisor, if available and qualified.

Why Counsel?

Counseling should be done for the purpose of helping to alleviate the counselee's distress. In schoolchildren, the symptoms of distress are often manifested in disobeying teachers, poor achievement, and breaking school rules. Children, if unhappy, may act-out their distress or refuse to do what is asked of them in school, and not necessarily become the stereotypical lethargic, withdrawn adult depressant. This active behavior by unhappy children is the reason why clinicians have hesitated to formally label children as depressed. Yet, acting-out children can be very depressed and could ultimately become self-destructive if their psychological pain is not alleviated. Therefore, many potential counselees who come to the attention of the school psychologist are initially reported as being a "behavior management problem" and often as also having "learning problems."

Cross-cultural Counseling

Although this writer believes that a competent counselor can be effective with a client from any background or heritage, there are certain factors to consider. Probably the two most important considerations are that (a) certain groups have definitely been oppressed by the dominant American host culture, and (b) different ethnic groups have customs which are at odds with the majority of Americans. (Caution must be taken to ensure that children from non-English speaking homes are not placed cavalierly in special communications handicapped classes, or that poor and minority children are not too quickly labeled mildly retarded or learning disabled.) If you, as the counselor, are sensitive to and can accept these facts, then you should succeed. Work by Derald Wing Sue (1981) as well as Comas-Diaz and Griffith (1988), among others, are good resources.

Referrals

There will be few self-referrals by young schoolchildren. However, at the secondary level many students may seek the counsel of the school psychologist (Shaffer, 1985), especially one who has a reputation for being accessible, nonthreatening, and worthwhile seeing. Students who already know the school psychologist may request sessions at a later time after the initial termination merely to "say hello" or "touch base." Occasionally, the psychologist, while in a school, may spot a student that appears distressed, disoriented, excessively withdrawn, highly agitated or aggressive and make arrangements to see such a pupil. Invariably, though, referrals will originate from teachers, guidance counselors, or administrators who handle discipline problems. Moreover, the expectation is not usually that such youngsters be aided in their adjustment so much as it is that they will be placed in a special education program, preferably out of their present school. Building administrators can exert much pressure on the psychologist in an effort to make this happen. It is at this point where the psychologist has to muster one's professional courage by saying that the situation will be looked into without promising a special placement. A review of the student's records, an unobtrusive classroom observation, and a teacher conference/consultation —which may include parental involvement at a greater level than before—is in order. If teacher consultation does not help or is not feasible, an exploratory face-to-face interview with the student is indicated.

Individual and Group Counseling

In spite of time constraints, there are certain cases where individual counseling is preferable to group work. Examples of this are: extremely shy students who will not speak in group situations; rather intimate concerns, perhaps of a medical or interpersonal nature; no compatible school groups; and in some cases, age disparity. If there are other students with similar adjustment problems of approximately the same age, a counseling group should be initiated. In essence, the school psychologist should counsel to alleviate the distress of as many students as time permits; and therefore, selectivity and grouping are necessary. The effective group counselor must understand the natural course of groups, their dynamics, and the group leader's role (see Claiborn & Strong, 1982; Rosenbaum, 1976; Yalom, 1975). The leader must be directive with typical groups of young children, but with adolescents a nonjudgmental or "interview method" (Croake, 1986) often is better.

When to Counsel?

The primary goal of the school psychologist should be to facilitate the emotional adjustment of as many students as possible so that they can have a pleasant and therefore productive school experience. Moreover, inasmuch as counseling is a time consuming direct intervention, only those students for whom the process appears productive should be seen on a regular basis. And when seen, short-term counseling (Barbanel, 1982; Barten & Barten, 1973; Bellak & Siegel, 1983; Brown, 1986; Fisch, Weakland, & Segal, 1982; Sifneos, 1972; Weakland, Fisch, Watzlawick, & Bodin, 1974; Wolberg, 1965), which lasts from two to forty sessions, should be utilized. Finally, for an in-depth discussion on case management and when school counseling psychology is most appropriate, see Sigmon (1988; Appendix A, this book).

Conclusion

It is hoped that the ability to competently do counseling will become part of the many skills already held by school psychologists—who are too well rounded to merely fulfill the role of psychometrician/special education gate-keeper. Moreover, it is proposed that effective school counseling will change attitudes, and in so doing, reduce the practice of placing quickly into special education a child with an adjustment problem who has not yet received counseling. The school is a social organization that is usually changed by external forces, but it is possible to alter its functioning from within as well. Finally, such practice will not only provide more job satisfaction and enable the school psychologist to become a child advocate in greater measure, but also, the school psychologist will have changed one's role oneself—without having to wait for others to make systemic modifications.

Chapter 14

New Conceptualizations for Special Education*

*Alan Gartner and
Dorothy Kerzner Lipsky*

Current special education practices in the USA have failed to produce satisfactory results for students in terms of their learning, return to general education settings, graduation or preparation for post-secondary education, employment or citizenship. Minor changes at the margin will not produce the necessary educational reforms. What is needed is a new paradigm based upon a different set of premises. These include new conceptualizations in terms of: (1) the relationship between the individual, his or her impairment and the resulting handicap; (2) the understanding of intelligence; (3) the location of the problem; (4) the role of the individual as learner; (5) the relationship between location of learning and level of services; (6) the roles of parents; and (7) the relationship of special to general education. Only with new understandings in these (and other) areas can we build an educational system that provides quality education for students labeled as handicapped, one that sees them as "capable of achievement and worthy of respect."

Introduction

The current practice of special education has been the subject of increasing attention in the USA and elsewhere.[1] Data are

*This chapter first appeared in the *European Journal of Special Needs Education* (1989), Vol. 4, No. 1, pp. 16–22. Copyright © 1989 NFER-Nelson (Windsor, England).

increasingly available challenging the efficacy of present arrangements. Whatever the metric used—student academic or social skills
learning, return to general education from special education,
graduation with a regular diploma, preparation for post-secondary
employment, education or citizenship—the results of the current
practice of special education in the USA are not acceptable. Of
course, there are islands of quality, particular programs of excellence. But in the large, the quality of services offered is at best
mediocre, despite dedicated efforts of many and the expenditure
of vast sums of money. While there is increasing recognition of
this harsh reality, most efforts have involved changes at the
margin—the improvement of this or that practice, the issuance
of a new guideline or waiver of a regulation or tinkering with a
particular procedure.

New Conceptualizations

Towards the futherance of the more systematic and root
changes that are necessary, we suggest the need for reform in
several areas. Without pretending to be exhaustive, we will suggest
seven areas for new conceptualization, identify current special
education practices and the alternative potential of future reforms.

The Individual, his/her Impairment and Resulting Handicap

The current practice of special education, with its inheritance
of the medical model and its use of categorical descriptions of
students, both equates the child with the impairment and fails to
see that the handicap comes not from the impairment (alone),
but from the societal response to it. Handicap is a social construct,
created and built by an attitudinal environment. For example, the
youngster who is mobility impaired suffers a handicap when the
school has no ramps. Or the student who is blind becomes handicapped when this impairment leads others to think she cannot
learn. Too frequently special education practice is addressed solely
to the impairment, teaching those who are labeled alike in the
same way, as if there were "spina bifida" spelling, or teaching those
who are mobility impaired, for example, to maneuver a wheelchair
but never how to advocate for accessible public transportation.

The new conceptualization will require understanding of the relationship between impairment and handicap; that is, preparing the student both to overcome or cope with the impairment and to become an advocate for needed services against the handicapping response of society.

The Nature of Intelligence

The current practice of special education construes intelligence as unidimensional, for example, cognitive knowledge as measured by an IQ test, fixed once and for all and fully known. Instead educators need to recognize that there are various types of intelligence (Gardner, 1983); and that these change over dimensions and time. Furthermore, until we remove the barriers of inaccessibility, we will never know the extent to which the limits as measured by current intelligence tests are a function of those instruments and/or environments or "true" or "real" limits.

The new conceptualization will require greater openness to the range, extent and changeability of intelligence; the designing of programs based upon such understanding; and the consequence of the concept of multiple intelligences for the education of students currently labeled as handicapped (see Goldman & Gardner, 1989). Most particularly, this will require schools both to broaden their concept of intelligence and to extend the range and variety of instructional strategies employed.

The Location of the Problem

The current practice of special education operates on a deficit model; that is, it identifies something as wrong or missing in the student. When a student has a learning or behavior deficit, the current model conduces towards finding cause in terms of an impairment of the child.[2]

The new conceptualization will frame the "problem" in a different context. It will see the problem as the result of a mismatch between learner needs and instructional or management systems, and therefore will see the child not as a disabled person, but as a learner whose potential is being thwarted by the educational mismatch.

The Individual as Learner

The current practice of education sees students as recipients and instruction as given to the student who is the active participant in learning, that while the adult may teach, it is the student who must be engaged in the learning—to be, if you will, a worker in his/her own learning (Gartner & Riessman, 1974). To be involved in this way, the student must be engaged, interested and respected.

The new conceptualization will see the student as able to participate both in his/her own learning but also to join with others in mutual learning, in programs such as co-operative learning (Slavin, 1986, 1987) and learning through teaching. Such instructional strategies are not only expressions of a different conceptualization of the role of the student as learner, they also are means towards the integration of students with a wide range of capacities and needs.

The Place of Learning and the Level of Services

The current practice of special education can be seen as organized as follows:

Degree of impairment	*Intensity of service*	*Location of service*
Mild or moderate	Low	In or near the mainstream
Profound or severe	High	Separate or distant from mainstream

This is, in effect, the cascade (Deno, 1970) or continuum of services model (Reynolds, 1962). As Taylor (1988) urges, a different formulation starts with the commitment to all students being educated in an integrated setting and then varying the level of services. Thus a new educational model can be seen as follows:

Degree of impairment	*Intensity of service*	*Location of service*
Mild or moderate	Low	Fully integrated
Profound or severe	High	Fully integrated

The new special education direction will start with placement in an integrated setting, what we call a "refashioned mainstream," as the most appropriate location for the essential social and academic learning necessary for all children to grow and develop and to be prepared for a life of full involvement and participation in the larger community. In such a refashioned mainstream, the amount and range of services will vary depending upon individual students' needs which, of course, will vary by topic or subject-matter over time.

Parental Roles

The current practice of special education has not involved parents to the full extent envisioned by the law. In practice, Individualized Education Plans (IEP's) are written with limited parental input, often with only a "sign off" obtained (*Ninth Annual Report*, 1987); actual contact between school and parents is limited (Meyers & Blacher, 1987); and the emphasis is more on procedural obligations rather than on substantive involvement (Lipsky & Gartner, 1989). In part, this is due to the general school culture that presents a cool if not hostile face to parental involvement. More particularly, in special education, parents are seen as part of the problem (Lipsky, 1985). Indeed the remedy to the lack of parental participation is often counseling for the parents—to overcome guilt or shame or chronic sadness, and training of them to become, in effect, semi-professionals.

The new conceptualization of parental involvement will see parents as partners—not as ignorant persons to be trained by professionals, but as possessors of valuable knowledge and legitimate interests. Their role is different from, but no less important than, that of the professional.

Relationship to Broad School Reform Efforts

The current practice of special education is largely separate from general education. Of course, the current structure of special education is a function of the extrusion of students labeled as handicapped by general education (Lipsky & Gartner, 1987). And this continues to be true in the day-to-day life of the school (Allington & Johnston, 1986; Allington & McGill-Franzen, 1989;

Jenkins, 1987) and in the ignoring of special education in the concerns of the school reform movement. The response of the special education establishment is to decry being ignored and to indicate that until general educators are more open to closer relationships, special education should keep itself separate.

The new conceptualization will recognize that the issues facing special education cannot be addressed, no less solved, in isolation from broader school reform. For those concerned with the education of students labeled as handicapped, failure to insist that the school reform movement encompasses the needs of all students will leave special education further apart, consigned now more permanently to a separate and second-class status.

New Challenges

The Education of All Handicapped Children Act (P.L. 94–142) was exceptional for its time in history and has produced achievements of great magnitude. In its implementation, it has assured near-universal access to educational services for all handicapped children. What it has not done is to provide quality education in ways to assure full integration in society. The placement data for the most recent school years show no increase in students served in integrated settings; indeed, for some categories of handicapping conditions, the extent of segregation has increased (Lipsky & Gartner, 1989).

There are increasing challenges to the current design (Biklen, 1985; Gartner & Lipsky, 1987; Lipsky & Gartner, 1989; Skrtic, 1987; Stainback & Stainback, 1984). We call our approach a "refashioned mainstream" for all students. A refashioned mainstream will have two fundamental constructs. First, from the perspective of students now "in" special education, there will be no "dumping," that is, the "mainstreaming" of students labeled as handicapped into inappropriate programs. Secondly, from the perspective of all students, there will be improved instructional programs. A refashioned mainstream builds upon the belief that children are more alike than different, and do not need separate *educational systems,* and that all children have individual needs, and *school programs* must be organized to address those needs. The effect is not to ignore individual differences, nor is it to see them as characteristics of only a special group of students or the basis for the establishment of separate systems and unequal programs. Rather, the differences are welcomed and seen as opportunities to enhance the social and academic learning opportunities of all children. A refashioned mainstream will be fundamentally different than the present special and general education programs; it will be one where the idea of choosing between equity and excellence is inappropriate. Towards the goal of a refashioned educational system, outcomes-based legislation is called for—i.e. a national effective schools Act that will focus on student academic and social development rather than procedural requirements.

To this point, we have framed the issues as matters of school organization and pedagogy. But at bottom, they are ultimately issues of values, a question of the type of people we are and the nature of the society that we wish to build. Is it to be a society that separates and sorts people, relegating some to permanent second-class status, or is it to be one that incorporates an alternative vision, one of an open and inclusive society?

In his opening address to the first International Conference on Special Education in 1988,[3] Deng Pu Fang, President of the China Welfare Fund for the Disabled, talked of the purpose of special education as preparing persons with disabilities to fulfill social obligations. To do so, we need to see persons labeled as handicapped in new ways—as "capable of achievement and worthy of respect" (Lipsky & Gartner, 1987, p. 69); and we must adopt new conceptualizations as the basis for a different way to educate children with impairments, indeed to educate all children.

Notes

1. We are aware of the debates in the UK and elsewhere in Western Europe, Australia, New Zealand and Canada. Our knowledge, however, is limited to the USA, and therefore we will restrict our descriptions to the USA. We do believe, however, that the assumptions which we describe as undergirding US practices are not limited to the USA alone. Further, we hope the new conceptualizations presented have some applicability to other countries.

2. There is an abundant body of literature describing the inadequacy of the assessment and evaluation procedures, both as to reliability and validity. For a current summary of this literature, see Ysseldyke (1987).

3. This chapter derives from a paper presented by the first author at the International Conference on Special Education, Beijing, China, June 1988. The order of authors does not represent seniority.

Conclusion: A Critique of Special Education's Major Problems with Suggested Solutions

Scott B. Sigmon

> It obviously makes a difference whether we consider ourselves as pawns in a game whose rules we call reality or as players of the game who know that the rules are "real" only to the extent that we have created or accepted them, and that we can change them.
>
> Watzlawick, Weakland, & Fisch (1974, p. 26)

Special education, like ordinary education, is steeped with social problems. In fact, special education's relationship to the difficulties of society at large are more complex because they are often camouflaged by misguided "scientific" theories and practices. The most confused aspect of special education today is the treatment of the so-called mildly handicapped student—the type usually considered learning disabled. However, it is the current multitude of mildly handicapped that has been the major impetus for us to re-examine how we determine whether someone is educationally handicapped, and more importantly, what we then shall do. The first part of this chapter deals with the problematic issues, the second with procedural solutions, and the last with differences between the schooling process and learning.

The Issues

There are a number of issues in special education that require careful scrutiny. We must ensure that minorities are not disproportionately placed into special education—regardless of the label or program. Ignorant or unethical administrators should not be allowed to use federally funded special education in lieu of locally funded remedial education, as the need to remediate does not necessitate labeling a student as being handicapped. Instruction, learning strategies, teacher consultation, and guidance/counseling, all of the highest possible caliber, must be utilized prior to special education consideration. Unless the special education programs are definitively and qualitatively better for the student than the ordinary education available, special placement should not be made. And finally, we must be critical of psychoeducational tests, because, as most were designed to search for pathology, they can virtually find some disability in anyone.

Because of increasing special education enrollments, local, state, and the federal governments have become concerned over student misidentification, but more so over the expense involved. The federal government has begun a general education initiative (Will, 1986) to have students with learning problems remain in their regular education classes. Currently, the state of California is studying an alternative to the traditional "pull-out" resource room program whereby, under a "consultative model," the "resource specialists would predominantly provide advice and assistance to regular classroom teachers rather than direct instruction to students" (Office of the Legislative Analyst, 1987, p. 4). California views this "consultative model" as an example of "cost-effective" alternatives "which result in a greater level of student outcomes when compared to other alternatives of similar cost" (p. 4).

It is noteworthy that as far back as 1959, when New Jersey enacted major new special education legislation, the (State Department of Education) certified position of "remedial instructor" (later changed to "learning disabilities specialist," and then to "learning disabilities teacher-consultant") was created. The remedial instructor—in addition to serving as the third member of a "child study team," alongside of the school psychologist and school social worker—was to serve as a learning consultant to classroom teachers.

The main focus of the remedial instructor's efforts was to be the improvement of the quality of the classroom teacher's work with all pupils, not only with the handicapped. In so functioning, the remedial instructor would be instrumental in planning an individualized educational program for a specific child to be carried out in the regular classroom setting. Thus, all students would benefit from a teacher who had recourse to a remedial instructor.

Working in this manner, the remedial instructor would be expected to observe the learning disabled pupil as he or she functioned in the classroom. The remedial instructor might, in certain cases, work for a short period of time on a one-to-one basis with a handicapped pupil to test the effectiveness of a proposed method or material before recommending it to the classroom teacher.

As a full member of the Child Study Team, the remedial instructor was to play an equal part in the diagnosis of the student's learning disability and a major part in determining the individualized educational program needed. The remedial instructor would assume, also, a major role in the on-going re-evaluation of the learner's progress and educational status. (Jan-Tausch, 1985, p. 2)

The California report, mentioned earlier, cited a study done in Colorado (Shepard & Smith, 1981) which found that "42 percent of all expenditures on learning disabled children were devoted to such noninstructional activities as assessment"; and went on to say that "If the same percentage holds true for California, we estimate that as much as $300 million statewide is now being expended on the identification and assessment of individuals suspected of being learning disabled" (Office of the Legislative Analyst, 1987, p. 4).

The identification, assessment, and placement activities associated with providing students special education—no matter how minimal, e.g., supplemental instruction—are very expensive as well as time-consuming. The process is also seriously flawed. Previous instructional factors such as quality and appropriateness are usually overlooked. Moreover, it is assumed that the problem emanates from within the child and that the results of a one-time "comprehensive" (multidisciplinary) psychoeducational assessment are valid. Almost all students referred by teachers for consideration as educationally handicapped are tested; and the overwhelming majority of those tested are found eligible for special education. From an earlier three-year national survey of local education agency directors of special education (Algozzine, Christenson, & Ysseldyke, 1982), it was found that "3% to 6% of the school-age population is referred each year for psycho-educational evaluation. Of those referred, 92% are tested; of those tested, 73% are declared eligible for special education services" (Ysseldyke et al., 1983, p. 80). In poor urban areas in America, it is likely the percentage referred is in line with what Ysseldyke and his colleagues found, but the percentages of those actually tested and found eligible for special education are much higher. The basis for reasoning that the percentages are greater within poor urban areas is that so many more children will have more severe problems; and therefore, it is easier to validate their handicaps. Also, years of first-hand experience have shown me that this is true. Nevertheless, "A referral should not mean that a child is automatically tested and placed, as current research indicates" (Ysseldyke et al., 1983, p. 87); more should be done first.

The multidisciplinary team (MDT) or child study team—as it may be called either in the various states—should function as a safeguard, but it does not. (The Team, after a formal referral usually initiated by a regular classroom teacher, determines through the use of a psychoeducational assessment a student's eligibility for special education.) There is great pressure from administrators, teachers, and sometimes parents to classify students who do not fit well into the regular educational system, and the local school district receives (from the federal government through the states) additional funding for each student classified as educationally handicapped. In addition, the Teams know there is not much they can do to help the referred children educationally because of a paucity of programs associated with the lock-step regular curriculum, so the Teams take a nurturing position by placing such students into various special education programs.

The psychoeducational assessment, paperwork (written reports related to the assessment), and conferences (with parents and school personnel) relative to the placement of students into special education is a very time-consuming, expensive process. After the placement of a student into a special program occurs, the MDT must continue to monitor that student. And although the monitoring procedures are not as complex as the initial placement activities, they too require resources—additional professional time and more paperwork.

In most situations, the local school districts hire only enough Team personnel to meet within the required timelines the legal mandates for evaluations and monitoring reviews; and this leaves virtually no extra time for Team members to do things that really help children; i.e., pre-referral interventions. That is, school psychologists are unable to counsel children, learning consultants cannot spend time in classrooms helping teachers teach children with learning problems and school social workers cannot work as a true liaison between the school and the student's family. It is ironic that those professionals best trained to provide special services to schoolchildren with problems in most cases today are unable to do so.

Many minority children in poor urban areas are placed into special education programs that are nothing more than holding tanks where hardly any learning takes place, and where expectations for achievement are virtually non-existent. Yet, simultaneously, affluent districts continue to abuse in growing numbers the special education apparatus by using it for remedial education with children having no real handicaps. In both cases, this is merely substandard tracking. This is what can be expected from a society that talks much about concern for the poor and children in general but really does little of significance for either—especially if one is both; i.e., a poor child. Although there are well intentioned educators who would prefer to believe schooling is separate from socio-political concerns, it is not. The misuse of special education will end when there is an empowerment of oppressed groups, especially poor minorities, and at which time regular education will accept the fact that low academic achievers and social non-conformists are in most cases not truly handicapped in their ability to learn.

There is continuing debate as to what percentage of the population at large is educationally handicapped. This is especially problematic when dealing with handicaps that are not obviously sensory (blindness or deafness) or physical (orthopedic) in nature. The areas of greatest disagreement are those where subjective opinions are made (emotional disturbance, mild mental retardation and learning disability).

When emotional disturbance is discussed, we are often dealing with value judgements. Many times a clash of social class values is confused with purely intrapsychic pathology. Perhaps if school personnel were more sensitive to social class differences they would find less psychopathology in their students. Most teachers have so-called middle class values, while many students in urban American public schools today are poor. Students, thought to have such severe emotional disturbance that special education is considered for them, should first be provided counseling or alternative regular education programs—unless of course they are assaultive or suicidal.

The Interagency Committee on Learning Disabilities (1987) stated that "Learning disabilities. . . are intrinsic to the individual and presumed to be due to central nervous system dysfunction" (p. 222). This presumption is usually based upon inferential testing whose validity is highly questionable (Sigmon, 1987). The inferential, or so-called mildly handicapped, learning disabled students have no definitive medical problem, and yet, they constitute the largest special education group. This should be interpreted that there is today something seriously wrong with most of the special educational programming of pupils.

Even where we have strong evidence that a student may actually have a learning disability caused by central nervous system (CNS) disorder, there is nothing that can be done to reverse the condition. "Are the causes of learning disabilities in children known at a biological level? Can anything be done to reverse the brain state causing such disorders? The answer is 'no' to both questions" (Interagency Committee, 1987, p. 135). Therefore, we must develop more sophisticated instructional methods for the truly handicapped learners with CNS disorder.

Interventions and Assessment Prior to Special Education Placement

Before placing a child into special education, certain pre-placement interventions must be attempted. These intervention assistance activities are so important because such a high percentage of those students formally referred—for a psycho-educational evaluation to determine their special education eligibility—are classified as educationally handicapped, and yet most are considered to be "only mildly" impaired. Essential global pre-placement interventions are: up-grading instruction, providing "meta-instruction" (the teaching of learning strategies), doing counseling, and offering consultation from specialists to teachers to help improve their effectiveness with individual students or whole classrooms.

If it is believed that special education should be for those with intrapsychic/internal handicaps, then the quality and quantity of instruction previously provided to the student must be assessed—even before the individual is evaluated to determine eligibility for special education. *Direct instruction, precision teaching,* and *peer tutoring* are highly recommended. These three, and other instructional techniques, should be implemented before a child is assessed.

The *interaction* of the individual pupil with the problematic aspects of the curriculum, the social relationship with the teacher, and the school as an institution representing dominant cultural influences (hegemony) must all be examined. Take reading for example, as it is so important to the school curriculum.

> An interactionist perspective is well suited to the understanding of reading (dis)ability because it predicts variability in performance within individuals across texts, tasks, and settings. In this context, a child's performance on various reading measures is considered an indication of what he or she can and will do under a specific set of conditions, rather than a set of fixed abilities and disabilities. Therefore, the necessity for identifying the "disability" is eliminated, and our attention is refocused on how each child performs under different conditions and which set of conditions is most likely to facilitate learning. (Lipson & Wixson, 1986, pp. 120–121)

After doing an interactional analysis of the student's problem, an "intervention plan" including counseling and/or instruction within the regular education apparatus should be developed and implemented. Should this fail, a non-special education alternative program with smaller groupings, including but not limited to motivation and/or vocational training, could be tried. If none of this has succeeded, only then would we be justified in considering a student for special education. Because, by now, we can feel more assured that the problem probably emanates from within the student, and therefore, the student might actually be handicapped.

Traditional psychoeducational tests (such as the WISC-R, WRAT, PIAT, etc.) are "norm-referenced" in that an individual's score is compared to normative data from the original general population sampled. On the other hand, "curriculum based assessment" (CBA), which is a form of criterion-referenced assessment, compares a child's test results with the school curriculum being utilized. There is currently an emphasis on CBA so that evaluation can better aid in instructing children who have academic problems, rather than to merely certify their eligibility for special education. As long as the curriculum is sensible, this seems reasonable. This is related to the general education initiative (GEI) whereby those with mild learning disabilities spend more or all of their time in regular classes, and are provided better "individualized" instruction. It should be kept in mind that although the possibility of bias is not eliminated, assessment in this way is related more to instruction.

After having done all the possible/feasible pre-referral interventions, the next step is the formal referral. This is the time for a last safeguard. At this stage, a "test-teach-test" evaluation should be conducted. This would ensure that a child is not misdiagnosed because of previous lack of exposure to what the test is measuring. This is especially essential when using cognitive tests so that a false positive for mild retardation does not occur. Moreover, perhaps practice with a visual-motor test may help prevent a pupil from being mislabeled as having a learning disability. The test-teach-test approach has generally been associated with Budoff and associates' "learning potential status" (see Budoff & Pagell, 1968) or the Feuerstein group's "dynamic assessment" (see Feuerstein, 1979). Although the work by Feuerstein as well as Budoff was associated primarily with preventing a mistaken diagnosis of mild or educable retardation at a time when too much emphasis for such classification was placed on IQ tests, I am insisting that test-teach-test be used to prevent the misdiagnosis of learning disabilities. Assessment must be linked to teaching, and not to labeling and segregation.

Special Education: School Process vs. Learning Process

Special Education, with a capital E, is the school process; while special education, with a small e, is the learning process. One (E) is institutionalized and custodial, which equals schooling; yet the other (e) is individualized and personal, and is equated with learning. The point is, because so many millions of schoolchildren have been deemed unsuitable for ordinary eduation, Special Education serves more a warehousing function for society than as a means of educating children. Real special education should be for individual edification, and not to serve society's need to segregate the mildly atypical learner. The position here is not that Special Education teachers do not try to teach their students, but rather, too much energy has been spent justifying the current placement of over four million USA students into Special Education (U.S. Office of Special Education, 1987) —and this *is* certainly hard to justify. We must expend more resources in educating students.

Within the past few years, the recently deceased psychiatrist Milton H. Erickson (1902–1980) has become recognized as a gifted psychotherapist. Erickson had a knack for succeeding with the hard-to-reach. Using the same basic premise in which he did psychotherapy, Erickson taught a seventy year old to read within three weeks—whereas various school teachers could not do the same with this elderly person over several months (see Haley, 1985). The key is using "satisfaction that can be derived from dissatisfaction" (p. 243); or, "You try to get him to learn to enjoy his satisfactions" (p. 245; in Haley, 1985). The reason this satisfaction notion sounds paradoxical is because it is a primary technique in the out-of-the ordinary process of hypnosis, and Erickson is now considered to have been one of the greatest medical hypnotists. Perhaps Erickson's satisfaction principle should be used to ensure that a student receives real special education, and is not merely being warehoused in Special Education.

Now that some concerted effort has finally been put forth to examine Special Education as a significant societal process, it can be seen that any kind of special schooling for the educationally handicapped is an arrangement which is not entirely benefical and it is often help that hurts (Carrier, 1986; Coles, 1987; Sigmon, 1987; Tomlinson, 1982). Special Education currently constitutes a vast cultural panorama within the total school scene. It has inappropriately included the millions of misdiagnosed so-called mildly handicapped children. Make no mistake, we are not merely dealing with curriculum, teaching methodology, and helping children learn. On the contrary, Special Education's present superstructure is dysfunctional, and it cannot meet adequately the real educational needs of most of those within its domain. Rather than debating their particular special placement and its justification, the so-called mildly handicapped, as well as the moderately and severely impaired (blind, orthopedically handicapped, etc.) not in need of special schooling, must be de-institutionalized from it as soon as possible. Thus, the debate need only be on how best to teach them, and not where to put them. Because, at this time, Special Education for most students is a form of low level tracking functioning under the pretense of scientific theory and practice.

Schooling serves a societal need to reproduce culture. Special Education aids that goal. On the other hand, the aim of any true type of education is to cultivate individual growth while instilling simultaneously an understanding of and an appreciation for a democratic society.

Appendix A

A Framework to Determine
When the School Psychologist Should Counsel*

Scott B. Sigmon

The major goal of this piece is to identify a "five-level framework of psychological adjustment" specifically for use by school psychologists. The levels range from one of excellent adjustment to severe psychopathology. The school psychologist is guided toward interaction with clients based on a differential scale of adjustment.

Those students for whom short-term counseling appears productive should be seen in school. Others, in need of psychotherapy, should be referred to outside professional resources. Counseling is a time-consuming direct intervention. Thus, short-term counseling (Barbanel, 1982; Barten & Barten, 1973; Brown, 1986; Fisch, Weakland, & Segal, 1982; Sifneos, 1972; Watzlawick, Weakland, & Fisch, 1974; Weakland, Fisch, Watzlawick, & Bodin, 1974; Wolberg, 1965), which constitutes two to forty sessions, is recommended for school practice.

Prior to selection, the counselor must try to determine the level of distress of the prospective client. Once a corresponding prognosis can be made, the counselor can then make a decision as to whether to proceed with a particular client or make an outside referral. This decision is made from knowledge about the student from a single in-depth interview, if possible; but also from

*This piece first appeared in *Psychology in the Schools* (1988), Vol. 25, No. 1, pp. 62–64. Copyright © 1988 Clinical Psychology Publishing Company (CPPC).

193

the use of the student's school records, and if necessary, through conferences with school staff who know the pupil.

A five-level schema of psychological adjustment is proposed to aid the counselor in determining case management. There are three levels that require the psychologist's attention. The five levels are described as follows:

Level V: A severe or "crisis situation," in which the person has been traumatized or is threatening suicide and requires immediate attention. This situation is always the psychologist's highest priority. Knowledge of crisis intervention is important (Bellak & Siegel, 1983; Golan, 1978; Slaikeu, 1984; Smead, 1985). The seriously traumatized and the suicidal often will require hospitalization and medical attention. The school psychologist is required to provide "psychological first aid," quickly notify parents, and help arrange for psychiatric treatment.

Students who are unhappy may threaten suicide and are always taken seriously. They may not necessarily follow through with their threat. The school psychologist must be able to differentiate by observing affect and inquiring about the suicide strategy: when it will be done and by what method. If the student is not depressed, if the proposed suicide is planned for a distant time or the method has not been decided upon, and the student denies that a suicide was really planned, identification has been made of someone seeking help, but who may not be physically self-destructive.

According to Kenneth Rubin, President of the New Jersey Psychiatric Association, the "overwhelming majority of teen-age suicide attempts are impulsive, ill-considered, spur-of-the-moment behavior" (1987, p.5). This is what makes a level V state so potentially dangerous. Traits to look for in an impulsive level V are anger, antisocial behavior, alienation, regularly "in trouble," and frequent alcohol or drug usage. The most likely occurrence for adolescent self-destructive behavior is immediately "after getting into trouble at home or with the law, or after breaking up or fighting with a boyfriend or girlfriend" (Rubin, p. 5).

There are, however, certain classic warning signs for which the counselor can look to determine if a suicide is imminent. These include such things as giving away prized possessions, a decrease in the amount as well as the quality of schoolwork, and extreme changes in behavior—manic, withdrawn, or both. Moreover, in addition to the classic signs, if the counselee explicitly or implicitly affectively expresses being helpless, hopeless, and worthless, such an individual should not be left alone—probably requiring 24-hour hospital observation.

A *level IV* represents a moderate to severe problem where there is a "deep-seated adjustment problem of some duration," for which long-term psychotherapeutic intervention and/or medical management appear warranted. The student may have hallucinations, delusions, or exaggerated phobias. This is not the type of case that would generally be handled within a regular public school. It is outside the expertise of most school psychologists. This type of student may already be attending a special school.

Level IV types may be most at risk for life threat crisis at any point in their social-emotional development. Thus, any professional responsible for level IVs must diligently monitor them; and it is essential that the school practitioner—regardless of the institutional setting—be aware of this. Being serious, long-term cases, they should already be under supervision; yet they might not have been identified. So, as the psychologist working in the schools must usually rely upon the regular school staff (teachers, administrators, and guidance counselors) to initially identify troubled students, staff in-service training for the identification of those at-risk would be very helpful—especially because a number of pupils with these kinds of problems are not acting-out enough to receive teacher attention.

The youngster having a mild to moderate "adjustment reaction" is the ideal candidate for school psychological counseling. This is a *level III* situation. The term reaction connotes the result of behavior that is situational and transient. The school counselor is likely to be effective in this type of intervention. Level IIIs are children who may refuse to do schoolwork. They can be withdrawn or act-out; but they are ordinarily not physically self-destructive (level V), nor are they severely pathological, and they reveal no pathognomonic signs on personality assessment (level IV). Such students may have problems with interpersonal relationships, may attend various special education programs—at various times— within regular public schools, and frequently are classified emotionally disturbed.

Within the five-level schema, a *level II* suggests a mild problem that is occasional—perhaps the sort of child who has become known as "difficult" and who previously was called "high-strung." A level II youngster may have intermittent personal problems or episodes of misbehavior in school, but, as a general rule, should not be considered for special education due to emotional factors, as counseling is more efficacious for this child's needs.

Level I is the normal child who, although there may be a noteworthy but minor problem, is not considered to be in need of psychological counseling. The counselor must understand what constitutes normal behavior and development (Neubauer, 1972; Schecter, Toussieng, & Sternlof, 1972).

Regardless of the level of a student's problem, when the psychologist first becomes aware of it, there is a professional obligation to inform the parents. With level IV students, the parents will be referred to outside agencies or private psychotherapists. Good professional practice dictates recommending a minimum of two (or possibly three) suitable resources from which the parents may choose. If the counselor decides to see a level III child for ongoing short-term counseling, informed consent, in writing, should be obtained from the parents before a second session with that child occurs. The school psychologist ordinarily need not be concerned about legalities if a child is seen once. A second session without parental permission can result in complicated and unnecessary problems for the counselor.

Knowledge of this proposed framework will help the counselor to conceptualize degrees of psychopathology that will be encountered in schools. (It is to be noted that, as a person's emotional adjustment changes, one's designated level will also change.) Knowing this, the school psychologist will be able to make more informed recommendations, as well as referrals, and be a better prepared counselor.

Appendix B

Black and Male in Special Education: A Brief Local/NJ State Analysis

——————————————————————— *Scott B. Sigmon*

Special education statistical data from a northern urban New Jersey school district, whose student population is virtually all Afro-American, parallels the NJ state averages. Particularly significant is the fact that the low incidence (physical or sensory or very low cognitive) handicaps are nearly equal by gender; but the inferential, high incidence classifications (notably, learning disabilities and emotional disturbance) result in a disproportionate placement of males in special education—both locally and statewide. Being black adds greatly to the likelihood of a pupil being classified emotionally disturbed in New Jersey for males especially, but also for females. The author attributes this to socio-cultural factors.

It has long been thought and occasionally quite dramatically shown that there are more boys than girls in special education programs. The data from this particular study once again confirm that fact. The reasons for this present disproportion, however, remain speculative, but based upon the categories with a large number of students with great disproportion by gender and race, the primary reason would seem to be socio-cultural. The latter point is highlighted by the fact that 80% of New Jersey's students classified as emotionally disturbed (ED) are males and the New Jersey ED prevalence rate for blacks is twice that of whites.

The local data—presented within this paragraph—for this study came from one urban New Jersey school district with approximately 12,000 students where almost all the pupils are Afro-Americans.

Those categories that comprise low incidence handicaps—which are all obviously physical (orthopedic, 56% boys, n=9); sensory (auditory, 60% boys, n=15); and cognitive (moderate-severe retardation, 50%, n=18)—show a relatively equal distribution by sex. On the other hand, high incidence handicaps—which are predominantly based upon inferential psychoeducational test results and overt behavior—have a much larger percentage of boys with a percentage range of 63% (mild mental retardation) to 79% (emotional disturbance), with learning disabilities and speech/communication problems residing between the extremes (see Table 1). (An interesting note is that from this same population at the identical point in time, the proportion of school suspension is 70% boys and the drop-out rate is 55% males.)

The local figures parallel those of the state of New Jersey (New Jersey State Department of Education, 1987). However, on the national level, "Males are three times as likely as females to be found in programs for the seriously emotionally disturbed. Males are two and one half times as likely as females to be in learning disabled programs" (Comptroller General of the United States, 1981, p. iv). Thus, NJ's special education male prevalence ratios differ somewhat from those nationally: The New Jersey ED ratio for males is higher (4:1), while the NJ male learning disabled (LD) ratio is lower (2.1:1).

To the extent that the percentage of males classified ED is the same for the local district under study as it is for NJ (80%) as a whole, the factor of gender disproportion is more problematic than race—although the latter is also a serious concern. The NJ prevalence rate in which black males are classified ED is 3.2, and this is much higher than any other NJ cohort—white males and Hispanic males 1.6, black females .8, and white females and Hispanic females .4 (NJ Dept. of Education, 1987, p. 8). The data suggest that more blacks than whites would be classified ED in mixed racial NJ school districts. Further comparison should be made with other school districts where the student population is almost all black or all white to determine their classified ED male percentage.

The females who do poorly in school or leave school early usually exhibit more passive behaviors than males. Contradistinctively, and for whatever reason(s), boys seem to be more active and are therefore more problematic for schools—where docility

Table 1
Special Education Students by Classification and Gender[a]

Classification	Male				Female				Total Number	
	Number		Percent		Number		Percent			
Educable Mentally Retarded	26	(2,253)	63%	(52%)	15	(2,101)	37%	(48%)	41	(4,354)
Trainable Mentally Retarded	9	(1,413)	50%	(56%)	9	(1,093)	50%	(44%)	18	(2,506)
Neurologically Impaired (NI)[b]	130	(10,471)	76%	(72%)	42	(4,102)	24%	(28%)	172	(14,573)
Perceptually Impaired (PI)[b]	250	(37,536)	64%	(68%)	141	(17,614)	36%	(32%)	391	(55,150)
Emotionally Disturbed	126	(10,851)	79%	(80%)	34	(2,659)	21%	(20%)	160	(13,510)
Multiply Handicapped	49	(3,132)	68%	(68%)	23	(1,445)	32%	(32%)	72	(4,577)
Socially Maladjusted (SM)[c]	1	(540)	100%	(80%)	0	(132)	0%	(20%)	1	(672)
Auditorily Handicapped	9	(655)	60%	(52%)	6	(606)	40%	(48%)	15	(1,261)
Orthopedically Handicapped	5	(385)	56%	(58%)	4	(274)	44%	(42%)	9	(659)
Chronically Ill (CI)[d]	2	(253)	67%	(35%)	1	(476)	33%	(65%)	3	(729)
Visually Handicapped	1	(103)	100%	(52%)	0	(95)	0%	(48%)	1	(198)
Communication Handicapped	16	(1,622)	67%	(67%)	8	(782)	33%	(33%)	24	(2,404)
Preschool Handicapped	28	(2,313)	70%	(67%)	12	(1,156)	30%	(33%)	40	(3,469)
Subtotal	652	(71,527)	69%	(69%)	295	(32,535)	31%	(31%)	947	(104,062)
Speech Correction Services	278	(29,712)	65%	(62%)	147	(18,419)	35%	(38%)	425	(48,131)
Total	930	(101,239)	68%	(67%)	442	(50,954)	32%	(33%)	1,372	(152,193)

[a] The local data are as of December 1, 1987. NJ state figures, in parentheses, are for the 1985–86 schoolyear and are the latest available. The classifications are those currently in use in NJ.
[b] PI and NI categories in NJ are degrees of Specific Learning Disability (LD).
[c] NJ and some other states use the SM classification; the US federal government does not.
[d] Pregnant students in NJ may be classified CI.

and submissiveness are rewarded. Perhaps boys encounter problems upon entering school because they are socialized to be assertive from a very young age; moreover, males, especially adolescents, appear prone biologically to be more aggressive, more frequently, than females (see Sigmon, 1987). Thus, it is not surprising that young lads are driven into classes or schools for the emotionally disturbed/behavior disordered, and young men are forced out of school before graduating. Unless boys are socialized differently, the schools must adjust rather than stigmatize (with special education programs and/or labels) or force out males from school.

It is the opinion here that, related to special education, race and gender results very similar to this local/NJ study would be found throughout America. As an example, Shinn, Tindal, and Spira (1987) recently found in a "large Midwestern city" that teachers referred more boys than girls, and more black students than others. The Shinn et al. study resulted in the finding that "teacher tolerance"—or, more accurately, teacher intolerance— appeared to be a major factor in decisions to refer students for special education. In essence, it appears that throughout the United States, boys are consistently less well-tolerated in school than girls, and Afro-American males least of all.

Appendix C

Questioning Elementary Urban Public School Teachers on Classroom Rules for Control*

Scott B. Sigmon

[The tiny article reproduced here is an example of pragmatic *practitioner research*. It was done by a practicing school psychologist employed by a public school district. Most of the literature in special education and school psychology has been written by non-school practitioners (i.e., university professors)— whose suggested methods and theory are often non-translatable into practice (see Sigmon, 1984, 1985). It was thought that when the methods by which teachers who easily maintained a good learning environment (classroom climate) were compiled, school support staff (e.g., learning consultants, school psychologists, etc.) could come equipped with more realistic (consultative) suggestions to the aid of other teachers requesting assistance. Therefore, the ultimate intent of this research was to be able to do more effective consultation with teachers.

Besides learning problems per se, teachers are obviously most disturbed by disruptive students. Thus, teachers faced with classroom disruption want support and, naturally, often have a need to ventilate their feelings. Disturbing pupils have been too often and too quickly placed in special education, usually into classes for the emotionally disturbed or socially maladjusted. Rather than making immediate arrangements for special place-

*This short piece first appeared in *Psychological Reports* (1983), Vol. 53, No. 1, page 58. Copyright © 1983 Psychological Reports. (A longer version, written in 1982, is available through the U.S. Department of Education: ERIC Document Reproduction Service No. ED 269 528.)

ment, the consultant should attempt to help change the teacher-student interaction. Should this fail, perhaps placement with another mainstream teacher may be the solution. Sometimes personality conflicts occur—as they can in any type of interpersonal relationship—between teachers and students which may reach an intolerable point where change is absolutely necessary. (The tension generated by such negative teacher-student interaction often troubles other students, and prevents them from learning. Many times they have told me so!) Moreover, counseling, regular administrative disciplinary procedures, and working with the children's families are options to be utilized in such cases. Only when these possibilities are exhausted should special education placement, as a last resort, be considered.

On the term control, one final note. When sought in an ideological sense, social control is indoctrination. If a student is placed in special education as punishment, which is unethical and illegal, this is a form of negative student control. On the other hand, if used so that *real learning* can take place, I view this form of control as positive. Debate need not be about control, but instead over what type of schooling a child receives if a society makes school attendance mandatory.]

In the classroom, preventing violations of rules and the method of dealing with violators are extremely important. This was studied by surveying teachers and searching the literature.

All general education classroom teachers in one Northeastern urban (K-8) public elementary school whose median class size was 31 (range of 23 to 36) were requested to complete a questionnaire on classroom rules for control. Twenty of the 25 did. Only two (from the upper levels) posted written rules. Verbal rules regarding inappropriate talking and leaving one's seat were the most frequently issued across all grades (37% of the total teacher responses when asked for their three most emphasized rules). Getting younger students to attend aurally and older ones to refrain from gum chewing or eating were also quite problematic. Also issued but at a lower frequency were rules regarding courteousness ("The Golden Rule") in the hope it would generalize to other situations. Techniques to avoid or eliminate problem behaviors were offered by half the teachers to an optional open-ended question, with some being rather traditional while others are unique. Some are: Reviewing rules at year's beginning for all, then discussing specifics openly in class with offenders (7th grade), Using detention and later parent conferences (4th grade), Incorporating rules into social studies lessons about harmonious community life (5th), The use of "large words" for impact, private student "conferences" in the hallway for the blatantly defiant to avoid snickering from classmates, "long-stare" eye contact with those caught in the act, and desk-attached behavioral checklists (2nd), A clapping sequence or the snapping of fingers by teacher which the entire group must in turn duplicate (3rd), Turning off lights (1st). The most positive of all, perhaps, is teacher-prompted clapping to acknowledge good work and for following proper procedures (K). Most agreed, though, that instructor must start the schoolyear being firm, stick to rules so that a pattern of students' taking advantage of teacher does not commence, and grant privileges as they are earned.

Literature indicated that most work focused on behavior modification while many studies examined teachers' characteristics and over-all teaching styles. The efficacy of such studies for use in practical control of a classroom especially with rule violators is questioned by this author. Behavioral baseline data seem difficult to obtain mainly in terms of professional time (for the psychologist and/or teacher, especially for the latter with large groups) while teachers' attributes appear primarily preventive as well as ingrained. Behavior modification may be effective up to a certain point before negative returns accrue depending on class size, amount of support, and skill. Specific techniques suggested to teachers to eliminate or prevent a recurrence of rule violations in the classroom and increasing students' awareness for internalization purposes are considered valuable. Further study is needed.

Appendix D

Rights Without Labels*

— National Coalition of Advocates for Students, National Association of School Psychologists, and National Association of Social Workers

The Rights Without Labels concept has been developed to address problems associated with the classification and labeling of children as "handicapped" for educational purposes. This classification establishes certain legal rights for children and parents, often including funds for schools offering specialized services.

Problems permeate this system: unreliability of classification; lack of instructional relevance for some classifications; exclusion of children from regular education; and the stigmatization of classified children. Moreover, removing these classifications and labels to return a student to regular education has proved very difficult.

The Rights Without Labels guidelines presented here have special significance for children with academic and/or behavioral difficulties who are frequently classified as learning disabled, educable mentally retarded or behavior disordered/emotionally disturbed. Our intention, however, is to apply these guidelines to as broad a range of exceptionalities as is feasible and in no way to diminish opportunities for even the severely/profoundly handicapped student to be served in settings with their non-handicapped peers.

The Rights Without Labels guidelines are based on the assumption that it would be desirable at this time to conduct programs

---

*Appeared in the "Forum" section of *Education Week* (May 27, 1987; page 22).

wherein efforts are made to serve children who have special needs without labeling them or removing them from regular education programs. Research indicates that several factors are critical to the success of such experimental programs.

Pre-referral Screening/Intervention

Attempts must be made at the very outset to ameliorate educational difficulties through the use of pre-referral screening/intervention methods conducted by regular school personnel with the support of resources typically limited to special education (i.e. school psychologists, teachers, social workers, speech therapists, etc.). This benefits all children, especially those experiencing educational problems, while helping to identify students with characteristics consonant with legal definitions of handicapped conditions. Such practices will engender an abiding respect for students' rights under the law not to be evaluated in the absence of genuine suspicion of a handicap.

Curriculum Based Assessment

Secondly, identification and evaluation methods must include curriculum based assessment procedures. Research demonstrates these procedures provide reliable measures of student performance and produce relevant information for instructional planning. Most importantly, they fulfill the evaluation protection criteria set out in P.L. 94–142. The primary purpose of these procedures is *not* to classify or label children, but rather to identify specific curriculum and instructional deficits and strengths in order to provide a framework to develop appropriate educational programs. Individualized Educational Programs (IEPs) continue to be required, as well as related services provided in accordance with current legal guidelines.

Special Resources In Regular Settings

The traditional array of special education supplementary aids, services and resources (including teachers/aides) are available to children only outside the regular classroom. Our goal is to broaden the classroom situation within which special education resources can be used and to reverse the practice of moving handicapped students to special education situations outside regular classes and schools. Instead, special education resources can be transferred into the non-categorically identified students' regular classroom setting.

RIGHTS WITHOUT LABELS GUIDELINES

These guidelines are stated positively as principles for programs which professionals, advocates and parents may wish to examine. The checklist format is provided for use in developing experimental programs in local or state systems.

GUIDELINES FOR ASSURING RIGHTS WITHOUT LABELS IN REGULAR/SPECIAL EDUCATION PROGRAMS

I. ASSURANCES: Any proposed alternatives, non-categorical program or system shall:
A. Ensure that the fundamental rights afforded handicapped students and their parents under P.L. 94–142 are maintained and safeguarded. These include, but are not limited to:

(1) Standards for fair and unbiased identification and evaluation of children who would qualify as "handicapped" in a categorical system.

(2) Individualized Education Programs (IEPs) for all students who would otherwise qualify under a categorical system.

(3) Specialized instruction and related services for students who would otherwise qualify under a categorical system.

(4) Least Restrictive Environment (LRE) standards in determining educational placements.

(5) Appointment of surrogate parents when appropriate.

(6) Non-discriminatory discipline procedures.

(7) All timeline standards governing the above practices and procedures.

(8) Parental rights in the identification, evaluation, IEPs and placement of students who would otherwise qualify under a categorical system.

(9) Due Process Rights for parents and students who wish to pursue concerns/complaints regarding educational evaluations, programs and placements.

(10) Local advisory boards to assist (LEAs) in planning for the provision of appropriate educational services.

B. Provide parents of handicapped students with an alternative to selecting a traditional categorical approach to classification.

C. Provide full disclosure of the non-categorical system to parents including an explanation of resources, services and rights that will be afforded students in this system.**

II. GENERAL QUALITY OF ALTERNATIVE PROGRAM: Any proposed non-categorical program or system shall:

A. Employ pre-referral screening/intervention measures and utilize evaluation procedures that include curriculum based assessments.

B. Employ methodology known to be associated with effective teaching/learning (for example, provide students with orderly and productive environments, ample learning/teaching time, systematic and objective feedback on performance, well sequenced curricula, etc.).

C. Focus attention on basic skills as priority areas for instruction (for example, language, self-dependence, reasonable social behavior, mathematics, health and safety, etc.).

D. Provide procedures to identify and respond to the individual needs of all students, and in particular, those who may need modifications in their school programs.

E. Provide for special education aids, services and resources to be delivered in regular education settings.

III. ASSESSMENT OF OUTCOMES: Any proposed non-categorical program shall:

A. Have an objective methodology for assessing the educational progress of students in major curriculum domains (including academic, social, motivational and attitudinal variables) and for comparing such progress with results in traditional programs.

B. Contain and utilize a cost-benefit analysis to compare costs with traditional programs.

IV. TEACHING STAFF AND FACILITIES: Any proposed non-categorical program shall:

A. Include instruction and services by teachers and staff who are qualified in accordance with current state certification standards.

B. Include a delivery system that provides continuing staff development responsive to the training needs of the teaching staff and administrative personnel who will be implementing the requirements of the non-categorical program.

C. Include appropriate instructional materials and other resources.

D. Include assurances that funding levels and personnel allocations will not be decreased during the experimental period or as a result of successful alternative service delivery.

**To provide these assurances, it is assumed that as part of the experimental procedures, it would be common to conduct a dual classification system, whereby, for example, a student who might be classified as "learning disabled" in a traditional system would actually be so identified. Although the student's record would reflect the traditional classification, the student would be considered in need of "supplemental services" (i.e, regular and special education services) for purposes of his/her participation in the non-categorical program. Only by such a dual system could assurances concerning "rights" be offered and safeguarded. Over the long term, the traditional classification system might be modified if all stake-holders are satisfied about the new procedure.

Appendix E

Enlarged Special Education Group Creates "Problems"*

--- *Scott B. Sigmon*

To the Editor:

The Forum statement "Rights Without Labels" (*May 27, 1987*), by the National Coalition of Advocates for Students, the National Association of School Psychologists, and the National Association of Social Workers Inc. is an excellent document on child advocacy and special education. Nevertheless, two related points require comment.

First, too many children, usually labeled "learning disabled," are placed in special education settings, when instead they should receive remedial instruction within a regular education program. Thus, for such students, the type of special education program into which they are placed is not the main problem. It is the stigma of "special" education itself.

Second, since the special education population has been massively expanded by the inclusion of the alleged mildly handicapped, attention and funds have been diverted from moderately and severely handicapped youngsters, resulting in their receiving a much less than ideal education.

When these main policy problems are rectified, the other concerns addressed in the "Rights Without Labels" manifesto will be much less problematic.

---

*This "letter to the editor" of *Education Week (EW)* was published on page 21 of its June 24, 1987 issue. It is a comment on "Rights Without Labels" (Appendix D, this book) which appeared a month earlier in *EW.*

Appendix F

Position Statement: Advocacy for Appropriate Educational Services for All Children*

National Association of School Psychologists (NASP) and National Coalition of Advocates for Students (NCAS)

P.L. 94–142 (The Education of All Handicapped Children Act) has achieved major goals in serving handicapped children, many of whom had been previously excluded from appropriate educational programs. Since its enactment in 1975, all handicapped children have been guaranteed a free and appropriate education, the right to due process, and individualization of program according to need. We strongly support the continuation of legislation which has mandated these guarantees.

We also recognize that serious problems have been encountered as school districts strive to meet these mandates and that quality education is still an elusive goal. Some of these problems reflect difficulties within special education; others appear to be special education issues but have their origins in the regular education system.

One major set of problems involves reverse sides of the issue of access to appropriate education: (1) On the one hand, access to special education must be assured for all significantly handicapped children who need and can benefit from it. (2) Conversely, children are being inappropriately diagnosed as handicapped and placed in special education because of: (a) a lack of regular education options designed to meet the needs of children with diverse

*Circa 1985.

213

learning styles, (b) a lack of understanding, at times, of diverse cultural and linguistic backgrounds, and (c) inadequate measurement technologies which focus on labels for placement rather than providing information for program development.

It is not a benign action to label as "handicapped" children who are low achievers but are not, in fact, handicapped, even when this is done in order to provide them with services unavailable in general education. School personnel often resort to labeling because it seems the only way to obtain needed services for children. This is an unfortunate result of categorical models which attach funding to classifications. Other problems originating in the classification system include:

- Labels that are often irrelevant to instructional needs.
- Categories, based on deficit labels, that are rather arbitrarily defined, particularly for mildly handicapped and low achieving students, but which come to be accepted as "real" and may prevent more meaningful understanding of the child's psycho-educational needs. The intent of this statement is not necessarily to endorse mixing children with different moderate to severe handicaps in a single special education classroom.
- Reduced expectations for children who are placed in special needs programs.
- Assessment processes aimed at determining eligibility which often deflects limited resources from the determination of functional educational needs and the development of effective psychoeducational programs.
- A decreased willingness on the part of regular education, at times bordering on abdication of responsibility to modify curricula and programs in order to better meet the diverse needs of all children.

As increasing numbers of children are classified as handicapped and removed from regular classrooms for special instruction, there has been a dramatic reduction in the range of abilities among children who remain within the general education system. Concurrently, as national standards for excellence are being raised, the number of children at risk for school failure is growing dramatically. Without provisions to prepare students for higher expectations through effective instructional programs, many of these children may also be identified as handicapped and placed in special education. This climate, in which children are tested and labeled as failures or as handicapped in increasing numbers, creates an urgent need for reexamination and change in the system which provides access to services.

In view of these problems, and based upon the commitment to see that all children receive effective and appropriate education irrespective of race, cultural background, linguistic background, socioeconomic status, or educational need, we believe:

- All children can learn. Schools have responsibility to teach them, and school personnel and parents should work together to assure every child a free and appropriate education in a positive social environment.

- Instructional options, based on the individual psycho-educational needs of each child, must be maximized within the general education system. Necessary support services should be provided within general education, eliminating the need to classify children as handicapped in order to receive these services.

- Psychoeducational needs of children should be determined through a multi-dimensional, nonbiased assessment process. This must evaluate the match between the learner and his or her educational environment, assessing the compatibility of curriculum and system as they interact with the child, rather than relying on the deficit based model which places the blame for failure within the child. Referral to the assessment and placement process must always relate directly to services designed to meet psychoeducational needs.

- In addition to maintaining current protection for handicapped children, protections and safeguards must be developed to assure the rights of children who are at risk for school failure and require services while remaining in general education without classification as handicapped.

We propose a new national initiative to meet the educational needs of all children:

We propose the development and piloting of alternatives to the current categorical system. This requires reevalutaion of funding mechanisms, and advocacy for policy and funding waivers needed for the piloting of alternative service delivery models. It also requires the development of increased support systems and extensive retraining of all school personnel to enable them to work effectively with a broad range of children with special needs within the regular education system.

This initiative will encourage greater independence for children by enabling them to function within the broadest possible environment, and independence for school personnel by providing them with training and support so they can help a wide range of children.

The types and extent of change we are suggesting should be made cautiously. Targeted funds intended for children with moderate and severe handicapping conditions must be protected. Similarly, resources for children who are not handicapped, but who experience learning difficulties, must be protected even though these children are served within general education. We need to assure that no child is put at risk for loss of services while the change process is occurring.

Our task is to reduce the rigidities of the current system without taking away the protections offered by P.L. 94–142. All experimentation and research must take place within a framework of maximum protection for children. It is highly likely that this may require the development of temporary parallel systems—the traditional system of classification and placement under P.L. 94–142, and a system of experimental programs, primarily within general education—until satisfactory models can be developed which meet the requirements of accountability, due process, and protection of students' and parents' rights, and provide funding for students in need of services. In addition, while these recommended modifications might reduce the risk of misclassification due to cultural or linguistic differences, we caution that these issues must continue to be monitored and discussed during the transition period and beyond.

Because of the complexity of these issues, the generation of effective solutions will require a national effort of interested persons and organizations which we hope to generate through this task force. We will actively work toward the collaboration of a wide variety of individuals and organizations, joining together to develop a strong base of knowledge, research, and experience in order to establish new frameworks and conceptualizations on which to base decisions, design feasible service delivery options, advocate for policy and funding changes needed to implement these alternatives, and coordinate efforts and share information for positive change. We invite you to join with us.

References

Preface

Johnson, J. L. (1969). Special education and the inner city: A challenge for the future or another means for cooling the mark out? *Journal of Special Eduation, 3,* 241–251.

Kuhn, T. S. (1962). *The structure of scientific revolutions.* Chicago, IL: University of Chicago Press.

Ryan, W. (1971). *Blaming the victim.* New York: Pantheon.

Sigmon, S. B. (1987). *Radical analysis of special education: Focus on historical development and learning disabilities.* London, New York, & Philadelphia: The Falmer Press/Taylor & Francis.

Tomlinson, S. (1982). *A sociology of special education.* London: Routledge & Kegan Paul.

Introduction

Illich, I. (1970). *Deschooling society.* New York: Harper & Row.

Schumaker, J. B., Deshler, D. D., Alley, G. R., & Warner, M. M. (1983). Toward the development of an intervention model for learning disabled adolescents: The University of Kansas Institute. *Exceptional Education Quarterly, 4*(1), 45–74.

Sigmon, S. B. (1987a). *Radical analysis of special education: Focus on historical development and learning disabilities.* London, New York, & Philadelphia: The Falmer Press/Taylor & Francis.

Sigmon, S. B. (1987b). The essence of curriculum. *Reading Improvement, 24*(1), back two cover pages.

219

Chapter 1

Bernstein, B. (1960). Language and social class. *British Journal of Sociology, 11*, 271–276.

Bloom, B. S. (1980). *All our children learning.* New York: McGraw-Hill.

Blumberg, P. (Ed.). (1972). *The impact of social class: A book of readings.* New York: Harper & Row.

Boocock, S. S. (1980). *Sociology of education: An introduction* (2nd ed.). Boston: Houghton Mifflin.

Bowles, S., & Gintis, H. (1976). *Schooling in capitalist America: Educational reform and the contradictions of economic life.* New York: Basic Books.

Clark, K. B. (1965). *Dark ghetto: Dilemmas of social power.* New York: Harper & Row.

College Entrance Examination Board, The. (1974). *College-bound seniors, 1973–4.* New York: Author.

Collins, R., & Camblin, L. D., Jr. (1983). The politics and science of learning disability classification: Implications for black children. *Contemporary Education, 54,* 113–118.

de Lone, R. (1979). *Small futures: Children, inequality, and the limits of liberal reform.* New York: Harcourt Brace Jovanovich.

Entwisle, D. R. (1970). Semantic systems of children: Some assessments of social class and ethnic differences. In F. Williams (Ed.), *Language and poverty: Perspectives on a theme* (pp. 123–139). Chicago: Markham.

Goldthorpe, J. H., Lockwood, D., Bechhofer, F., & Platt, J. (1967). The affluent worker and the thesis of "embourgeoisement": Some preliminary research findings. *Sociology, 1,* 11–31.

Grier, W. H., & Cobbs, P. M. (1968). *Black rage.* New York: Basic Books.

Jencks, C., & Riesman, D. (1968). *The academic revolution.* Garden City, NY: Doubleday.

Jencks, C., Smith, M., Acland, H., Bane, M. J., Cohen, D., Gintis, H., Heyns, B., & Michelson, S. (1972). *Inequality: A reassessment of the effect of family and schooling in America.* New York: Basic Books.

Johnson, J. L. (1969). Special education and the inner city: A challenge for the future or another means for cooling the mark out? *Journal of Special Education, 3,* 241–251.

Larry P. vs. Wilson Riles. (1979). U.S. District Court for the Northern District of California. No. C–71–2270.

Lasch, C. (1975). Inequality and education. In D. M. Levine & M. J. Bane (Eds.), *The "inequality" controversy: Schooling and distributive justice* (pp. 45–62). New York: Basic Books.

McKnight, T. S. (1982). The learning disability myth in American education. *Journal of Education, 164,* 351–359.

Manni, J. L., Winikur, D. W., & Keller, M. (1980). *The status of minority group representation in special education programs in the state of New Jersey.* Trenton, NJ: NJ State Department of Education. (ERIC Document Reproduction Service No. ED 203 575).

Massachusetts Advocacy Center. (1978). *Double jeopardy: The plight of minority students in special education.* Boston: Author.

Mattie T. et al. vs. Charles E. Holliday et al. (1979). U.S. District Court for the Northern District of Mississippi. No. DC–75–31–S.

Nisbet, R. A. (1959). The decline and fall of social class. *Pacific Sociological Review, 2,* 11–17.

Racial balance eyed in special education. (1981, February 22). Hackensack, NJ: *The Record,* p. A3.

Sigmon, S. B. (1983a). The history and future of educational segregation. *Journal for Special Educators, 19*(4), 1–15.

Sigmon, S. B. (1983b). Performance of American schoolchildren on Raven's Colored Progressive Matrices Scale. *Perceptual and Motor Skills, 56,* 484–486.

Sigmon, S. B. (1984). Comments on the so-called learning disability myth in American education. *Reading Improvement, 21,* 103–104.

Tyler, L. E. (1965). *The psychology of human differences* (3rd ed.). New York: Appleton-Century-Crofts.

United States Office of Special Education and Rehabilitative Services. (1987). *Ninth annual report to Congress on the implementation of the education of the handicapped act.* Washington, DC: U.S. Department of Education.

Williams, R. L. (1972). Abuses and misuses in testing black children. In R. L. Jones (Ed.), *Black psychology* (pp. 77–91). New York: Harper & Row.

Williams, R. L. (Ed.). (1975). *Ebonics: The true language of black folks.* St. Louis: Robert L. Williams & Associates.

Chapter 2

Anyon, J. (1981). Elementary schooling and distinctions of social class. *Interchange, 12,* 118–132.

Apple, M. W. (Ed.). (1981). *Cultural and economic reproduction in education.* Boston: Routledge & Kegan Paul.

Back to the 3 R's? (1957, March 15). *U.S. News and World Report,* pp. 38–44.

Bender, L. (1957). Specific reading disability as a maturational lag. *Bulletin of the Orton Society, 7,* 9–18.

Bloom, B. S., Davis, A., & Hess, R. (1965). *Compensatory education for the culturally deprived.* New York: Holt, Rinehart & Winston.

Boyer, E. L. (1983). *High school.* New York: Harper & Row.

Brookover, W. B., Beady, C., Flood, P., Schweitzer, J., & Wisenbaker, J. (1979). *School social systems and student achievement: Schools can make a difference.* New York: Praeger.

CEC (Council for Exceptional Children) Ad Hoc Committee to Study and Respond to the 1983 Report of the National Commission on Excellence in Education. (1984). Reply to 'A Nation at Risk'. *Exceptional Children, 52,* 484–494.

Chall, J. S. (1977). *An analysis of textbooks in relation to declining SAT scores.* Princeton, NJ: College Entrance Examination Board.

Chall, J. S. (1983). *Stages of reading development.* New York: McGraw-Hill.

Coles, G. S. (1978). The learning–disabilities test battery: Empirical and social issues. *Harvard Educational Review, 48,* 313–340.

Cruickshank, W. M., Bentzen, F. A., Ratzeburg, F. H., & Tannhauser, M. T. (1961). *A teaching method for brain-injured and hyperactive children.* Syracuse, NY: Syracuse University Press.

Delacato, C. H. (1959). *The treatment and prevention of reading problems.* Springfield, IL: Charles C. Thomas.

Deutsch, M. (1963). The disadvantaged child and the learning process. In A. H. Passow (Ed.), *Education in depressed areas* (pp. 163–179). New York: Teachers College Press.

Doman, G., Delacato, C., & Doman, R. (1964). *The Doman-Delacato developmental profile*. Philadelphia: Institutes for the Achievement of Human Potential.

Dunn, L. M. (1963). *Exceptional children in the schools*. New York: Holt, Rinehart & Winston.

Education and the disadvantaged American. (1962, May 19). *Saturday Review*, p. 58.

Famous educator's plan for a school that will advance students according to ability. (1958, April 14). *Life*, pp. 120–121.

Farber, B. (1968). *Mental retardation: Its social context and social consequences*. Boston, MA: Houghton Mifflin.

Feingold, B. F. (1975). *Why your child is hyperactive*. New York: Random House.

Foster, G., & Ysseldyke, J. (1976). Expectancy and halo effects as a result of artificially induced teacher bias. *Contemporary Educational Psychology, 1*, 37–45.

Franks, D. J. (1971). Ethnic and social status characteristics of children in EMR and LD classes. *Exceptional Children, 37*, 537–538.

Frostig, M., & Horne, D. (1964). *The Frostig program for the development of visual perception*. Chicago: Follett.

Goldstein, H. (1962). *The educable mentally retarded child in the elementary school*. Washington, DC: National Education Association.

Goodlad, J. I. (1984). *A place called school*. New York: McGraw-Hill.

Grossman, H. (Ed.). (1973). *Manual on terminology and classification in mental retardation* (rev. ed.). Washington, DC: American Association on Mental Deficiency.

Grotberg, E. H. (1970). Neurological aspects of learning disabilities: A case for the disadvantaged. *Journal of Learning Disabilities, 3*, 25–31.

Harder work for students. (1961, Sept. 4). *U.S. News and World Report*, p. 45.

Hieronymus, A. N., & Lindquist, E. G. (1974). *Manual for administrators, supervisors, and counselors, Forms 5 & 6, Iowa tests of basic skills.* Boston: Houghton Mifflin.

Jackson, G., & Cosca, C. (1974). The inequality of educational opportunity in the Southwest: An observational study of ethnically mixed classrooms. *American Educational Research Journal, 11,* 219–229.

Learning to read. (1959, October 12). *Newsweek,* p. 110.

Maisel, A. Q. (1964). Hope for brain-injured children. *The Reader's Digest, 11,* 219–229.

Moore, J., & Fine, M. J. (1978). Regular and special class teachers' perceptions of normal and exceptional children and their attitudes toward mainstreaming. *Psychology in the Schools, 15,* 253–259.

National Commission on Excellence in Education. (1983). *A nation at risk.* Washington, DC: U.S. Government Printing Office.

Orton, S. T. (1937). *Reading, writing, and speech problems in children.* New York: W. W. Norton.

Persell, C. A. (1977). *Education and inequality.* New York: The Free Press.

Rabinovitch, R. D. (1962). Dyslexia: Psychiatric considerations. In J. Money (Ed.), *Reading disability: Progress and research needs in dyslexia.* Baltimore: Johns Hopkins University Press.

Resnick, D. P., & Resnick, L. B. (1977). The nature of literacy: An historical exploration. *Harvard Educational Review, 47,* 370–385.

Rickover, H. G. (1957, March 2). Let's stop wasting our greatest resources. *Saturday Evening Post,* pp. 19, 108–111.

Riessman, F. (1962). *The culturally deprived child.* New York: Harper & Row.

Rist, R. C. (1970). Student social class and teacher expectations in ghetto education. *Harvard Educational Review, 40,* 411–451.

Rosenbaum, J. E. (1976). *Making inequality.* New York: John Wiley & Sons.

Rosenthal, R., & Jacobson, L. (1968). *Pygmalion in the classroom.* NYC: Holt, Rinehart & Winston.

Salvia, J., Clark, G., & Ysseldyke, J. (1973). Teacher retention of stereotypes of exceptionality. *Exceptional Children, 39,* 651–652.

Sarason, S. B., & Doris, J. (1979). *Educational handicap, public policy, and social history.* New York: The Free Press.

School boys point up a U.S. weakness. (1958, March 24). *Life,* pp. 26–37.

Shafer, W. E., & Olexa, C. (1971). *Tracking and opportunity.* Scranton, PA: Chandler.

Shaw, C. R., & McKay, H. D. (1942). *Juvenile delinquency and urban areas.* Chicago: University of Chicago Press.

Shotel, J. R., Iano, R. P., & McGettigan, J. F. (1972). Teacher attitudes associated with the integration of handicapped children. *Exceptional Children, 38,* 677–683.

Slow learners. (1962, Feb. 17). *Saturday Review,* pp. 53–54.

Special Report No. 7. (1971). *Guidelines for standardization sampling: Metropolitan achievement tests special report.* New York: Harcourt Brace Jovanovich.

Spring, J. (1976). *The sorting machine.* New York: Longman.

Sroufe, L. A., & Stewart, M. A. (1973). Treating problem children with stimulant drugs. *New England Journal of Medicine, 289,* 407–413.

Strauss, A. A., & Kephart, N. C. (1955). *Psychopathology and education of the brain-injured child: Vol. II.* New York: Grune & Stratton.

Strauss, A. A., & Lehtinen, L. E. (1947). *Psychopathology and education of the brain-injured child.* New York: Grune & Stratton.

Tarnopol, L. (1970). Delinquency and minimal brain dysfunction. *Journal of Learning Disabilities, 3,* 200–207.

Task Force on Education for Economic Growth. (1983). *Action for excellence.* Denver: Education Commission of the States.

Trace, A. S., Jr. (1961, May 27). Can Ivan read better than Johnny? *Saturday Evening Post,* pp. 30+.

Tucker, J. A. (1980). Ethnic proportions in classes for the learning disabled: Issues in nonbiased assessment. *Journal of Special Education, 14,* 93–105.

What went wrong with U.S. schools: An interview with professor Arthur Bestor, University of Illinois. (1958, January 24). *U.S. News and World Report, 44,* 68–80.

White, M. A., & Charry, J. (1966). *School disorder, intelligence, and social class.* New York: Teachers College Press.

226 REFERENCES

Williams, R. J., & Algozzine, B. (1979). Teachers' attitudes toward mainstreaming. *Elementary School Journal, 80,* 63–67.

Woodring, P. (1957, Sept. 2). Reform plan for schools. *Life,* pp. 123–136.

Ysseldyke, J. E., & Algozzine, B. (1982). *Critical issues in special and remedial education.* Boston: Houghton Mifflin.

Ysseldyke, J. E., Algozzine, B., Shinn, M. R., & McGue, M. (1982). Similarities and differences between low achievers and students classified as learning disabled. *Journal of Special Education, 16,* 73–85.

Ysseldyke, J. E., & Foster, G. G. (1978). Bias in teachers' observations of emotionally disturbed and learning disabled children. *Exceptional Children, 44,* 613–615.

The following LD textbooks were reviewed in preparing this chapter: Adelman, H. S. and Taylor, L. (1983) *Learning Disabilities in Perspective* (Scott Foresman, Dallas, TX); DeRuiter, J. A. and Wansart, W. L. (1982) *Psychology of Learning Disabilities* (Aspen, Rockville, MD); Gearheart, B. R. (1981) *Learning Disabilities: Educational Strategies* (Mosby, St. Louis, MO); Hallahan, D. P., Kauffman, J. M. and Lloyd, J. W. (1985) *Introduction to Learning Disabilities* (Prentice-Hall, Englewood Cliffs, NJ); Johnson, S. W. and Morasky, R. L. (1980) *Learning Disabilities,* 2nd ed. (Allyn and Bacon, Boston, MA); Kirk, S. A. and Chalfant, J. C. (1984) *Academic and Developmental Learning Disabilities* (Love Pub. Co., Denver, CO); Lerner, J. (1981) *Learning Disabilities* 3rd ed. (Houghton Mifflin, Boston, MA); Mercer, C. D. (1983) *Students with Learning Disabilities,* 2nd ed. (Charles E. Merrill, Columbus, OH); Reid, D. K. and Hresko, W. P. (1981) *A Cognitive Approach to Learning Disabilities* (McGraw-Hill, New York, NY); Sabatino, D. A., Miller, T. L., and Schmidt, C. (1981) *Learning Disabilities* (Aspen, Rockville, MD); Siegel, E. and Gold, R. (1982) *Educating the Learning Disabled* (Macmillan, New York); Sloan, H. A. (1982) *The Treatment and Management of Children with Learning Disabilities* (Charles C. Thomas, Springfield, IL); Smith, C. R. (1983) *Learning Disabilities* (Little, Brown and Co., Boston, MA); Smith, D. D. (1981) *Teaching the Learning Disabled* (Prentice-Hall, Englewood Cliffs, NJ); Woodward, D. M. and Peters, D. J. (1983) *The Learning Disabled Adolescents* (Aspen, Rockville, MD).

Chapter 3

Apple, M. W. (1979). *Ideology and curriculum.* Boston & London: Routledge & Kegan Paul.

Bowles, S., & Gintis, H. (1976). *Schooling in capitalist America: Educational reform and the contradictions of economic life.* New York: Basic Books.

Brann, E. T. (1979). *Paradoxes of education in a republic.* Chicago: University of Chicago Press.

Buss, A. R. (1979). *A dialectical psychology.* New York: Irvington Publishers.

Comptroller General of the United States. (1981). *Disparities still exist in who gets special education.* Washington, DC: U.S. General Accounting Office.

Endler, N. S., & Magnusson, D. (1976). *Interactional psychology & personality.* Washington, DC & London: Hemisphere.

Epps, S., McGue, M., & Ysseldyke, J. E. (1982). Interjudge agreement in classifying students as learning disabled. *Psychology in the Schools, 19,* 209-220.

Fromm, E. (1955). *The sane society.* New York: Rinehart.

Gill, G. R. (1980). *Meanness mania: The changed mood.* Washington, DC: Howard University Press.

Giroux, H. A. (1981). *Ideology culture & the process of schooling.* Philadelphia: Temple University Press.

Giroux, H. A. (1983a). Theories of reproduction and resistance in the new sociology of education: A critical analysis. *Harvard Educational Review, 53,* 257-293.

Giroux, H. A. (1983b). *Theory and resistance in education: A pedagogy for the opposition.* South Hadley, MA: Bergin & Garvey.

Harris, K. (1979). *Education and knowledge: The structured misrepresentation of reality.* London: Routledge & Kegan Paul.

Hoffman, E. (1974). The treatment of deviance by the educational system: History. In W. C. Rhodes & S. Head (Eds.), *A study of child variance: Vol. 3, Service delivery systems* (pp. 41-79). Franklin, TN: New Academic Village.

Hurn, C. J. (1978). *The limits and possibilities of schooling: An introduction to the sociology of education.* Boston: Allyn & Bacon.

Karabel, J., & Halsey, A. H. (Eds.). (1977). *Power and ideology in education.* New York: Oxford University Press.

Levitas, M. (1974). *Marxist perspectives in the sociology of education.* London: Routledge & Kegan Paul.

Nahem, J. (1981). *Psychology & psychiatry today: A Marxist view.* New York: International Publishers.

Pervin, L., & Lewis, M. (Eds.). (1978). *Perspectives in interactional psychology.* New York: Plenum.

Riegel, K. F. (1979). *Foundations of dialectical psychology.* New York: Academic Press.

Rippa, S. A. (1980). *Education in a free society: An American history* (4th ed.). New York: Longman. (Original work published 1967).

Sarup, M. (1978). *Marxism and education: A study of phenomenological and Marxist approaches to education.* London: Routledge & Kegan Paul.

Shapiro, H. S. (1980). Society, ideology and the reform of special education: A study in the limits of educational change. *Educational Theory, 30,* 211-223.

Sharp, R. (1980). *Knowledge, ideology and the politics of schooling: Towards a Marxist analysis of education.* London: Routledge & Kegan Paul.

Sigmon, S. B. (1984a). Interactionistic psychology: A fourth force? *Psychological Reports, 54,* 156.

Sigmon, S. B. (1984b). Force four psychology: Interactionism. *Professional Psychology: Research and Practice, 15,* 470-471.

Sigmon, S. B. (1985). *A radical perspective on the development of American special education with a focus on the concept of "learning disabilities."* Doctoral dissertation; Rutgers, The State University of New Jersey.

Tomlinson, S. (1982). *A sociology of special education.* London: Routledge & Kegan Paul.

United States Office of Special Education and Rehabilitative Services. (1987). *Ninth annual report to Congress on the implementation of the education of the handicapped act.* Washington, DC: U.S. Department of Education.

Willis, P. (1977). *Learning to labour: How working-class kids get working-class jobs.* Westmead, England: Saxon House.

Young, M. F. D. (Ed.). (1971). *Knowledge and control: New directions for the sociology of education.* London: Routledge & Kegan Paul.

Ysseldyke, J. E., Algozzine, B., Shinn, M. R., & McGue, M. (1982). Similarities and differences between low achievers and students classified learning disabled. *Journal of Special Education, 16,* 73-85.

Chapter 4

Bickel, W. E. (1982). Classifying mentally retarded students: A review of placement practices in special education. In K. A. Heller, W. H. Holtzman, & S. Messick (Eds.), *Placing children in special education: A strategy for equity* (pp. 182-229). Washington, DC: National Academy Press.

Bogdan, R., & Kugelmass, J. (1984). Case studies in mainstreaming: A symbolic interactionist approach to special schooling. In L. Barton & S. Tomlinson (Eds.), *Special education and social interests* (pp. 173-191). New York: Nichols Publishing.

Cantrell, R. P., & Cantrell, M. L. (1976). Preventive mainstreaming: Impact of a supportive services program on pupils. *Exceptional Children, 42,* 381-386.

Chalfant, J. C. (1984). *Identifying learning disabled students: Guidelines for decision making.* Burlington, VT: Northeast Regional Resource Center.

Chalfant, J. C., Pysh, M. V., & Moultrie, R. (1979). Teacher assistance teams: A model for within-building problem solving. *Learning Disability Quarterly, 2,* 85-96.

Croll, P., & Moses, D. (1985). *One in five: The assessment and incidence of special educational needs.* London: Routledge & Kegan Paul.

Edgerton, R. B. (1979). *Mental retardation.* Cambridge, MA: Harvard University Press.

Frassinelli, L., Superior, K., & Meyers, J. (1983). A consultation model for speech and language intervention. *ASHA, 25*(11), 25-30.

Gerber, M. M., & Semmel, M. J. (1984). Teacher as imperfect test: Reconceptualizing the referral process. *Educational Psychologist, 19,* 137-148.

Geschwind, N. (1984). The brain of a learning-disabled individual. *Annals of Dyslexia, 34,* 319-327.

Gliedman, J., & Roth, W. (1980). *The unexpected minority: Handicapped children in America.* New York: Harcourt Brace Jovanovich.

Graden, J. L., Casey, A., & Bonstrom, O. (1985). Implementing a prereferral intervention system: Part II, the data. *Exceptional Children, 51,* 487-496.

Grossman, H. J. (1973). *Manual on terminology and classification in mental retardation* (1973 revision, special publication series no. 2). Washington, DC: American Association on Mental Deficiency.

Heber, R. (1959). A manual on terminology and classification in mental retardation. *American Journal of Mental Deficiency, Monograph Supplement, 64*(2).

Heller, K. A., Holtzman, W. H., & Messick, S. (Eds.). (1982). *Placing children in special education: A strategy for equity.* Washington, DC: National Academy Press.

Horn, W. F., O'Donnell, J. P., & Vitulano, L. A. (1983). Long-term follow-up studies of learning-disabled persons. *Journal of Learning Disabilities, 16,* 542-555.

Lazarus, B. (1985, April). *Getting a special education identity: How an experienced teacher decides.* Paper presented at the annual meeting of the American Educational Research Association, Chicago, IL.

Meyers, J. (1973). A consultation model for school psychological services. *Journal of School Psychology, 11,* 5-15.

Pear, R. (1985, March 10). U.S. is reviewing benefits stance. *The New York Times,* p. 33.

Ritter, D. R. (1978). Effects of a school consultation program upon referral patterns of teachers. *Psychology in the Schools, 15,* 239-243.

Rogers, E. M., & Shoemaker, F. F. (1971). *Communication of innovation: A cross cultural approach* (2nd ed.). New York: Free Press.

Rosenholtz, S. J., & Rosenholtz, S. H. (1981). Classroom organization and the perception of ability. *Sociology of Education, 54,* 132-140.

Sarason, S. B. (1971). *The culture of school and the problem of change.* Boston: Allyn & Bacon.

Sarason, S. B., & Doris, J. (1979). *Educational handicap, public policy, and social history: A broadened perspective on mental retardation.* New York: Macmillan.

Shepard, L. A., Smith, M. L., & Vojir, C. P. (1983). Characteristics of pupils identified as learning disabled. *American Educational Research Journal, 20,* 309-331.

Slavin, R. D. (1984). Team assisted individualization: Cooperative learning and individualized instruction in the mainstream classroom. *Remedial and Special Education, 5,* 33-42.

Smith, M. L. (1982). *How educators decide who is learning disabled.* Springfield, IL: Charles C. Thomas.

Trifiletti, J. J., Frith, G. H., & Armstrong, S. (1984). Microcomputers versus resource room for LD students: A preliminary investigation of the effects on math skills. *Learning Disability Quarterly, 7,* 69-76.

U.S. Department of Education. (1984). Executive summary, 6th annual report to Congress on the implementation of Public Law 94-142: The education for all handicapped children act. *Exceptional Children, 51,* 199-202.

Wang, M. C., Peverly, S., & Randolph, R. (1984). An investigation of the implementation and effects of a full-time mainstreaming program. *Remedial and Special Education, 5,* 21-32.

Ysseldyke, J. E. (1983). Current practices in making psychoeducational decisions about learning disabled students. *Journal of Learning Disabilities, 16,* 226-233.

Ysseldyke, J. E., & Thurlow, M. L. (1984). Assessment practices in special education: Adequacy and appropriateness. *Educational Psychologist, 9,* 123-136.

Chapter 5

Abramson, M., Wilson, V., Yoshida, R. K., & Hagerty, G. (1983). Parents' perceptions of their learning disabled child's educational performance. *Learning Disability Quarterly, 6*(2), 184–194.

Algozzine, R., Salvia, J., & Ysseldyke, J. E. (1983). Who should teach the difficult to teach students? *Educators Forum, 3*(1), 37–39.

Bloomer, R., Bates, H., Brown, S., & Norlander, K. (1982). *Mainstreaming in Vermont: A study of the identification process.* Livonia, NY: Brador Publications.

Chalfant, J. (1984). *Identifying learning disabled students: Guidelines for decision making.* Burlington, VT: Northeast Regional Resource Center (NERRC).

General Accounting Office. (1981). *Disparities still exist in who gets special education.* Washington, DC: U.S. Government Printing Office.

Gerber, M. (1984). Is Congress getting the full story? *Exceptional Children, 51*(3), 209–224.

Glass, G. (1983). Effectiveness of special education. *Policy Studies Review, 2*(1), 65–78.

Hagerty, G., Behrens, T., & Abramson, M. (1983). Fostering an agenda of shared responsibility in teacher education. In B. Sharp (Ed.), *Challenge and change in teacher education* (pp. 11–25). Washington, DC: AACTE Publications.

Hersh, R., & Walker, H. (1983). Great expectations: Making schools effective for all students. *Policy Studies Review, 2*(1), 147–188.

Howe, C., & Keele, L. (1982). Responsibility for the mildly handicapped: A proposal for change. *The Executive Review, 2*(6), 27–32.

Kakalik, J. S., Furry, W. S., Thomas, M. A., & Carney, M. F. (1981). *The cost of special education.* Santa Monica, CA: The Rand Corporation. (Sponsored under Contract No. 300–79–0733, USDE).

Kennedy, M. (1982). *Report of the Division H task force on special education evaluation: American Educational Research Association.* Washington, DC: ERIC Clearinghouse.

Little, J. W. (1982). Collegiality and improvement norms: The school as workplace. *American Educational Research Journal, 19*, 197–203.

Pugach, M., & Lilly, M. S. (1984). Reconceptualizing support services for classroom teachers: Implications for teacher education. *Journal of Teacher Education, 35*(5), 48–55.

Shepard, L. (1983). The role of measurement in educational policy: Lessons from the identification of learning disabilities. *Educational Measurement: Issues and Practices, 2*(1), 4–8.

Shepard, L., & Smith, M. (1981). *Evaluation of the identification of perceptual–communicative disorders in Colorado* (Final Report). Boulder, CO: University of Colorado.

Sontag, E., Hagerty, G., & Button, J. (1983). Perspectives on the status and future of special education and regular education. In M. C. Reynolds (Ed.), *The future of mainstreaming* (pp. 65-73). Washington, DC: AACTE Publications.

Stainback, W., & Stainback, S. (1984). A rationale for the merger of special and regular education. *Exceptional Children, 51*(2), 102–111.

U. S. Department of Education. (1984). *1984 annual report to Congress on the implementation of the Education of the Handicapped Act.* Washington, DC: Government Printing Office.

U. S. Department of Education. (1985). *1985 annual report to Congress on the implementation of the Education of the Handicapped Act.* Washington, DC: Government Printing Office.

U. S. Government. (1984). *Code of federal regulations: Parts 300 to 399, revised as of July 1984.* Washington, DC: Government Printing Office.

Wang, M., & Reynolds, M. (1985). Avoiding the "catch 22" in special education reform. *Exceptional Children, 51,* 497–502.

Wilson, V. L., & Reynolds, C. (1984). Another look at evaluating aptitude–achievement discrepancies in the diagnosis of LD. *Journal of Special Education, 18*(4), 217–236.

Chapter 6

Angeles, P. A. (1981). *Dictionary of philosophy.* New York: Barnes & Noble.

Bernstein, R. J. (1971). *Praxis and action.* Philadelphia: University of Pennsylvania Press.

Buss, A. R. (1979). *A dialectical psychology.* New York: Irvington Publishers.

Carrier, J. G. (1983). Masking the social in educational knowledge: The case of learning disability theory. *American Journal of Sociology, 88,* 948–974.

Endler, N. S., & Magnusson, D. (1976). *Interactional psychology and personality.* Washington, DC and London: Hemisphere.

Giarelli, J. M. (1982). [Review of *Progressive education: A Marxist interpretation*]. *Educational Studies, 13,* 464–471.

Giroux, H. A. (1981). *Ideology culture & the process of schooling.* Philadelphia: Temple University Press.

Hall, R. (1967). Dialectic. In *The encyclopedia of philosophy* (Vol. 1–2, pp. 385–389). New York: Macmillan & The Free Press.

Hurn, C. J. (1978). *The limits and possibilities of schooling: An introduction to the sociology of education.* Boston: Allyn & Bacon.

Kaufmann, W. (1966). Hegel: A reinterpretation. New York: Anchor.

Kuhn, T. S. (1962). *The structure of scientific revolutions.* Chicago: University of Chicago Press.

Kuhn, T. S. (1970). *The structure of scientific revolutions* (2nd ed.). Chicago: University of Chicago Press.

Pacheco, A. (1978). Marx, philosophy, and education. *Philosophy of Education 1978: Proceedings of the Thirty-Fourth Annual Meeting of the Philosophy of Education Society, 34,* 208–220.

Pervin, L., & Lewis, M. (Eds.). (1978). *Perspectives in interactional psychology.* New York: Plenum.

Riegel, K. F. (1979). *Foundations of dialectical psychology.* New York: Academic Press.

Sarup, M. (1978). *Marxism and education: A study of phenomenological and Marxist approaches to education.* London: Routledge & Kegan Paul.

Shapiro, H. S. (1980). Society, ideology and the reform of special education: A study in the limits of educational change. *Educational Theory, 30,* 211–223.

Sharp, R. (1980). *Knowledge, ideology and the politics of schooling: Towards a Marxist analysis of education.* London: Routledge & Kegan Paul.

Sigmon, S. B. (1983). The history and future of educational segregation. *Journal for Special Educators, 19*(4), 1–15.

Sigmon, S. B. (1984a). Interactionistic psychology: A fourth force? *Psychological Reports, 54,* 156.

Sigmon, S. B. (1984b). Force four psychology: Interactionism. *Professional Psychology: Research and Practice, 25,* 470–471.

Tolman, C. (1983). Further comments on the meaning of 'dialectic'. *Human Development, 26,* 320–324.

Vygotsky, L. S. (1978). *Mind in society: The development of higher psychological processes* (A. R. Luria, M. Lopez-Morillas, M. Cole, & J. Wertsch, Trans.; M. Cole, V. John-Steiner, S. Scribner, & E. Souberman, Eds.). Cambridge, MA: Harvard University Press. (The material quoted herein was written in 1931).

Young, M. F. D. (Ed.). (1971). *Knowledge and control: New directions for the sociology of education.* London: Routledge & Kegan Paul.

Chapter 7

Adler, A. (1917). *A study of organ inferiority and its psychical compensation* (S. E. Jelliffe, Trans.). New York: Nervous & Mental Disease Publishing Co.; Monograph Series, No. 24. (Original work published 1907).

Bradley, R. C. (1970). *The education of exceptional children.* Wolfe City, TX: The University [of Texas] Press.

Diller, L. (1972). Psychological aspects of physically handicapped children. In B. B. Wolman (Ed.), *Manual of child psychopathology* (pp. 591–623). New York: McGraw-Hill.

Dreikurs, R. (1948). The socio-psychological dynamics of physical disability: A review of the Adlerian concept. *Journal of Social Issues, 4*(4), 39–54.

Lewin, K. (1936). *Principles of topological psychology* (F. Heider & G. M. Heider, Trans.). New York: McGraw-Hill.

Livingston, R. H., Korn, T. A., & McAlees, D. C. (1982). Alternative strategies in vocational rehabilitation. In C. R. Reynolds & T. B. Gutkin (Eds.), *The handbook of school psychology* (pp. 721–747). New York: John Wiley & Sons.

Meyerson, L. (1971). Somatopsychology of physical disability. In W. M. Cruickshank (Ed.), *Psychology of exceptional children and youth* (3rd ed., pp. 1–74). Englewood Cliffs, NJ: Prentice-Hall.

236 REFERENCES

Mussen, P. H., & Newman, D. K. (1958). Acceptance of handicap, motivation, and adjustment in physically disabled children. *Exceptional Children, 24*, 255–260, 277–279.

Wolman, B. B. (Ed.). (1973). *Dictionary of behavioral science.* New York: Van Nostrand Reinhold.

Wright, B. A. (1960). *Physical disability — A psychological approach.* New York: Harper & Row.

Chapter 8

Abt Associates. (1976). *Education as experimentation: A planned variation model* (Vol. III). Cambridge, MA: Author.

Abt Associates. (1977). *Education as experimentation: A planned variation model* (Vol. IV). Cambridge, MA: Author.

Bailey, D. B., Jr., & Harbin, G. L. (1980). Nondiscriminatory evaluation. *Exceptional Children, 46*, 590–596.

Beck, R. (1983, May). *Direct instruction, opportunity to respond and precision teaching: What can each offer the others?* Symposium presented at the 9th annual convention of the Association for Behavior Analysis, Milwaukee, Wisconsin.

Beck, R. (1979). *Report for the Office of Education: Joint Dissemination Review Panel.* Great Falls, MT.

Becker, W. C., & Carnine, D. W. (1980). Direct instruction: An effective approach to educational intervention with the disadvantaged and low performers. In B. B. Lahey & A. E. Kazdin (Eds.), *Advances in clinical and child psychology* (Vol. 3). New York: Plenum Press.

Bereiter, C., & Engelmann, S. (1966). *Teaching disadvantaged children in the preschool.* Englewood Cliffs, NJ: Prentice-Hall.

Bickel, W. E. (1983). Effective schools: Knowledge, dissemination, inquiry. *Educational Researcher, 12*(4), 3–5.

Delquadri, J., Whorton, D., Elliott, M., Greenwood, C., & Hall, R. (1981). *The Juniper Gardens classroom peer tutoring program for oral reading* (Draft 1). Kansas City, KS: Juniper Gardens Children's Project, Bureau of Child Research, University of Kansas.

Dunn, L. M. (1968). Special education for the mildly retarded—Is much of it justifiable? *Exceptional Children, 35,* 5–22.

Engelmann, S. (1971). The effectiveness of direct instruction on IQ performance and achievement in reading and math. In J. Hellmuth (Ed.), *Disadvantaged child* (Vol. 3). New York: Brunner/Mazel.

Exemplary Center for Reading Instruction. (1981). *Joint Dissemination and Review Panel Report No. 74–78.*

Gersten, R. (1982). *Direct instruction with special education students: A review of evaluation research.* Unpublished manuscript, College of Education, University of Oregon.

Greenwood, C., Delquadri, J., & Hall, R. (1982a, September). *The opportunity to respond and student academic performance in school.* Paper presented at the conference on Behavior Analysis in Education, Ohio State University, Columbus, OH.

Greenwood, C. R., Preston, D., & Harris, J. (1982b). *Minority issues in the education of handicapped children.* Unpublished manuscript, Department of Special Education, University of Kansas.

Heller, K. A., Holtzman, W. H., & Messick, S. (Eds.). (1982). *Placing children in special education: A strategy for equity.* Washington, DC: National Academy Press.

House, E. R., Glass, G. V., McLean, L. D., & Walker, D. C. (1978). No simple answer: Critique of the "follow–through" evaluation. *Harvard Educational Review, 48,* 128–160.

Linn, W. (1980, December). ECRI everywhere. *ECRI Newsletter,* p. 3.

Marshall, H. (1976). *Dimensions of classroom structure and functioning project: Summary of final report.* Berkeley, CA: University of California.

Oakland, T. (Ed.). (1977). *Psychological and educational assessment of minority students.* New York: Brunner/Mazel.

Reid, E. (undated). *ECRI: A success-proven method for reading instruction.* Salt Lake City, UT: ECRI publication.

Reschly, D. (1979). Nonbiased assessment. In G. Phye & D. Reschly (Eds.), *School psychology: Perspectives and issues.* New York: Academic Press.

Reschly, D. J. (1980). *Nonbiased assessment.* Ames, IA: Iowa Department of Public Instruction/Iowa State University.

Reynolds, M. C., & Wang, M. C. (1983). Restructuring "special" school programs. *Policy Studies Review, 2*(Special #1), 189–212.

Rosenshine, B. V., & Berliner, D. C. (1978). Academic engaged time. *British Journal of Teacher Education, 4,* 3–16.

Sattler, J. M. (1982). *Assessment of children's intelligence and special abilities* (2nd ed.). Boston: Allyn & Bacon.

Stallings, J. A., & Kaskowitz, D. (1974). *Follow-through classroom observation evaluation, 1972–73.* Menlo Park, CA: Stanford Research Institute.

Stevens, R., & Rosenshine, B. (1981). Advances in research on teaching. *Exceptional Education Quarterly, 2*(1), 1–9.

Tucker, J. A. (1980). Ethnic proportions in classes for the learning disabled: Issues in nonbiased assessment. *Journal of Special Education, 14,* 93–105.

Wang, M. C. (1981). *The adaptive learning environments model.* Pittsburgh, PA: University of Pittsburgh, Learning Research and Development Center.

Williams, R. L. (1970). Black pride, academic relevance, and individual achievement. *Counseling Psychologist, 2,* 18–22.

Ysseldyke, J. E., & Algozzine, B. (1982). *Critical issues in special and remedial education.* Boston, MA: Houghton Mifflin.

Chapter 9

Allington, R. (1980). Teacher interruption behaviors during primary grade oral reading. *Journal of Educational Psychology, 72,* 371–377.

Ames, C. (1983). Competitive, cooperative and individualistic goal structures: A motivational analysis. In R. Ames & C. Ames (Eds.), *Research on motivation in education: Student motivation* (Vol. 1, pp. 177–207). New York: Academic Press.

Brown, A., Palincsar, A., & Armbruster, B. (1984). Inducing comprehension-fostering activities in interactive learning situations. In H. Mandl, N. Stein, & T. Trabasso (Eds.), *Learning from texts* (pp. 255–286). Hillsdale, NJ: Erlbaum.

Clay, M. (1979). *The early detection of reading difficulties: A diagnostic survey with recovery procedures* (2nd ed.). Auckland, New Zealand: Heinemann.

Coltheart, M., Patterson, K., & Marshall, J. (1980). *Deep dyslexia.* London: Routledge & Kegan Paul.

Crooks, T. (1982, April). *Generalization in educational research: Through a glass darkly.* Paper presented at the annual meeting of the American Educational Research Association, New York.

Dunn, L. M., & Markwardt, F. C. (1970). *Peabody individual achievement test.* Circle Pines, MN: American Guidance Service.

Dweck, C. S., & Bempechat, J. K. (1983). Children's theories of intelligence: Consequences for learning. In S. G. Paris, G. M. Olson, & H. W. Stevenson (Eds.), *Learning and motivation in the classroom* (pp. 239–256). Hillsdale, NJ: Erlbaum.

Easley, J., & Zwoyer, R. (1975). Teaching by listening — toward a new day in math classes. *Contemporary Education, 47,* 19–25.

Harste, J., & Burke, C. (1979, December). *Reexamining retellings as comprehension devices.* Paper presented at the annual meeting of the National Reading Conference, San Antonio.

Holdaway, D. (1979). *Foundations of literacy.* Gosford, Australia: Scholastic.

Holt, J. (1964). *How children fail.* New York: Pittman.

Jastak, J. F., Bijou, S. W., & Jastak, S. R. (1965). *Wide range achievement test.* Wilmington, DE: Guidance Associates of Delaware.

Johnston, P. (1984). Assessment in reading: The emperor has no clothes. In P. D. Pearson (Ed.), *Handbook of reading research* (pp. 147–182). New York: Longman.

Johnston, P. (1985). Understanding reading disability: A case study approach. *Harvard Educational Review, 55,* 153–177.

Johnston, P., & Winograd, P. (1985). Passive failure in reading. *Journal of Reading Behavior, 17,* 279–301.

Karlsen, B., Madden, R., & Gardner, E. (1976). *Stanford diagnostic reading test manual.* New York: Harcourt Brace Jovanovich.

Leont'ev, A. (1979). The problem of activity in Soviet psychology. In J. V. Wertsch (Ed.), *The concept of activity in Soviet psychology* (pp. 37–71). Armonk, NY: Sharpe, Inc.

Lahey, B., McNees, M., & Brown, C. (1973). Modification of deficits in reading for comprehension. *Journal of Applied Behavior Analysis, 6,* 475–480.

McConkie, G., Tavakoli, R., Wolverton, G., & Zola, D. (1983, December). *Computer aided reading: A help for illiterate adults.* Paper presented at the annual meeting of the National Reading Conference, Austin.

McGill-Franzen, A., & McDermott, P. (1978, December). *Negotiating a reading diagnosis.* Paper presented at the annual meeting of the National Reading Conference, St. Petersburg.

McNaughton, S. (1981). The influence of immediate teacher correction on self-correction and proficient oral reading. *Journal of Reading Behavior, 13,* 367–371.

Mehan, H. (1978). Structuring school structure. *Harvard Educational Review, 48,* 32–64.

Nicholls, J. (1983). Conceptions of ability and achievement motivation: A theory and its implications for education. In S. Paris, G. Olsen, & H. Stevenson (Eds.), *Learning and motivation in the classroom* (pp. 211–237). Hillsdale, NJ: Erlbaum.

Nurss, J., & McGauvrin, M. (1976). *Teacher's manual (Part Two): Interpretation and use of test results.* New York: Harcourt Brace.

Palincsar, M. (1982). *Improving the reading comprehension of junior high students through the reciprocal teaching of comprehension monitoring strategies.* Unpublished doctoral dissertation, University of Illinois at Urbana-Champaign.

Paris, S. G., Lipson, M. Y., & Wixson, K. K. (1983). Becoming a strategic reader. *Contemporary Educational Psychology, 8,* 293–316.

Prescott, G. A., Balow, I. H., Hogan, T. P., & Farr, R. C. (1985). *Metropolitan achievement tests.* Cleveland, OH: Psychological Corporation.

Resnick, D. (1982). History of educational testing. In A. K. Wigdor & W. R. Garner (Eds.), *Ability testing: Uses, consequences and controversies* (Part II, pp. 173–194). Washington, DC: National Academy Press.

Rohrkemper, M. M., & Brophy, J. E. (1983). Teachers thinking about students. In J. M. Levine & M. C. Wang (Eds.), *Teacher and student perceptions: Implications for learning* (pp.75–104). Hillsdale, NJ: Erlbaum.

Scriven, M. (1972). Objectivity and subjectivity in educational research. In L. G. Thomas (Ed.), *Philosophical redirection of educational research: 71st Yearbook of the National Society for the Study of Education* (Part One, pp. 94–142). Chicago, IL: University of Chicago Press.

Spache, G. (1981). *Diagnostic reading scales.* Monterey, CA: McGraw-Hill.

Vygotsky, L. (1979). The genesis of higher mental functions. In J. V. Wertsch (Ed.), *The concept of activity in Soviet psychology* (pp. 134–162). Armonk, NY: Sharpe, Inc.

Vygotsky, L. (1978). *Mind in society* (M. Cole, V. John-Steiner, S. Scribner, & E. Souberman, Eds.). Cambridge, MA: Harvard U. Press.

Vygotsky, L. (1962). *Thought and language* (E. Hanfmann & G. Vakar, Trans.). Cambridge, MA: MIT Press.

Walmsley, S. (1978–79). The criterion referenced measurement of an early reading behavior. *Reading Research Quarterly, 14,* 574–604.

Wertsch, J. V. (1979a). The concept of activity in Soviet psychology: An introduction. In J. V. Wertsch (Ed.), *The concept of activity in Soviet psychology* (pp. 3–36). Armonk, NY: Sharpe, Inc.

Wertsch, J. V. (1979b). From social interaction to higher psychological processes. *Human Development, 22,* 1–22.

Woodcock, R. W. (1973). *Woodcock reading mastery tests, forms A and B.* Circle Pines, MN: American Guidance Service.

Zinchenko, V. P., & Gordon, V. M. (1979). Methodological problems in the psychological analysis of activity. In J. V. Wertsch (Ed.), *The concept of activity in Soviet psychology* (pp. 72–133). Armonk, NY: Sharpe, Inc.

Chapter 10

Algozzine, R. (1979). *The disturbing child: A validation report* (Research Report No. 8). Minneapolis, MN: University of Minnesota, Institute for Research on Learning Disabilities.

Algozzine, B., & Ysseldyke, J. E. (1980). Decision makers' prediction of students' academic difficulties as a function of referral information. *Journal of Educational Research, 73,* 145–150.

Ashlock, R. B. (1976). *Error patterns in computation: A semi-programmed approach* (2nd ed.). Columbus, OH: Merrill.

Bachor, D. G. (1979). Using work samples as diagnostic information. *Learning Disability Quarterly, 2*(1), 45–52.

Bennett, R. E. (1982). The use of grade and age equivalents in the schools. *Diagnostique, 7*, 139–146.

Bennett, R. E. (1983). A multimethod approach to assessment in special education. *Diagnostique, 8*, 88–97.

Bennett, R. E., & Shepherd, M. J. (1982). Basic measurement proficiency of learning disability specialists. *Learning Disability Quarterly, 5*, 177–184.

Burstein, A. (1985). *The turning point: New directions for special education* (Report of the New Jersey Special Education Study Commission). Trenton, N.J.: Division of Special Education, New Jersey Department of Education.

Deno, S. L., Marston, D., & Mirkin, P. (1982). Valid measurement procedures for continuous evaluation of written expression. *Exceptional Children, 48*, 368–371.

Deno, S. L., Marston, D., Shinn, M., & Tindal, G. (1983). Oral reading fluency: A simple datum for scaling reading disability. *Topics in Learning and Learning Disabilities, 2*(4), 53–59.

Eaton, M., & Lovitt, T. (1972). Achievement tests vs. direct and daily measurement. In G. Semb (Ed.), *Behavior analysis and education*. Lawrence, KS: University of Kansas.

Eaves, R. C., & McLaughlin, P. (1977). A systems approach for the assessment of the child and his environment: Getting back to basics. *Journal of Special Education, 11*, 99–111.

Howell, K. W., & Kaplan, J. S. (1980). Diagnosing basic skills: A handbook for deciding what to teach. Columbus, OH: Merrill.

Howell, K. W., Kaplan, J. S., & O'Connell, C. Y. (1979). *Evaluating exceptional children: A task analysis approach*. Columbus, OH: Merrill.

Salvia, J., & Ysseldyke, J. E. (1981). *Assessment in special and remedial education* (2nd ed.). Boston: Houghton Mifflin.

Shepard, L. A., Smith, M. L., & Vojir, C. P. (1983). Characteristics of pupils identified as learning disabled. *American Educational Research Journal, 20*, 309–331.

Thurlow, M. L., & Ysseldyke, J. E. (1979). Current assessment and decision-making practices in model LD programs. *Learning Disability Quarterly, 2*(4), 15–24.

U.S. Office of Education. (1977). Education of handicapped children: Implementation of part B of the education of the handicapped act. *Federal Register, 42*, 42474–42518.

Wesson, C. L., King, R. P., & Deno, S. L. (1984). Direct and frequent measurement of student performance: If it's good for us, why don't we do it? *Learning Disability Quarterly, 7*(1), 45–48.

Zigmond, N., Vallecorsa, A., & Silverman, R. (1983). *Assessment for instructional planning in special education.* Englewood Cliffs, NJ: Prentice-Hall.

Chapter 11

Alley, G. R., & Deshler, D. D. (1979). *Teaching the learning disabled adolescent: Strategies and methods.* Denver: Love Publishing Co.

Brown, A. L. (1982). Learning how to learn from reading. In J. A. Langer & M. T. Smith-Burke (Eds.), *Reader meets author/bridging the gap.* Newark, DE: International Reading Association.

Brown, A. L., Campione, J. C., & Day, J. D. (1981, February). Learning to learn: On training students to learn from texts. *Educational Researcher*, 14–21.

Carlson, S. A., & Alley, G. R. (1981). *Performance and competence of learning disabled and high-achieving high school students on essential cognitive skills* (Res. Rep. No. 53). Lawrence: University of Kansas Institute for Research in Learning Disabilities.

Clark, F. L., Warner, M. M., Alley, G. R., Deshler, D. D., Schumaker, J. B., Vetter, A. F., & Nolan, S. M. (in press). Visual imagery and self-questioning: Strategies to improve comprehension of written material. *Journal of Learning Disabilities.*

den Uyl, M., & van Oostendorp, H. (1980). The use of scripts in text comprehension. *Poetics, 9*, 275–294.

Deshler, D. D., Alley, G. R., Warner, M. M., & Schumaker, J. B. (1981). Instructional practices for promoting skills acquisition and generalization in severely learning disabled adolescents. *Learning Disability Quarterly, 4*, 415–421.

Deshler, D. D., Schumaker, J. B., Alley, G. R., Warner, M. M., & Clark, F. L. (1981). Social interaction deficits in learning disabled adolescents—Another myth? In W. M. Cruickshank & A. A. Silver (Eds.), *Bridges to tomorrow (Vol. 2): The best of ACLD.* Syracuse, NY: Syracuse University Press.

Deshler, D. D., Schumaker, J. B., Warner, M. M., Alley, G. R., & Clark, F. L. (1980). *An epidemiological study of learning disabled adolescents in secondary schools: Social status, peer relationships, activities in and out of school, and time use* (Res. Rep. No. 18). Lawrence: University of Kansas Institute for Research in Learning Disabilities.

Deshler, D. D., Warner, M. M., Schumaker, J. B., & Alley, G. R. (1983). Learning strategies intervention model: Key components and current status. In J. McKinney & L. Feagans (Eds.), *Current topics in learning disabilities: Vol. 1.* Norwood, NJ: Ablex Publishing Corp.

Ellis, E. S. (1983). *The effects of teaching learning disabled adolescents an executive strategy to facilitate self-generation of task-specific strategies.* Unpublished doctoral dissertation, University of Kansas, Lawrence.

Flanagan, J. (1962). *Measuring human performance.* Pittsburgh: American Institute for Research.

Fry, E. (1977). *Elementary reading instruction.* New York: McGraw-Hill.

Hazel, J. S., Schumaker, J. B., Nolan, S., & Pederson, C. S. (in preparation). *Training the generalized use of social skills through "the social skills curriculum"* (Research Report). Lawrence: University of Kansas Institute for Research in Learning Disabilities.

Hunt, K. W. (1970). Syntactic maturity in school children and adults. *Monograph of the Society for Research in Child Development, 134,* 1–44.

Jenkins, J. J. (1979). Four points to remember: A tetrahedral model and memory experiments. In L. S. Cermak & F. I. M. Craik (Eds.), *Levels and processing in human memory.* Hillsdale, NJ: Erlbaum.

Kintsch, W., Kozminsky, E., Streby, J., McKoon, G., & Keena, J. M. (1975). Comprehension and recall as a function of content variables. *Journal of Verbal Behavior, 14,* 190–214.

Knowlton, E. K. (1983). *Secondary regular classroom teachers' expectations of learning disabled students* (Research Report No. 75).

Lawrence: University of Kansas Institute for Research in Learning Disabilities.

Knowlton, H. E., & Schlick, L. (in preparation). *Secondary regular classroom teachers' expectations of learning disabled students: The critical incident technique.* Lawrence: University of Kansas Institute for Research in Learning Disabilities.

Lewin, K. (1935). *A dynamic theory of personality: Selected papers* (Translated by Donald K. Adams & K. E. Zener). New York: McGraw-Hill.

Link, D. B. (1980). *Essential learning skills and the low-achieving student at the secondary level: A rating of the importance of 24 academic abilities.* Unpublished master's thesis, University of Kansas.

Marshall, N., & Glock, M. (1978). Comprehension of connected discourse: A study into the relationship between structure of text and information recalled. *Reading Research Quarterly, 14,* 10–56.

Mathews, R. M., Whang, P. L., & Fawcett, S. B. (1982). Behavioral assessment of occupational skills of learning disabled adolescents. *Journal of Learning Disabilities, 11,* 38–41.

McClenaghan, W. A. (1979). *Magruder's American government.* Boston: Allyn & Bacon.

Meyen, E. L., Alley, G. R., Scannell, D. P., Harnden, G. M., & Miller, K. F. (1982). *A mandated minimum competency testing program and its impact on learning disabled students: Curricular validity and comparative performance* (Res. Rep. No. 63). Lawrence: University of Kansas Institute for Research in Learning Disabilities.

Moran, M. R. (1980). *An investigation of the demands on oral language skills of learning disabled students in secondary classrooms* (Res. Rep. No. 1). Lawrence: University of Kansas Institute for Research in Learning Disabilities.

Moran, M. R. (1981). *A comparison of formal features of written language of learning disabled, low-achieving, and achieving secondary students* (Res. Rep. No. 34). Lawrence: University of Kansas Institute for Research in Learning Disabilities.

Moran, M. R., & DeLoach, T. F. (1982). *Mainstream teachers' responses to formal features of writing by secondary learning disabled students* (Res. Rep. No. 61). Lawrence: University of Kansas Institute for Research in Learning Disabilities.

Otto, J. H., Towle, A., & Bradley, J. V. (1981). *Modern biology*. New York: Holt, Rinehart & Winston.

Powell, L., Suzuki, K., Atwater, J., Gorney-Krupsaw, B., & Morris, E. K. (1981). *Interactions between teachers and learning disabled and non-learning disabled students* (Res. Rep. No. 44). Lawrence: University of Kansas Institute for Research in Learning Disabilities.

Pullin, D. (1980). Mandated minimum competency testing: Its impact on handicapped adolescents. *Exceptional Education Quarterly, 1*(2), 107–116.

Schank, R. (1983). A conversation with Roger Schank. *Psychology Today, 17*(4), 28–36.

Schlick, A. R., Gall, M., & Riegel, R. H. (1981). Modifying study guides, practice and tests for students with learning difficulties at the secondary level. In T. Shaw (Ed.), *Teaching handicapped students in social studies*. Washington, DC: National Education Association.

Schmidt, J. (1983). *The effects of four generalization conditions on learning disabled adolescents' written language performance in the regular classroom*. Unpublished doctoral dissertation, University of Kansas, Lawrence.

Schumaker, J. B., Alley, G. R., Warner, M. M., & Deshler, D. D. (1980). *A research strategy for studying learning disabled adolescents and young adults* (Res. Mono. No. 6). Lawrence: University of Kansas Institute for Research in Learning Disabilities.

Schumaker, J. B., Deshler, D. D., Alley, G. R., Warner, M. M., Clark, F. L., & Nolan, S. (1982). Error monitoring: A learning strategy for improving adolescent academic performance. In W. M. Cruickshank & J. W. Lerner (Eds.), *Best of ACLD, Vol. 3*. Syracuse, NY: Syracuse University Press.

Schumaker, J. B., Deshler, D. D., Denton, P. H., Alley, G. R., Clark, F. L., & Warner, M. M. (1982). Multipass: A learning strategy for improving reading comprehension. *Learning Disability Quarterly, 5*, 295–304.

Schumaker, J. B., Hazel, J. S., Sherman, J. A., & Sheldon, J. (1982). Social skill performances of learning disabled, non-learning disabled, and delinquent adolescents. *Learning Disability Quarterly, 5*, 388–397.

Schumaker, J. B., Sheldon-Wildgen, J., & Sherman, J. A. (1980). *An observational study of the academic and social behaviors of learning disabled adolescents in the regular classroom* (Res. Rep. No. 22). Lawrence: University of Kansas Institute for Research in Learning Disabilities.

Skrtic, T. M. (1980). *The regular classroom interactions of learning disabled adolescents and their teachers* (Res. Rep. No. 8). Lawrence: University of Kansas Institute for Research in Learning Disabilities.

Spiro, R. J. (1980). Prior knowledge and story processing: Integration, selection, and variation. *Poetics, 9,* 313–327.

Todd, L. P., & Curti, M. (1982). *Rise of the American nation.* New York: Harcourt Brace Jovanovich.

Vetter, A. (1983). *A comparison of the characteristics of learning disabled and non-learning disabled young adults.* Unpublished doctoral dissertation, University of Kansas, Lawrence.

Warner, M. M. (in preparation). *Analysis of Woodcock-Johnson psycho-educational battery written language cluster scores for LD and low-achieving adolescents.* Lawrence: University of Kansas Institute for Research in Learning Disabilities.

Warner, M. M., Alley, G. R., Deshler, D. D., & Schumaker, J. B. (1980). *An epidemiological study of learning disabled adolescents in secondary schools: Classification and discrimination of learning disabled and low-achieving adolescents* (Research Report No. 20). Lawrence: University of Kansas Institute for Research in Learning Disabilities.

Warner, M. M., Alley, G. R., Schumaker, J. B., Deshler, D. D., & Clark, F. L. (1980). *An epidemiological study of learning disabled adolescents in secondary schools: Achievement and ability, socioeconomic status, and school experiences* (Research Report No. 13). Lawrence: University of Kansas Institute for Research in Learning Disabilities.

Westendorf, D. K., Cape, E. L., & Skrtic, T. M. (in preparation). *A naturalistic study of post-secondary setting demands* (Res. Rep.). Lawrence: University of Kansas Institute for Research in Learning Disabilities.

Whitaker, K. K. (1982). *Development and field testing of an assignment strategy for learning disabled adolescents.* Unpublished master's thesis, University of Kansas, Lawrence.

Chapter 12

Alley, G. R., & Deshler, D. D. (1979). *Teaching the learning disabled adolescent: Strategies and methods*. Denver: Love Publishing.

Armbruster, B. B., Echols, C. H., & Brown, A. L. (1984). The role of metacognition in reading to learn: A developmental perspective. *The Volta Review*, *84*(5), 79–101.

Brown, A. L. (1980). Metacognitive development and reading. In R. J. Spiro, B. B. Bruce, & W. F. Brewer (Eds.), *Theoretical issues in reading comprehension*. Hillsdale, NJ: Lawrence Erlbaum Associates.

Bulgren, J. A., & Schumaker, J. B. (in preparation). *Learning strategies curriculum: The paired-associates strategy*. Lawrence: University of Kansas Institute for Research in Learning Disabilities.

Clark, F. L., Deshler, D. D., Schumaker, J. B., & Alley, G. R. (1984). Visual imagery and self-questioning: Strategies to improve comprehension of written materials. *Journal of Learning Disabilities*, *17*(3), 145–149.

Deshler, D. D., Alley, G. R., Warner, M. M., & Schumaker, J. B. (1981). Instructional practices for promoting skill acquisition and generalization in severely learning disabled adolescents. *Learning Disabilities Quarterly*, *4*(4), 415–421.

Deshler, D. D., Denton, P. H., & Schumaker, J. B. (in press). *Learning strategies curriculum: The listening and notetaking strategy*. Lawrence: University of Kansas.

Deshler, D. D., Lowrey, N. J., & Alley, G. R. (1979). Programming alternatives for learning disabled adolescents: A nationwide survey. *Academic Therapy*, *14*, 54–63.

Deshler, D. D., & Schumaker, J. B. (1983). Social skills of learning disabled adolescents: A review of characteristics and interventions. *Topics in Learning and Learning Disabilities*, *3*(2), 15–23.

Deshler, D. D., & Schumaker, J. B. (1984). *Strategies instruction: A new way to teach*. Salt Lake City: Worldwide Media, Inc.

Deshler, D. D., Schumaker, J. B., Alley, G. R., Warner, M. M., & Clark, F. L. (1982). Learning disabilities in adolescent and young adult populations: Research implications (Part I). *Focus on Exceptional Children*, *15*(1), 1–12.

Deshler, D. D., Schumaker, J. B., Lenz, B. K., & Ellis, E. S. (1984). Academic and cognitive interventions for LD adolescents (Part II). *Journal of Learning Disabilities, 17*(3), 170–187.

Deshler, D. D., Warner, M. M., Schumaker, J. B., & Alley, G. R. (1983). The learning strategies intervention model: Key components and current status. In J. D. McKinney & L. Feagans (Eds.), *Current topics in learning disabilities* (Vol. 1). Norwood, NJ: Ablex Publishing.

Ellis, E. S. (1985). *The effects of teaching learning disabled adolescents an executive problem solving strategy.* Unpublished dissertation. Lawrence: University of Kansas.

Goodlad, J. (1984). *A place called school.* New York: McGraw-Hill.

Haring, N. G., Lovitt, T. C., Eaton, M. D., & Hanson, C. L. (1978). *The fourth R: Research in the classroom.* Columbus: Charles E. Merrill.

Hughes, C. (1985). *A test taking strategy for emotionally handicapped disabled adolescents.* Unpublished doctoral dissertation. Gainesville: University of Florida.

Kea, C. D., Deshler, D. D., & Schumaker, J. B. (in preparation). *An analysis of critical teaching behaviors as applied by secondary special education teachers.* Lawrence: University of Kansas Institute for Research in Learning Disabilities.

Lenz, B. K., Schumaker, J. B., & Deshler, D. D. (in press). *Learning strategies curriculum: The interpreting visual aids strategy.* Lawrence: University of Kansas.

Lenz, B. K., Schumaker, J. B., Deshler, D. D., & Beals, V. L. (1984). *Learning strategies curriculum: The word identification strategy.* Lawrence: University of Kansas.

Meyen, E. L., & Deshler, D. D. (1978). The Kansas Research Institute in Learning Disabilities. *Learning Disability Quarterly, 1,* 73–75.

Reid, D. K., & Hresko, W. P. (1981). *A cognitive approach to learning disabilities.* New York: McGraw-Hill.

Robbins, D. A. (1982). *FIRST—letter mnemonic strategy: A memorization technique for learning disabled high school students.* Unpublished master's thesis. Lawrence: University of Kansas.

Schumaker, J. B. (in preparation [a]). *Learning strategies curriculum: The paragraph writing strategy.* Lawrence: University of Kansas.

Schumaker, J. B. (in preparation [b]). *Learning strategies curriculum: The theme writing strategy*. Lawrence: University of Kansas.

Schumaker, J. B., Denton, P. H., & Deshler, D. D. (1984). *Learning strategies curriculum: The paraphrasing strategy*. Lawrence: University of Kansas.

Schumaker, J. B., & Deshler, D. D. (1984). Setting demand variables: A major factor in program planning for the LD adolescent. *Topics in Language Disorders*, *4*(2), 22–40.

Schumaker, J. B., Deshler, D. D., Alley, G. R., & Denton, P. H. (1982). Multipass: A learning strategy for improving reading comprehension. *Learning Disability Quarterly*, *5*(3), 295–304.

Schumaker, J. B., Deshler, D. D., Alley, G. R., & Warner, M. M. (1983). Toward the development of an intervention model for learning disabled adolescents. *Exceptional Education Quarterly*, *3*(4), 45–50.

Schumaker, J. B., Deshler, D. D., & Ellis, E. S. (1986). Intervention issues related to the education of LD adolescents. In J. K. Torgeson & B. Y. L. Wong (Eds.), *Learning disabilities: Some new perspectives*. New York: Academic Press.

Schumaker, J. B., Nolan, S., & Deshler, D. D. (1985). *Learning strategies curriculum: The error monitoring strategy*. Lawrence: University of Kansas.

Schumaker, J. B., & Sheldon, J. (1985). *Learning strategies curriculum: The sentence writing strategy*. Lawrence: University of Kansas.

Seabaugh, G. O., & Schumaker, J. B. (1981). *The effects of self-regulation training on the academic productivity of LD and NLD adolescents* (Research Report No. 37). Lawrence: University of Kansas Institute for Research in Learning Disabilities.

Showers, B. (1985). Teachers coaching teachers. *Educational Leadership*, *47*(7), 43–48.

Stokes, T. F., & Baer, D. M. (1977). An implicit technology of generalization. *Journal of Applied Behavior Analysis*, *10*, 349–367.

Torgeson, J. K. (1977). The role of nonspecific factors in the task performance of learning disabled children: A theoretical assessment. *Journal of Learning Disabilities*, *10*(1), 17–34.

Van Reusen, A. K. (1985). *A study of the effects of training learning disabled adolescents in self-advocacy procedures for use in the IEP conference.* Unpublished doctoral dissertation. Lawrence: University of Kansas.

Whitaker, K. K. (1982). *Development and field test of an assignment completion strategy for learning disabled adolescents.* Unpublished master's thesis. Lawrence: University of Kansas.

Wong, B. Y. (1985). *Metacognition: Why should special educators attend to it?* Montreal: Canadian Society for the Study of Education.

Chapter 13

Barbanel, L. (1982). Short-term dynamic therapies with children. In C. R. Reynolds & T. B. Gutkin (Eds.), *The handbook of school psychology* (pp. 554–569). New York: Wiley.

Barten, H. H., & Barten, S. S. (Eds.). (1973). *Children and their parents in brief therapy.* New York: Behavioral Publications.

Bellak, L., & Siegel, H. (1983). *Brief and emergency psychotherapy.* Larchmont, NY: C.P.S.

Brown, S. L. (1986). A case of brief dynamic family therapy. *International Journal of Short-term Psychotherapy, 1,* 3–15.

Claiborn, C. D., & Strong, S. R. (1982). Group counseling in the schools. In C. R. Reynolds & T. B. Gutkin (Eds.), *The handbook of school psychology* (pp. 530–553). New York: Wiley.

Comas-Diaz, L., & Griffith, E. E. H. (Eds.). (1988). *Clinical guidelines in cross-cultural mental health.* New York: Wiley.

Croake, J. W. (1986). Treating conduct disorders in adolescents. *Individual Psychology: The Journal of Adlerian Theory, Research & Practice, 42,* 270–273.

Fisch, R., Weakland, J. H., & Segal, L. (1982). *The tactics of change: Doing therapy briefly.* San Francisco: Jossey-Bass.

Maddi, S. R. (1972). *Personality theories: A comparative analysis* (rev. ed.). Homewood, IL: Dorsey.

Rosenbaum, M. (1976). Group psychotherapies. In B. B. Wolman (Ed.), *The therapist's handbook: Treatment methods of mental disorders* (pp. 163–183). New York: Van Nostrand Reinhold.

Shaffer, M. B. (1985). Best practices in counseling high school students. In A. Thomas & J. Grimes (Eds.), *Best practices in school psychology* (pp. 393–400). Kent, OH: National Association of School Psychologists.

Sifneos, P. E. (1972). *Short-term psychotherapy and emotional crisis.* Cambridge, MA: Harvard University Press.

Sigmon, S. B. (1988). A framework to determine when the school psychologist should counsel. *Psychology in the Schools, 25,* 62–64.

Sue, D. W. (1981). *Counseling the culturally different: Theory and practice..* New York: Wiley.

Tharinger, D. (1985). Best practices in counseling elementary students. In A. Thomas & J. Grimes (Eds.), *Best practices in school psychology* (pp. 447–459). Kent, OH: National Association of School Psychologists.

Weakland, J. H., Fisch, R., Watzlawick, P., & Bodin, A. M. (1974). Brief therapy: Focused problem resolution. *Family Process, 13,* 141–168.

Wolberg, L. (Ed.). (1965). *Short-term psychotherapy.* New York: Grune & Stratton.

Wolman, B. B. (Ed.). (1973). *Dictionary of behavioral science.* New York: Van Nostrand Reinhold.

Yalom, I. D. (1975). *The theory and practice of group psychotherapy* (2nd ed.). New York: Basic Books.

Chapter 14

Allington, R. L., & Johnston, P. (1986). The coordination among regular classroom reading programs and targeted support programs. In B. I. Williams, P. A. Richmond, & B. J. Mason (Eds.), *Designing for compensatory education: Conference proceedings and papers* (pp. 3–40). Washington, DC: Research and Evaluation Associates.

Allington, R. L., & McGill-Franzen, A. (1989). Different programs, indifferent instruction. In D. K. Lipsky & A. Gartner (Eds.), *Beyond separate education: Quality education for all* (pp. 75–97). Baltimore, MD: Brookes.

Biklen, D. (1985). *Achieving the complete school: Strategies for effective mainstreaming.* New York: Teachers College Press.

Deno, E. (1970). Special education as developmental capital. *Exceptional Children, 37,* 229–237.

Gardner, H. (1983). *Frames of mind: The theory of multiple intelligences.* New York: Basic Books.

Gartner, A., & Lipsky, D. K. (1987). Beyond special education: Toward a quality system for all students. *Harvard Educational Review, 57,* 367–395.

Gartner, A., & Riessman, F. (1974). *The service society and the consumer vanguard.* New York: Harper & Row.

Goldman, J., & Gardner, H. (1989). Multiple paths to educational effectiveness. In D. K. Lipsky & A. Gartner (Eds.), *Beyond separate education: Quality education for all* (pp. 121–139). Baltimore, MD: Brookes.

Jenkins, J. R. (1987). Similarities in the achievement levels of learning disabled and remedial students. *Counterpoint, 7*(3), 16.

Lipsky, D. K. (1985). A parental perspective on stress and coping. *American Journal of Orthopsychiatry, 55,* 614–617.

Lipsky, D. K., & Gartner, A. (1987). Capable of achievement and worthy of respect: Education for handicapped students as if they were full-fledged human beings. *Exceptional Children, 54,* 69–74.

Lipsky, D. K., & Gartner, A. (Eds.). (1989). *Beyond separate education: Quality education for all.* Baltimore, MD: Brookes.

Meyers, C. E., & Blacher, J. (1987). Parents' perceptions of schooling for severely handicapped children: Home and family variables. *Exceptional Children, 53,* 441–449.

Ninth annual report to Congress on the implementation of The Education of the Handicapped Act. (1987). Washington, DC: U.S. Department of Education.

Reynolds, M. C. (1962). A framework for considering some issues in special education. *Exceptional Children, 28,* 367–370.

Skrtic, T. (1987, April). Preconditions for merger: An organizational analysis of special education reform. In *Prenuptial agreements necessary for wedding special education and general education.* Symposium conducted at the annual meeting of the American Educational Research Association, Washington, DC.

Slavin, R. E. (1986). Learning together. *American Educator: The Professional Journal of the American Federation of Teachers, 10*(2), 6–11.

Slavin, R. E. (1987). Cooperative learning and the cooperative school. *Educational Leadership, 45*(3), 7–13.

Stainback, W., & Stainback, S. (1984). A rationale for the merger of special and regular education. *Exceptional Children, 51*, 102–111.

Taylor, S. J. (1988). Caught in the continuum: A critical analysis of the principle of the least restrictive environment. *Journal of the Association for Persons with Severe Handicaps, 13*, 41–53.

Ysseldyke, J. E. (1987). Classification of handicapped students. In M. C. Wang, M. C. Reynolds, & H. J. Walberg (Eds.), *Handbook of special education: Research and practice. Vol. 1, Learner characteristics and adaptive education* (pp. 253–271). New York: Pergamon.

Conclusion

Algozzine, B., Christenson, S., & Ysseldyke, J. E. (1982). Probabilities associated with the referral to placement process. *Teacher Education and Special Education, 5*(3), 19–23.

Budoff, M., & Pagell, W. (1968). Learning potential and rigidity in the adolescent mentally retarded. *Journal of Abnormal Psychology, 73*, 479–486.

Carrier, J. G. (1986). *Learning disability: Social class and the construction of inequality in American education.* Westport, CT: Greenwood Press.

Coles, G. (1987). *The Learning mystique: A critical look at "learning disabilities."* New York: Pantheon.

Feuerstein, R. (1979). *The dynamic assessment of retarded performers: The learning potential device, theory, instruments, and techniques.* Baltimore: University Park Press.

Haley, J. (Ed.). (1985). *Conversations with Milton H. Erickson, M.D. (Vol. I): Changing individuals.* New York: Triangle Press/Norton.

Interagency Committee on Learning Disabilities. (1987). *Learning disabilities: A report to the U.S. Congress.* Washington, DC: U.S. Department of Health and Human Services.

Jan-Tausch, J. (1985). The origin and early development of the learning consultant. *Learning Consultant Journal, 6,* 1–4.

Lipson, M. Y., & Wixson, K. K. (1986). Reading disability research: An interactionist perspective. *Review of Educational Research, 56,* 111–136.

Office of the Legislative Analyst. (1987, September 14). *Request for proposals to evaluate alternative programs and strategies for serving pupils with learning disabilities.* Sacramento, CA: Joint Legislative Budget Committee, State of California.

Shepard, L., & Smith, M. L. (1981). *Evaluation of the identification of perceptual-communicative disorders in Colorado.* Boulder, CO: Laboratory of Educational Research, University of Colorado.

Sigmon, S. B. (1987). *Radical analysis of special education: Focus on historical development and learning disabilities.* London, New York, & Philadelphia: The Falmer Press/Taylor & Francis.

Tomlinson, S. (1982). *A sociology of special education.* London: Routledge & Kegan Paul.

U.S. Office of Special Education and Rehabilitative Services. (1987). *Ninth annual report to Congress on the implementation of The Education of the Handicapped Act.* Washington, DC: U.S. Department of Education.

Watzlawick, P., Weakland, J., & Fisch, R. (1974). *Change: Principles of problem formation and problem resolution.* New York: Norton.

Will, M. (1986, November). *Educating students with learning problems— A shared responsibility.* Washington, DC: Office of Special Education and Rehabilitative Services, U.S. Department of Education.

Ysseldyke, J. E., Thurlow, M., Graden, J., Wesson, C., Algozzine, B., & Deno, S. (1983). Generalizations from five years of research on assessment and decision making: The University of Minnesota Institute. *Exceptional Education Quarterly, 4*(1), 75–93.

Appendix A

Barbanel, L. (1982). Short-term dynamic therapies with children. In C. R. Reynolds & T. B. Gutkin (Eds.), *The handbook of school psychology* (pp.554–569). New York: Wiley.

256 REFERENCES

Barten, H. H., & Barten, S. S. (Eds.). (1973). *Children and their parents in brief therapy.* New York: Behavioral Publications.

Bellak, L., & Siegel, H. (1983). *Brief and emergency psychotherapy.* Larchmont, NY: C.P.S.

Brown, S. L. (1986). A case of brief dynamic family therapy. *International Journal of Short-term Psychotherapy, 1,* 3–15.

Fisch, R., Weakland, J. H., & Segal, L. (1982). *The tactics of change: Doing therapy briefly.* San Francisco: Jossey-Bass.

Golan, N. (1978). *Treatment in crisis situations.* New York: Free Press.

Neubauer, P. (1972). Normal development in childhood. In B. B. Wolman (Ed.), *Manual of child psychopathology* (pp. 3–21). New York: McGraw-Hill.

Rubin, K. (1987, May 14). What we need to know about teen suicide. Union, NJ: *Union Leader*, p.5.

Schecter, M. D., Toussieng, P. W., & Sternlof, R. E. (1972). Normal development in adolescence. In B. B. Wolman (Ed.), *Manual of child psychopathology* (pp. 22–45). New York: McGraw-Hill.

Sifneos, P. E. (1972). *Short-term psychotherapy and emotional crisis.* Cambridge, MA: Harvard University Press.

Slaikeu, K. A. (1984). *Crisis intervention: A handbook for practice and research.* Boston: Allyn & Bacon.

Smead, V. S. (1985). Best practices in crisis intervention. In A. Thomas & J. Grimes (Eds.), *Best practices in school psychology* (pp. 401–413). Kent, OH: National Association of School Psychologists.

Watzlawick, P., Weakland, J. H., & Fisch, R. (1974). *Change: Principles of problem formation and problem resolution.* New York: Norton.

Weakland, J. H., Fisch, R., Watzlawick, P., & Bodin, A. M. (1974). Brief therapy: Focused problem resolution. *Family Process, 13,* 141–168.

Wolberg, L. (Ed.). (1965). *Short-term psychotherapy.* New York: Grune & Stratton.

Appendix B

Comptroller General of the United States. (1981, September 30). *Disparities still exist in who gets special education* (IPE–81–1; Report to the chairman, subcommittee on select education, committee on education and labor, House of Representatives). Washington, DC: U.S. General Accounting Office.

New Jersey State Department of Education. (1987, April). *Special education: A statistical report for the 1985–1986 school year.* Trenton, NJ: Author.

Shinn, M. R., Tindal, G. A., & Spira, D. A. (1987). Special education referrals as an index of teacher tolerance: Are teachers imperfect tests? *Exceptional Children, 54,* 32–40.

Sigmon, S. B. (1987). Sex roles: Their relationship to cultural and biological determinants. *Sexual and Marital Therapy, 2*(1), 29–33.

Appendix C

Sigmon, S. B. (1984). Practitioners, trainers, and literature in school psychology. *New Jersey School Psychologist, 4*(1), 7 & 10.

Sigmon, S. B. (1985). Literature about school psychology: Who writes what for whom? *Professional Psychology: Research and Practice, 16,* 469–70.

Contributors

Scott B. Sigmon has for a number of years been a school psychologist. His doctorate from Rutgers University is in philosophy of education. He has taught graduate psychology and special education courses (most recently at Seton Hall University), served as supervisor of child study for a large urban school district, worked as a psychotherapist, and edited *The New Jersey School Psychologist*. In addition to being widely published in international education as well as psychology journals, Dr. Sigmon has authored two books—*Radical Socioeducational Analysis* (1985; New York: Irvington Publishers) and *Radical Analysis of Special Education: Focus on Historical Development and Learning Disabilities* (1987; London, New York, & Philadelphia: The Falmer Press/Taylor & Francis).

Marty Abramson is presently Associate Professor of Education, Grand Valley State University, Allendale, Michigan. He was formerly with the Office of Special Education Programs, U.S. Department of Education.

Bob Algozzine is presently Professor, University of North Carolina-Charlotte. He was formerly affiliated with the Institute for Research on Learning Disabilities, University of Minnesota, and later, University of Florida, Department of Special Education.

Steven A. Carlson is Director of Planning and Evaluation for the Beaverton, Oregon, Schools. He formerly taught or did research on learning disabilities at Rutgers University, Michigan State University, and the University of Kansas.

Donald D. Deshler is Director, University of Kansas Institute for Research in Learning Disabilities.

259

Alan Gartner is Professor and Director, Office of Sponsored Research, Graduate School and University Center, City University of New York; and, formerly, Executive Director, Division of Special Education, New York City Public Schools.

Lynn M. Gelzheiser is Assistant Professor, Department of Educational Psychology and Statistics, State University of New York at Albany.

George J. Hagerty is presently Director of Academic Development and Associate Professor of Political Science and Education at Stonehill College, North Easton, MA. He was formerly with the Office of Special Education Programs, U.S. Department of Education.

Peter H. Johnston is Associate Professor, Department of Reading, State University of New York at Albany.

Dorothy Kerzner Lipsky is Senior Research Scientist, Office of Sponsored Research, Graduate School and University Center, City University of New York; and, formerly, Chief of Program Administration, Division of Special Education, New York City Public Schools.

Larry Maheady is Associate Professor, Department of Education, State University of New York, College at Fredonia. He was previously with the Special Education Department, Michigan State University.

Jane Mercer is Professor, Department of Sociology, University of California at Riverside.

Jean B. Schumaker is Research Coordinator, University of Kansas Institute for Research in Learning Disabilities.

Christine E. Sleeter is Associate Professor, Education Department, University of Wisconsin-Parkside.

Richard Towne is Professor, Exceptional Child Education, State University of New York at Buffalo.

James Ysseldyke is Professor of Educational Psychology and Director, Institute for Research on Learning Disabilities, University of Minnesota.

Index

A

academic engaged time (AET), 93
adaptive: curriculum, 48; learning
  environments model (ALEM), 47,
  94, 100–101; physical education,
  84
Adler, A., 83, 85–86
affective needs, 70; *see* counseling
alternative systems, 207–209
alternative service delivery models,
  216

C

component steps, 160
computer assisted instruction, 47
consult/consultants, 47, 167
consultation, 168, 184, 189
consultative model, 184, 201
cooperative learning (teams), 47,
  178
counseling, 3, 5, 167–173, 193–196
criterion-referenced tests/assess-
  ment, 124–125, 127–128, 190
critical (social) theory, xii, 73–74
critical teaching behaviors, 162
curriculum expectations, 134, 155
curriculum based assessment (CBA),
  190, 206

D

differential scale of adjustment, 193
direct instruction, 93, 189

direct intervention, 169, 172
DISTAR, 94–96, 98–101
dynamic assessment, 190

E

educational: configurations, 1, 4, 39;
  microprocesses, 41;
  resisters, 42
Exemplary Center for Reading Instruction (ECRI), 96–101

G

general education initiative (GEI),
  184, 190

H

hard-to: –reach, 191; –teach, 50, 55,
  61
Hegel, 77–78
how to: learn, 155–156, perform
  tasks, 156

I

individualized instruction, 190
inferiority feeling, 85–86
institutional survival skills, 69
instructional: alternative, 155;
  techniques (tried), 130–131
interact, 47
interaction, environmental, 69, 83,
  85, 87, 111, 135, 141, 189

263

V

Vygotsky, L.S., 79, 103–119

W

Weber, M., 15
work samples, analysis of, 124–125

Z

zone of proximal development,
  106–108, 115